Guide to Kemetic Relationships:

Ancient Egyptian Maat Wisdom of Relationships, a Comprehensive Philosophical, Legal and Psychological Manual to Apply Ethical Conscience in All Relations in Life to Promote Peace, Progress and Spiritual Enlightenment by Muata Ashby

Sema Institute of Yoga

P. O. Box 570459
Miami, Florida, 33257
(305) 378-6253 Fax: (305) 378-6253

©**2017 By Sema Institute of Yoga**

The author is available for group lectures. For further information contact the publisher.

Guide to Kemetic Relationships: Ancient Egyptian Maat Wisdom of Relationships, a Comprehensive Philosophical, Legal and Psychological Manual to Apply Ethical Conscience in All Relations in Life to Promote Peace, Progress and Spiritual Enlightenment by Muata Ashby ISBN: 1-884564-95-X

Based on the books:

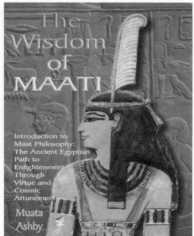

INTRODUCTION TO MAAT PHILOSOPHY: Spiritual Enlightenment Through the Path of Virtue

SACRED SEXUALITY: ANCIENT EGYPTIAN TANTRA YOGA: The Art of Sex Sublimation and Universal Consciousness

TABLE OF CONTENTS

Contents

Table of Questions and Answers

Table of Figures

ABOUT THE AUTHOR

Dr. Muata Ashby began studies in the area of religion and philosophy and achieved a doctorate degree in these areas while at the same time he began to collect his research into what would later become several books on the subject of the African History, religion and ethics, world mythology, origins of Yoga Philosophy and practice in ancient Africa (Ancient Egypt/Nubia) and also the origins of Christianity in Ancient Egypt. This was the catalyst for a successful book series on the subject called "Egyptian Yoga" begun in 1994. He has extensively studied mystical religious traditions from around the world and is an accomplished lecturer, musician, artist, poet, painter, screenwriter, playwright, and author of over 65 books on yoga philosophy, religious philosophy and social philosophy based on ancient African principles. A leading advocate of the concept of the existence of advanced social and religious philosophy in ancient Africa comparable to the Eastern traditions such as Vedanta, Buddhism, Confucianism, and Taoism, he has lectured and written extensively on the correlations of these with ancient African religion and philosophy.

Muata Abhaya Ashby holds a Doctor of Divinity Degree from the American Institute of Holistic Theology and a Master's degree in Liberal Arts and Religious Studies from Thomas Edison State College. He has performed extensive researched Ancient Egyptian philosophy and social order as well as Maat philosophy, the ethical foundation of Ancient Egyptian society.

Dr. Ashby has been an independent researcher and practitioner of Egyptian Yoga, Indian Yoga, Chinese Yoga, Buddhism and mystical psychology as well as Christian Mysticism. Dr. Ashby has engaged in Post Graduate research in advanced Jnana, Bhakti, and Kundalini Yogas at the Yoga Research Foundation.

Since 1999 he has researched Ancient Egyptian musical theory and created a series of musical compositions which explore this unique area of music from ancient Africa and its connection to world music. Dr. Ashby has lectured around the United States of America, Europe, and Africa.

In recent years he has researched the world economy in the last 300 years, focusing on the United States of America and western culture in general. He is also a Teacher of Yoga Philosophy and Discipline. Dr. Ashby is an adjunct professor at the American Institute of Holistic Theology and worked as an adjunct professor at the Florida International University.

In the last two years with the reorganization of the Kemet University and the introduction of the Egyptian Mystery School along with a tailored learning system making use of the Ancient Egyptian Temple teaching elements along with modern technologies Dr. Ashby has engendered a new phase of dissemination of the teachings introducing a new dynamism to the books as well as the live lectures given over the last 25 years.

Currently, he is focusing on projects related to the temples of Aset and of Asar, doing detailed photographic work and presenting new original translations of the related hieroglyphic scriptures while teaching those through the Kemet University Egyptian Mystery School online and through in person seminars and conferences.

KEMET UNIVERSITY
Egyptian Mysteries School

Dr. Muata Ashby began to function in the capacity of *Sebai* or Spiritual Preceptor of Shetaut Neter, Ancient Egyptian Religion [Including the Temple of Aset] and also as Ethics Philosopher and Religious Studies instructor. When operating as a professor in an academic setting he is addressed as Dr. Ashby. When operating in the capacity of temple priest he is addressed as Sebai MAA.

Through his studies of the teachings of the great philosophers of the world and meeting with and studying under spiritual masters and having practiced advanced meditative disciplines, Dr. Ashby began to function in the capacity of Sebai or Spiritual Preceptor of Shetaut Neter, Ancient Egyptian Religion and also as Ethics Philosopher and Religious Studies instructor. Thus his title is Sebai and the acronym of his Kemetic and western names is MAA. He believes that it is important to understand all religious teachings in the context of human historical, cultural and social development in order to promote greater understanding and the advancement of humanity.

TEMPLE OF SHETAUT NETER

The Sema Institute

Kemet University

www.Egyptianyoga.com

www.KemetUniversity.com

Introduction: Kemetic Maat Culture and Philosophy and Ancient African Relationships Wisdom

As originally explained in the book: MATRIX OF AFRICAN PROVERBS: Spiritual Ethics for Civilization based on African Proverbial Wisdom Teachings[2009], Chapter 1: The *Triune African Relationships:* An African Concept of Three Human Relations. There are three forms of relationships in African Culture and Ancient Egyptian culture is an African culture.

In African Ethics it is recognized that a human being is interconnected with the world, with other individuals, and with a subtle cosmic essence that permeates nature and the wider universe. Therefore, there are three important relationships that every human being needs to be concerned with. The quality of the relationships determines the quality of life and the outcome, the eschatology of the human journey of life and the fate after death. Some African religious traditions, for example, hold an eschatology of dying and becoming a revered ancestor, living forever in the realm of the Supreme Being, while others hold the ideal of becoming one with the Absolute and transcendental Supreme Being. In any case the triune ethical foundation for life promotes the desired goal. Thus, a human being works through three dimensions of experience in human life in order to seek fulfillment in life and after death. These foundations may be thought of as ethical constructs but in actuality, they are also aspects of African Religious practice. The three Fundamental Concepts of African Socio-spiritual Ethics are:

A. **The concept of relationship to family** -The human in relation to the human world.

B. **The concept of relationship to village** - The human in relation to the social world.

C. **The concept of relationship to the universal Spirit** -that expresses as all nature and transcendental of nature - The human in relation to the Spirit and the spiritual world.

Figure 1: The Triune Matrix of Human Relations

The *Matrix of African Proverbs* may be thought of as a triangle within which the individual (Self) exists in the world, connected to Spirit, Family and Community [society, politics, etc.]. So let's begin by looking at how this triune concept of African spiritual ethics manifests in the Proverbial Wisdom Teachings of Ancient Egypt. The Triune Conceptualizations of African Ethical Philosophy are readily discernible in the following statements contained in the Ancient Egyptian Wisdom Texts. One of the collections of aphorisms that are part of the greater tradition of African Proverbial Wisdom Teachings that may be found throughout African cultures and African History, come from Ancient Egyptian civilization, going back to 3,000 B.C.E. or earlier. Some authors refer to this triune concept as a system of religious morals.[1] The family and community relations are the foundation for being able to attain the proper relation with Spirit.

Figure 2: Movement of Human relations from Foundation to Spirit.

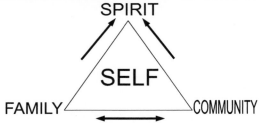

The *Matrix of African Proverbs* may also be conceptualized as a point in the center wherein the individual exists within ever expanding realms of relationships, to Family, Community, and God (Spirit). Each layer requires more expansion and with each expansion, there is a coming closer to the ultimate reality wherein all relationships are fulfilled.

---

[1] *Introduction to African Religion Second Edition* by John S. Mite, *Morals in African Religion,*

Figure 3: The Three Human Relations as Concentric Expanding Circles

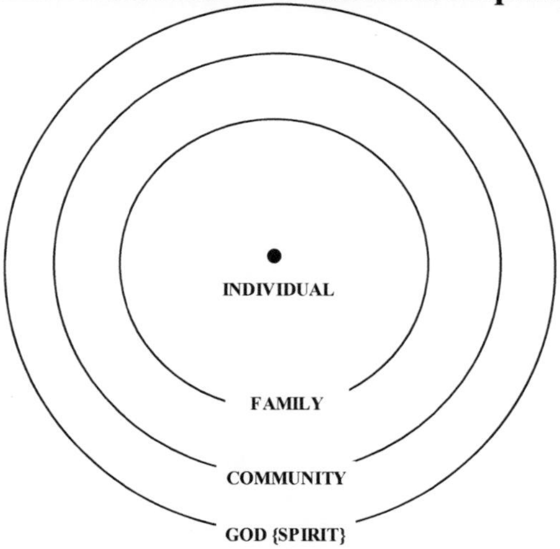

INDIVIDUAL

FAMILY

COMMUNITY

GOD {SPIRIT}

In this volume, we will be concentrating on the aspect or relationships in a family that relates to male/female relations in romantic, conjugal and philosophical contexts.

Ancient Egyptian Wisdom Foundations for Kemetic Relationships Philosophy

This program was, as I said before, it was instigated by the need to have a clearer understanding of the Kemetic concepts of relationships and marriage, specifically for anyone who wants to enter into marriage now but generally for everyone else especially those who are in a relationship at this time or who are contemplating and desiring to enter into a relationship.

This volume is not and was not intended as a sentimental kind of "how to" manual with instructions on how to make your relationship and or marriage work wonderfully and how you can be great partners and hold hands all the time and walk into the sunset forever and to the end of time, etc. I am being a little sarcastic but you get the point. This is not intended as a "New Age" just believe and everything will be perfect – program since in real life that sells books but does not work in relationships unless people are deluded, in which case why take this course?

This volume is going to be more related to a realistic and philosophical outlook which as some of you, people who have not attended lectures or do not know me from that standpoint or who are coming new or fresh to it may take it in the wrong way. I have given, in the past, some touchy-feely programs as appropriate. What I mean by this term is a program that caters to or emphasizes sentimentalities and feelings, which have their place. I refer you to the lecture that we did six years ago in Atlanta and also we did a previous lecture series, back in the 1990's within the Maat lecture series, there is a section on relationships and marriage also. So, I refer you to those. This present series will emphasize more of the philosophy and wisdom behind the Kemetic Marital Ethics but also the ethical Maatian principles as they are to be applied to other relationships such as with friends, parents, and children, nature, animals, other countries, etc.. The following principles will act as guides for our study of Kemetic Relationships.

THE KEMETIC PRINCIPLES OF MARRIAGE

- Ancient Egyptian proverbs and wisdom precepts on relationships and marriage:

- "Souls, Horus, son, are of the self-same nature, since they came from the same place where the Creator modeled them; nor male nor female are they. Sex is a thing of bodies not of Souls."

- "Take a wife while you are young,
  that she may make a son for you
  while you are youthful..." (Instructions of Ani)

- "When thou find sensibility of heart, joined with softness of manners, an accomplished mind, with a form agreeable to thy fancy, take her home to thy house; she is worthy to be thy friend, thy companion in life, the wife of thy bosom."

- "Remember thou art man's reasonable companion, not the slave of his passion; the end of thy being is not merely to gratify his loose desire, but to assist him in the toils of life, to soothe him with thy tenderness, and recompense his care and like treatment with soft endearments."

- "When you prosper and establish your home, love your wife with ardor. Then fill her belly and clothe her back. Caress her. Give her ointments to soothe her body. Fulfill her wishes for as long as you live. She is a fertile field for her husband. Do not be brutal. Good manners will influence her better than force. Do not contend with her in the courts. Keep her from the need to resort to outside powers. Her eye is her storm when she gazes. It is by such treatment that she will be compelled to stay in your house."

- "There is no happiness for the soul in the external worlds since these are perishable, true happiness lies in that which is eternal, within us."

- "Good things cease to be good in our wrong enjoyment of them. What nature meant to be pure sweetness, are then sources of bitterness to us; from such delights arise pain, from such joys, sorrows."

Some of what I will be discussing is contained in the book, *Sacred Sexuality: Egyptian Tantric Yoga*, and some of the images and things you will see come out of that book also. Additionally, other references will be the books *Introduction to Maat Philosophy* and *The Ancient Egyptian Wisdom Texts*.

So, with that basic caveat, I will go further now and say that some of the things that will be said are going to be undoubtedly, how should we say, designed to burst certain bubbles or certain concepts and delusions that you may have about relationships and marriage, so there's an element of poison in what will be taught here as opposed to the concepts you may have learned growing up in a decadent society of modern times. So, if you don't want your long held ideas or traditions to be poisoned, that is to say, if you don't want to give up your illusions about your concepts of relationship and your erroneous and futile ideals or your insatiable quest for fulfillment of desires as you may have come to believe those to be based on the general culture and worldly culture, and so on and so forth, if you do not want those ideas to be poisoned, to be dispelled, then you should not be listening to this program, or this series of talks. The reason is because that is one of the goals of the series, to dispel those delusions, to poison those erroneous concepts so that they will eventually die; not necessarily slowly and not necessarily fast but a progressive death.

And what is the purpose of doing that? The purpose of poisoning the illusions is so that it may be possible to fill the emptiness of illusory human desires with the fullness of spiritual enlightenment. This is the real purpose of relationships and not just for mindless pleasure or procreation, being in a family, etc. If you have any kind of illusions or delusions in life even be they wonderful ones, good ones, from a relative standpoint, positive ones, they will hold you back on your quest for spiritual enlightenment and even in your ideals of human relationships, that is to say if you have a wonderful person that you're partners with and they please you and they do everything you like and they provide for you, they never disappoint you, so called, that will be just as delusional, illusory as much as an obstacle if you have someone that you fight with all the time, that disappoints you, that annoys you.

Illusoriness of Relationships

And so, therefore, we come to the conception of the idea that this kind of talk is poison in the beginning and nectar in the end, whereas worldly pleasures and worldly sentimental relationships are nectar in the beginning and poison in the end because even those who say that they're happy in their relationships, and they may be so from a relative standpoint, they go out together and they may even finish each other's sentences and they take care of each other and so on and so forth; however, and there is always a however, in the end there is the pain of illness, of old age, letting go, death, and so on and so forth. This is what we might refer to as a worldly or egoistic, sentimental, deluded form of relationships. Those who live their lives thinking that that is the goal of life, they attain that limited goal. Those who live by a philosophical conception can have that goal in a correct way but also attain the higher goal of life which is attaining spiritual enlightenment.

So, throughout this document, there are some proverbs that we will look at, which cover the themes that I just discussed that will help us along the journey of Kemetic wisdom about relationships. One important Kemetic proverb is:

"Good things cease to be good in the wrong enjoyment of them. What nature meant to be pure sweetness are then sources of bitterness to us. From such delights our eyes pain, from such joys our eyes sorrows."

And that, in brief, is the predicament of worldly relationships. Not that you should not have pleasure, not that you should not have friendships, not that you should not get to enjoy holding hands and all that kind of thing, because seeking companionship and sex and all these kinds of things are parts of life, however, they are not all of life; the issue is the wrong enjoyment of them, the wrong understanding of them, the conception that they are the goal of life as if they were something real and abiding, whereas actually, the opposite is true. And if you were to have an understanding, you could have enjoyments and be free from the negative aspects of them and that happens if you determine yourself to follow the Maatian Path, and that is the philosophical foundation of this talk.

HOW DID MARRIAGE COME TO BE THOUGHT OF AS IT IS TODAY?

The idea of marriage as a sacred sacrament, which comes to us today in modern culture arises from the orthodox Catholic church. It comes in with the rise of Western culture especially, where the church took upon itself the task of organizing marriage so that there would not be disorder in the society. In the beginning of Christianity the church did not control or sanction marriage and some of the early church leaders actually shunned marriage in favor of the single and celibate life. However, most people could not maintain the vows of celibacy. They found there were too many bastards running around and men were not taking care of their families, things like that, so the church leaders decided to say, "Okay. Well, marriage is a sacrament and it is governed by God and you're going to have to come to church and be married or we excommunicate you and you go to hell, etc." So, the idea of marriage as being a holy sacrament of the church was invented out of necessity. That may come as a shock to some of you but that is actually the historical record. Over centuries people have been indoctrinated into the society and its ideas of marriage and that became the tradition people believe in today for the most part. Before that, there was no governance of marriage, as such in western culture or thought of marriage as an institution, shall we call it. So marriage by the church was not in the beginning of the Christian church; it began further along in history. In the beginning, the Christian church, which became dominant and forced people within the control of the Roman empire to convert to Christianity (including Ancient Egypt by this time) shunned marriage because they thought, in some respects rightly, that it was a way of intensifying worldliness. The early church leaders were trying to follow a more austere and devotional path [even as this form of following was deficient since they only practiced reverence of the myth of Jesus and rituals around that but not the mystical philosophy side of religion]. Nevertheless, most people (including the church leaders) could not follow that path. The leaders actually tried to get people to not marry and to stay away from having sex and even castrate themselves, but they found that it didn't work because people could not control themselves then just as they cannot today. They could not control themselves in ancient times and so, therefore, they decided that they needed to do something about the issue. Otherwise, they were going to have a mess in terms of wayward populations, promiscuous communities and a proliferation of out of wedlock births. Therefore, they decided to institute marriage as a church sacrament.

MARRIAGE IN ANCIENT EGYPT

Now, as we go on, I wanted to introduce a couple of other concepts. Firstly, I want to delineate between the understanding of Neterian (Ancient Egyptian Religion) culture as opposed to Kemetic culture. Neterian culture is the religious side of Ancient Egyptian life, the non-secular. It includes the Shetaut Neter (Ancient Egyptian Mysteries religion), the Sebait (ancient Egyptian Spiritual Philosophy), which is the mystical philosophy; it includes the gods and goddesses.

The Kemetic culture has a tendency more towards the secular side and this side is governed by Maat philosophy, by Maat law. And the first important lesson for you to understand about Kemetic marriage and, by extension, Kemetic relationships, is that it is covered by Kemetic culture as opposed to Neterian culture. So, in other words, you would not be expecting someone in Ancient Egypt to be going to a temple to be married by a priest. That did not happen. However, Maat secular culture and law formed a foundation for spiritual evolution as well as the secular married life.

So, how did marriage work in Ancient Egypt then? As I said before, marriage in Ancient Egypt was governed by the civil authorities and by the Maatian philosophy, the Maatian court, and essentially two people, a man, and a woman could be married by simply agreeing to do so. And it was very common to have a marriage contract that specified the legal, shall we say, the rights and sometimes responsibilities of each partner in the marital relationship. And this is very important to understand that in Ancient Egypt, the culture had developed to such a high degree that it was understood that the genders are equal and complementary in human existence; that is to say that male dominance or female dominance would be incompatible with Maatian culture, and this is part of the reason for the success of Ancient Egypt and that it allowed people to develop maturity and not to have undue stress and strain put on them by telling them that they have to get married and God is watching, if they don't stay married forever even though their family life and their personal life may be a mess and people are cheating on them and whatever, that they have to stay married because otherwise, they're going to go to hell; thus all that guilt and other nonsense was invented by the church.

As a human being, a male or a female, you are the supreme arbiter and responsible entity for your existence and therefore having that capacity you also are the architect of your destiny; you create your life, and what you create becomes your fate. If you create with a burden of ignorance and falsehood and stress, then what you create will be something less than ideal and the highest ideal of attaining enlightenment will be elusive in a given lifetime, then you have to come back and do it over again as we know, and so on and so forth.

So, the ideal of marriage then is for two people who are secure in their personhood, who do not have to be subservient to the other person, people who can be mature, who can be powerful and not just mature and powerful but also comfortable in their life to choose without undue stress and without having the choice forced on you by parents or forced on you by economics or all the different kinds of pressures, artificial pressures that a society or that one's own ignorance can place on one. This can be the internal pressure from the desire to find companionship like other peers but not out of maturity but instead out of codependency, the need, sometimes desperate, to be in a paired relationship due to feeling lack or incomplete or because society says if you are not married with children you are a loser, or a less than worthy human being, etc. There can be many psychological complexes used as reasons and they lead to misery and unfulfilled relations generally. Of course, when a decision is made out of stress, delusion or ignorance, the outcome will likely be negative in the short run (present lifetime) even when it serves the higher goal of purifying the personality in the long run, through suffering.

Therefore, if one chooses to be married and one chooses to cohabitate with someone or chooses to have children and so on, then one's life has a greater chance of being fulfilled. That is, if done by mature reflection, to fulfil ordinary and sane worldly desires and inclinations, in other words, with non-coerced, non-codependent (abnormal and unhealthy psychological dependencies) reasons and without undue pressures, since, in the mature choices, one can have freedom, and one will not be doing things out of fear, fear of loss, "I'm going to lose this person and I want them," or because "I don't know if I can go away, where am I going to go, where am I going to live, how am I going to live, alone" and all those kinds of fears and insecurities. In Ancient Egypt, everyone's rights and property were protected by contract and there is a maat law that all are provided with food, shelter, and sustenance. So no one needed to feel compelled to live with others for economic convenience or fear or being destitute.

What they call prenuptial agreements today were very common in Ancient Egypt. It avoids the issue of finances or it would tend to prevent as much as possible, not fully but as much as possible the uncertainty of finances, the uncertainty of legal issues in a marriage and other eventualities. So people could feel more comfortable to engage in a relationship or to leave a relationship, out of choice. When you have more freedom of choice you are more comfortable taking on the amount of responsibility for a higher good out of freedom and true caring instead of out of fear and weakness. Also, you tend to your responsibility knowing the partner also has a responsibility to do theirs or that person can leave you if they're perceiving that you're not fulfilling your responsibilities and without the undue stress of the society and the church being on top of them and saying, "No, you have to stay in the marriage even if it was a mistake or the two are causing each other constant misery, etc. Of course, back then also you had a situation where it was more of a village environment and no inflated currencies raising prices constantly keeping people's nose to grindstones and constant stress. Therefore, also, there was not so much concern for children or what's going to happen to the children and broken families, etc. Life was more natural and it was all easier in a sane culture with ethical values and a truly advanced society. Additionally, you also had extended families, you had other people who understood and who did not make more of it than was necessary. So, the legal aspects of the marriage were controlled by the Maatian ideal, founded in sanity, maturity and positive social support.

Another proverb that is to be understood is related to the teaching of Aset to Heru, which states that the souls have no gender. [highlighted section by Dr. Ashby for emphasis]

> "Sex is a thing of bodies, not of souls." pain, from such joys our eyes sorrow."

And I think this is the foundation of the equality of gender in Ancient Egypt. This is one of the pillars. It is extremely important for you to understand that the manifestation of the soul in gender form, in female or male form, is merely a tendency of cosmic forces, of *aryu* (sum total of a person's past actions, thoughts, feelings, desires and their results that direct a persons present day feelings, thoughts, and desires) within yourself. In other words, you're manifesting as a male or a female because of the tendency of the cosmic forces that you have engendered over time in this and past lifetimes and attached yourself to. So, in one incarnation you may manifest as a woman or as a man because of certain feelings and desires that you have engendered in a previous life. In Ancient Egyptian, this teaching is called "uhem ankh" – to live again, do over life once more. It is also taught in the Pert M Heru or Book of the Dead [real name Book of Enlightenment][2], and of course, if you're manifesting both in a more mixed way, you may come out physically as a hermaphrodite or you might come out as someone who's called gay or homosexual and if the aryu is of such nature you may be physically one way and mentally another, etc. The important thing to understand is all souls are beyond gender so gender is experienced the more intensely a person is attached to the physical realities of human existence and their complicated variations. That issue, of course, gets into many esoteric aspects of the Egyptian Mysteries and beyond the scope of this work at present.[3] You may go to the other books for details and extensive wisdom on those teachings. For now suffice to say that underneath it all, you're still a soul who has manifested as male and female in the past, and that is a higher reality than your physical existence and its attendant gender tendencies at present. Therefore your manifestation either as a male or female now is in no way any kind of determiner of your higher nature or a blight or a detriment to you as a human being and so, therefore, your value and higher nature as a soul being cannot be determined and or limited by gender.

So, with that brief historical introductory background, looking below you can see the Ancient Egyptian Hieroglyphs that are related to the Kemetic (Ancient Egyptian) concept of marriage. Let's go over those and then we'll continue to go over the other proverbs.

---

[2] An Ancient Egyptian treatise founded in Maat Philosophy for ethical social and spiritual life. For more on the issue, see the *EGYPTIAN BOOK OF THE DEAD* by Dr. Muata Ashby
[3] For more on the issue of gender and homosexuality see the book *Conversations with God* by Dr. Muata Ashby

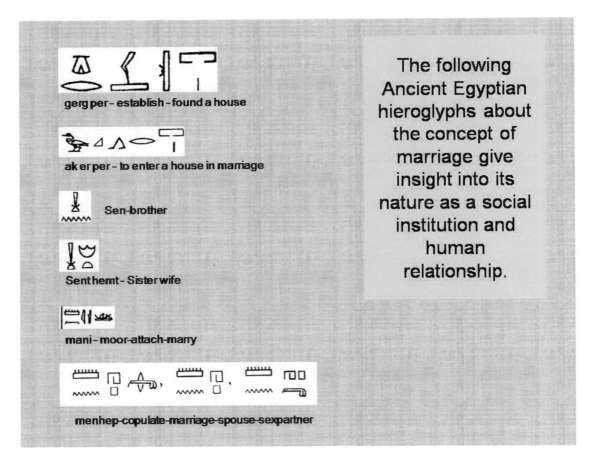

gerg per - establish - found a house

ak er per - to enter a house in marriage

Sen - brother

Sent hemt - Sister wife

mani - moor - attach - marry

menhep - copulate - marriage - spouse - sex partner

The following Ancient Egyptian hieroglyphs about the concept of marriage give insight into its nature as a social institution and human relationship.

The first hieroglyphic term we will look at is "gerg per", to establish or to found a house. When two people come together to create what we call today as a marriage, it's called "gerg per" which is like starting an organization, a foundation that does work in the community; you're like a founder or somebody founds an institution or they're a founder of some organization In this case you're the founders or co-founders of a house or a home and per means –building; it's something similar to the Per in *Per Heru*. The term *ak er per* means, to go into or to enter a building with the intent of going into a marriage or a house in the form of a marriage, meaning that you're accepting and you're willingly going into a relationship, a marital relationship. Those who are men and women who are married, then also can be referred to as brothers and sisters. That should not be confused with the concept, in other countries, of incest. All human beings are kin to each other so all are brothers and sisters. Also, in Ancient Egypt, there was no polygamy or polyandry (a man has several wives or the wife has several husbands).

In Ancient Egypt, it was customary to marry and one could also divorce. One could divorce for a myriad of reasons including you just don't want to be married anymore or the person committed adultery or some other breach of contract, etc.; so you have that freedom. It is to be understood that in certain cases like the pharaoh, polygamy might've been allowed especially due to political reasons because political alliances were made through marriage as much as by treaty in ancient times. But that was not a common practice of either the royalty or the general common folk of Ancient Egypt. The term for brother is *sen* and the term for a sister is *sent*. Another term that is used is *mani* depending on how it's pronounced which means to moor and it is a symbol of a boat that is wandering around, playing the field and doing whatever, but then a person who has decided to moor. So, it also means a commitment not to be promiscuous, not to be running around, and it is a choice that you're making to moor yourself as like a boat tying itself, mooring itself to a pier and not sailing the seas anymore. And then there's another term called *menhep* which means to have sexual relationships but this is in the context of a marriage. Here is an Ancient Kemetic proverb relating to sexuality:

> "Be circumspect in matters of sexual relations."

Going forward to the next proverbs now, these are actually either proverbs or they are teachings from the sages and this particular one comes from sage Ani where it says,

> "Take a wife while you're young, that she may make a son for you while you are youthful."

In Ancient Kemet, you have to realize that there is a teaching for the Initiates, the *Asaru,* and there's a teaching for the common folk, who are referred to as *rekhyt.* The rekhyt are encouraged to marry, have children and carry on a householder lifestyle if that's what they want. At some point, also, from the ranks of the rekhyt, there are going to be individuals developing spiritually, who may work for temple initiation and move beyond simple householder life. But there is no contradiction in the society, with the teaching and the worldly ideals of people. Priests and priestesses can marry and have families though, obviously, their outlook on life is dramatically different as it is guided by the Maatian teaching more closely and in a more non-secular form as opposed to that which is followed by the rekhyt. So, those who want to do more worldly things may do so within the limits of Maat secular philosophy and those who want to follow the path of the temple more closely may also do so by following the non-secular aspects of Maat Philosophy. In this context, we've shown that there were people in Ancient Egypt who ate meat and yet the teaching to the Initiates was to be vegetarian. So it is recognized that some people are at a particular level of human development while others are at another.

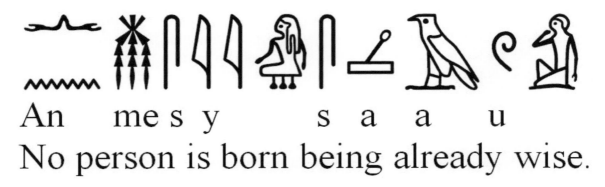

An   me s y   s   a   a   u

No person is born being already wise.

In the same way, since every new generation of human beings needs to explore and discover their path in life, they also need to be taught the wisdom that society has amassed and assisted to adopt it for the betterment of society as a whole. So, in order for the society to continue to forge ahead, it's necessary to have new human beings coming in because human beings are always dying as well, though this idea also recognizes that not everyone is sufficiently mature enough to adopt all the wisdom and best practices as discovered by the wise leaders of society and attain enlightenment in the present lifetime. So, that's one purpose for procreation, the continuation of society. And what is the purpose of continuing society? The purpose of continuing human society is for allowing individual human beings (ignorant souls) to have an entry point into time and space so as to be able to have human experiences; for them to be able to come in and to have a venue in order to gain knowledge of self through those human experiences. From a grander perspective, it is a capacity for physical life to exist so that spirit may have a vehicle for manifesting and experiencing itself in the form of creation and interacting with itself in the forms present throughout Creation.

Moving along with the next proverb,

"When thou find sensibility of heart, joined with softness of manners, an accomplished mind with the form agreeable to thy fancy, take her home to thy house; she is worthy to be thy friend, thy companion in life, the wife of thy bosom."

In this teaching, the sage is especially highlighting the sensibility of heart, joined with softness of manners, accomplished mind, accomplished intellect and agreeable form. So, it is giving some possible criteria for selecting a mate, not necessarily someone who is boisterous or worldly or running around all the time; and not someone who is dumb or who is like most people in this culture who revel in ignorance and faith-based culture, a culture of personality and sentimental nonsense values. An agreeable form implies someone who is appealing aesthetically, who cares about their body, which in turn means caring about health as well. However, one is not to seek a mate only on the basis of physical looks or physical appeal.

> "Remember thou art made man's reasonable companion, not the slave of his passion; the end of thy being is not merely to gratify his loose desire, but to assist him in the toils of life, to soothe him with thy tenderness and recompense his care and like treatment with soft endearments."

Now this one particularly seems to be directed to women although the other one may seem to be directed to men; it's still also directed to women as well, seeking a sensible and mature person in a man for marriage. But here, this particular proverb is reflective of the greatness of the Ancient Egyptian wisdom of marriage in that pretty much virtually, not exactly all, but virtually in every culture that we can think of, the reverse is either overtly or subtly encouraged, meaning that women are encouraged to be slaves of the passion of men and the ideal woman is the woman who doesn't nag and a woman who is ready to have sex all the time whenever the man wants to have sex, etc.; that's the male ideal that is projected in the male-oriented culture and so the woman should be a reasonable companion, a partner, and not a slave to the passions of man, and not just related to sexual passions but also whatever other passions the man may have. So in this society, it's not whatever the man wants they do, and whatever he says goes, etc. This proverb is also directed to men from the standpoint that they should not be seeking a woman who would allow themselves to be manipulated or diminished. Additionally, it means that the man better behaves because otherwise, the woman may leave him, so this again demonstrates the independence and personal sovereignty of women in Ancient Egyptian society as well as a certain level of independence and lack of over-dependency.

So the Ancient Egyptian marriage is supposed to be a partnership for people to help each other, on the path of life and the spiritual path to attain enlightenment, which in a higher sense is one and the same path. That's the highest goal of life, and some of the objectives towards that goal may include working so you can have a nice house that you can live in; nice from the standpoint of not expensive and big but nice that you're going to be comfortable, so that you have all your practical physical needs met and everyone works to do their part, not that one works and brings in income while the other sits around and neither should be a slave –to the other or to the work ethic of the Western culture that the male is supposed to work and produce the bread and the woman is supposed to stay at home or that both should work and have no life. Some cultures may go even further and still believe in the adage that, a "woman should stay barefoot and pregnant" all the time, etc.

That is all nonsense from the perspective of Kemetic Relationship wisdom; that is all ignorance, all concepts of an ignorant barbarous or worldly or primitive culture that has not matured to the level of Ancient Egyptian culture. This is how advanced Ancient Egyptian culture was and through us, it can resurge to a level that we can manifest even now. So, it's important for men to understand these principles and it's important for women to understand as well so that they can have a balanced and well-adjusted relationship, and so that they will not be relying on each other for happiness or for pleasures that are inordinate and thereby avoid the pitfalls of ignorant and immature relationships.

Naturally, people want to please each other; they want to make each other happy and things like that and that is a normal aspect of egoistic human existence, the desire to make another happy so that one can feel good about oneself by giving joy to another and receiving pleasure from a happy person, etc. On the receiving end, the joy felt by having someone care for one is also needed for certain aspects of the personality's evolution and development of self-worth, etc. But the inordinate pursuit of that pleasure-seeking and pleasure-giving so as to feel happy or fulfilled through egoistic human relations leads to emotional imbalance, intensification of ego either when things go well or when emotional support or pleasure is withdrawn for any reason (intentional or otherwise) and to ultimate disaster in terms of relationship deterioration. If people work together, they can produce great things; if one group of people try to impose themselves on others, try to enslave others, it leads to an emotional, ethical, and spiritual disaster for themselves and for the enslaved.

"When you prosper and establish your home, love your wife with ardor. Then fill her belly and clothe her back. Caress her. Give her ointments to soothe her body. Fulfill her wishes for as long as you live. She is a fertile field for her husband. Do not be brutal. Good manners will influence her better than force. Do not contend with her in the courts. Keep her from the need to resort to outside powers. Her eye is her storm when she gazes. It is by such treatment that she will be compelled to stay in your house."

Of course, these apply to the males and females, for the males and females to treat each other with warmth and with kindness and to doing what you can to meet the necessities, not necessarily the desires, of the other person. Necessities are a normal and "necessary" part of life while desires can be for inordinate and ultimately detrimental things. A child needs nutritious food but may desire candy. Providing the necessary nutrients is proper and will tend to perpetuate the relationship with health over a long time while providing the sweets for short-term pleasure and satisfaction will, in a short time, lead to disease and ultimately damage the relationship. And again, a caution is provided for men who are generally physically stronger than females; that difference in physical capacities is not meaningful as to the worth of either, as a human being, but rather a difference for complementary social interactions and progress. So it is a permission to physically dominate, hit women or be verbally abusive or otherwise hurtful. Instead, men should strive to use reason and or calm, during interactions, while trying to reach a resolution based on truth and justice (Maat) instead of egoistic personal desires or delusions of superiority. If these injunctions were to be followed honestly and forthrightly then there should be little reason to resort to going to court over disputes. Rather, the ethical conscience demands following the spirit of the Maatian wisdom as reflected in a Kemetic Marriage Contract and that should allow you to work things out in an amicable manner with reason and truth and Maatian (justice) order that will lead to HTP or peace before, during and after the relationship is over.

The aforesaid applies to those who are in a mature and balanced relationship, not for those of you who may be listening to this in the future or even now who are in relationships where you're imbalanced, where you are involved with a person who is worldly or who is unrighteous or mentally unstable. etc. You may have to go to court and let the court deal with things. But this is for those of you who may be entering into a relationship with a person who is initiated into this ideal philosophy and who agrees with this ideal, this culture of Maat wisdom. You should work to have amicable relations as you're entering into as well as exiting a relationship. For those who are in relationships already and only now becoming initiated into this Kemetic Marriage philosophy, you need to learn it well and work together, dealing with both of your egoisms, to a point where you can both agree to its benefits in principle, in spirit and legally also; so for anyone who wants to adopt this teaching, if you do and if you go all the way to creating a premarital Kemetic Marriage Contract, you should also agree that if a time comes when there is a need to break up that you will follow the parameters in the contract as your legal path instead of going to settle things with lawyers in the courts. In other words, the Kemetic Marriage Contract will be your legal agreement and it can be filed with the courts as well just as any regular "prenuptial" agreement would in the ordinary society.

In this context then, you should try to see the other person, as I said here, as a fertile field and yourself for that person as well. The relationship with the other person is a venue for theirs and your inner self to develop in. This is the real purpose of having a relationship. And the reason why you enter into a relationship is to fulfill a gap, to fulfill something that is missing, which is not filled by the other person but is filled by your discovering it within yourself by means of the experiences and wisdom attained through relationships. For example, discovering inner peace and self-worth may occur in a conducive relationship where one is confronted with experiences that necessitate exploring and cultivating those aspects of the personality, etc.

Now, of course, all this can get distorted in many different ways. Women can come to feel that men are dogs and they can come to feel that women are cats and men can feel that women are there mainly for their pleasure and women can feel that the men are there for their use, to take care of them and to provide for them so that they can live their lives, have children, etc., and to that extent, they service the needs of men. This is a selfish utilitarian view of relationships. It's a very degraded kind of conception of life and it's very ego intensifying as well which leads to people in such relationships moving farther away from enlightenment and more towards the creation of negative worldly *Aryu* that is full of sorrow and pain and discord.

Another Ancient Egyptian proverb that I would add to the list is,

"There is no happiness for the soul in the external worlds since these are perishable, indiscernible true happiness lies in that which is eternal, within us."

And, of course, that which is eternal within us is the soul. Since the gender of an individual is illusory and the soul is the true higher nature of self, you cannot expect to find abiding happiness in any relationship but with that same higher self. No matter how wonderful it may seem to work out; no matter how great, like I said before, you may seem to go hand in hand and you're soulmates and you finish each other's sentences and all that kind of thing, it's all illusory because it's perishable and changeable. Anything that is changeable and perishable is illusory. Anything that is illusory will inevitably lead to loss and pain if it is leaned upon as one's source of happiness and not treated with Maat, realizing its true nature and purpose. If it's treated, as I said before, with the correct understanding, then there will be a right enjoyment of it, there will be a positive experience through it and that is the ideal of the Kemetic Marriage and that will be a Maatian foundation for you to develop into a kind of personality that is capable and suitable for higher initiation and higher spiritual development. That is an introduction to the philosophy behind the Kemetic marriage. Now in this document, there is a sample of a Kemetic marriage contract or agreement.

Figure 4: An Ancient Egyptian Family

There is an important teaching relevant to Ancient Egyptian iconography related to the Kemetic family. In the image above you can see a husband and a wife and a little boy and a little girl. You'll notice that the males are painted in red and the females are painted in white and that is not at all to be taken to mean that the Ancient Egyptians were red and white. That is ridiculous. That is nonsense. The idea is that this is an idealistic portrayal. In iconographical portrayals you have idealistic and you have naturalistic portrayals. The naturalistic shows people in their original, true hues, their skin color and we find them in either dark black or brown or light brown as Ancient Egyptians. As for the red and white color, red symbolizes spirit in this context and white symbolizes creation. The union of the two, like the symbol of the ankh, a circle tied with a vertical line, relates to the coming together of spirit with matter to create life.

Figure 5: An Ancient Egyptian Ankh symbol

In this way, the male and female genders complement each other; the spirit that goes into matter and creates a living existence through a child. A child is seen in this context as an androgynous idea of life as opposed to a male or a female. As the child develops from an embryo, it differentiates into a gender.

HETEP-Peace

Chapter 1: Major Themes and Issues in Marriages and Solutions through Kemetic Marriage Philosophy

Major Themes

- Ancient Egyptian proverbs
- "Souls, Horus, son, are of the self-same nature, since they came from the same place where the Creator modeled them; nor male nor female are they. Sex is a thing of bodies not of Souls."

- "There is no happiness for the soul in the external worlds since these are perishable, true happiness lies in that which is eternal, within us."

- "Good things cease to be good in our wrong enjoyment of them. What nature meant to be pure sweetness, are then sources of bitterness to us; from such delights arise pain, from such joys, sorrows."

- "There are two roads traveled by humankind, those who seek to live MAAT and those who seek to satisfy their animal passions."

Recapping some major themes that are running through our program, these are the key teachings that undergird or act as the foundation for the entire understanding of the teaching of Kemetic relationships; they are as if the foundational philosophy behind Kemetic relationships.

The first one is the teaching of Aset to Heru where she explains to him that sex is a thing of bodies, not of souls. Souls come from the same place and have the same source so are not different. They're from the selfsame nature where they originated, where the creator modeled them. That is the first important principle to understand, that the souls of men and women are one and the same and not different or separate.

And there's another proverb we're going to be talking about later on which is the teaching from the wisdom text that body belongs to the earth and soul belongs to heaven.

The next proverb is that,
"There is no happiness for the soul in the external worlds since these are perishable. True happiness lies in that which is eternal within us."

And the next proverb,
"Good thing cease to be good in our wrong enjoyment of them. What nature meant to be pure, sweetness are then sources of bitterness to us. From such delights arise pain, from such joys, arise sorrows."

And the other important proverb is, "There are two roads traveled by humankind, those who seek to live Maat and those who seek to satisfy their animal passions." We've explored those teachings and perhaps now we're going to see some further dimensions to them.

In the slide above, we have various scenes of people being together, of people hugging, of people supposedly being happy.

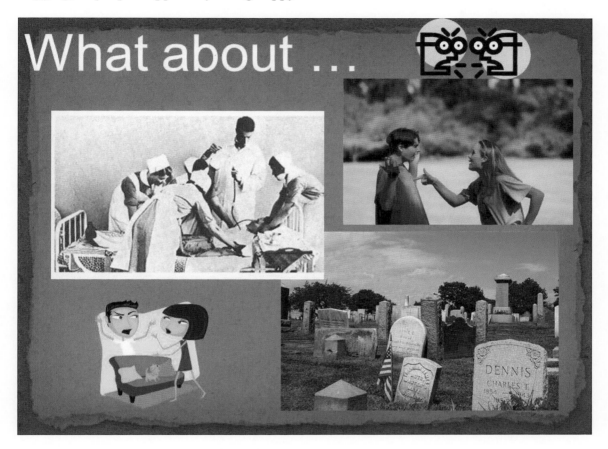

And on the next slide, we see the other side of things. These people are always hugging, they seem to be smiling, they seem to be satisfied and together but no one wants to think about, times of disagreement, not feeling well, old age, illness, and death. Many times people fool themselves into thinking they are happy when in reality they let things go in a relationship for the sake of keeping the peace, though when certain buttons are pushed, it all comes out anyway and many times with greater destructive force. And being so, people are living a lie, they're living a delusion, and in order to sustain that delusion, they have to 1- suppress thoughts, and feelings that point to higher wisdom about the nature of reality including the facing of worldly frustrations and finding the solutions to that instead of believing in deluded notions about finding happiness in any worldly situation or relationship, and 2- look for and seek out objects and ways of distracting themselves. And by objects, I mean anything outside of themselves in the world and other human beings to them are objects also. So, in other words, to you, your spouse is an object of the world of time and space. If you have an animal pet, that's an object. If you have a tree in front of your house, that's an object. If you have a car, that's an object. But you should realize also that in fact, your body is your object also, is your instrument. And what we're talking about is how really to find satisfaction, it's not to find fulfillment.

In the next slide, slide number five, we're going to talk about the illusion of relationships. This is kind of following along with the theme from the introduction, we're trying to introduce some further dimensions.

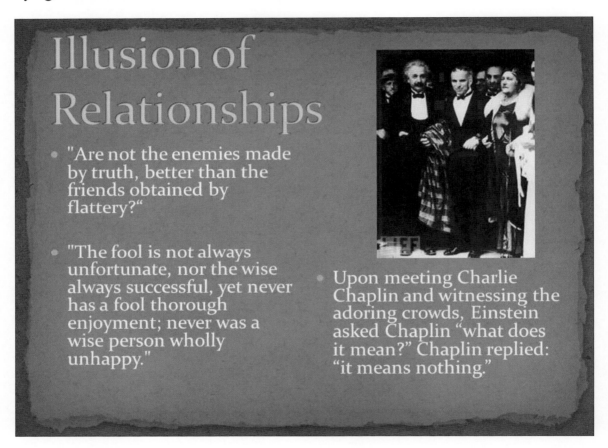

The proverbs here is,
"Are not the enemies made by truth better than the friends obtained by flattery?"
The fool is not always unfortunate…"

This second proverb is something that is discovered by people in Hollywood, many times, as they learn that while they are being flattered that people give them so many accolades and so much cheering; they cheer them on and the actors or personalities feel empowered to do things they would ordinarily not do and at the same time they internally know they are like everyone else and feel embarrassed or insecure or may even develop fear of being discovered as ordinary or having their mental issues revealed, etc. These may seem like extreme cases but they are emblematic, public examples of mental issues that actually operate in most every person in the world. They're complete disasters in their personal life but people adore them and so their disaster is sustained by the illusion of themselves and by the illusion of people praising them. They themselves know this deep down and this is why they turn to drugs, develop anxieties and other complexes, or turn to other distractions, trying to find a way to relieve their internal suffering, their internal pain, the void that they feel, that is not relieved or fulfilled by fame, fortune or mass adulation.

There is a wonderful example of how this problem of human beings operates. Charlie Chaplin was an extremely big movie star back in the '20s, as big as anyone today, and when Albert Einstein became famous, Charlie Chaplin, invited him to come to the USA and meet with him. Chaplin picked him up and they met a roaring, huge crowd that was at the port to meet the two of them, Charlie Chaplin and Albert Einstein. Einstein asked Charlie Chaplin "what does this mean, what does all this adulation, all these crowds, what does it all mean?", and Charlie Chaplin said, "it doesn't mean anything". Here was a man who was fabulously rich; he started Universal Studios which is still around today and he was world famous, Charlie Chaplin that is, and he was saying "it doesn't mean a thing." It didn't mean anything because he knew the illusion of life as well as the fickleness of fads and human desires. But most people don't understand this illusion and so they follow on, seeking it while believing in and reinforcing the deluded notions about themselves and the meaning of their relationships.

Before going forward, we should realize that the general Ancient Egyptian society was composed of human beings like us today. They had feelings and urges and desires as people do today. The following slides demonstrate that love poetry in ancient times was just as romantic and dreamy as the love poetry and music of the present age.

Romance and Illusion in Ancient Culture
Ancient History Sourcebook:
Egyptian Love Poetry, c. 2000 - 1100 BCE

- **I.** Your love has penetrated all within me
Like honey plunged into water,
Like an odor which penetrates spices,
As when one mixes juice in... ......
- **II.** Disturbed is the condition of my pool.
The mouth of my sister is a rosebud.
Her breast is a perfume.
Her arm is a............bough
Which offers a delusive seat.
Her forehead is a snare of *meryu-*wood.
- Never will I listen to their counsel
To abandon longing.
- My heart yearns for your breast,
I cannot sunder myself from your attractions.

- I have found my brother in his bed,
My heart is glad beyond all measure.
We each say:
"I will not tear myself away."
- My hand is in his hand.
I wander together with him
To every beautiful place.
He makes me the first of maidens,
Nor does he grieve my heart.
- Your hand in my hand,
My soul inspired
My heart in bliss,
Because we go together.
- New wine it is, to hear your voice;
I live for hearing it.
To see you with each look,
Is better than eating and drinking.

So why should we be considering Ancient Egyptian wisdom for insights into modern day issues with relationships? Because they discovered insights that helped them order their society in a way that promoted fruitful and balanced relationships which in turn also promoted positive order and balance in the society at large. We will see that even though there were people in ancient times who pursued worldly relations that there was another aspect which is lacking today that maintained available a stream of higher consciousness about life for those who become ready to listen and live in accordance with that higher wisdom and thereby discover the source of difficulties and dilemmas in relationships and move to discover the meaning of life and the deeper meaning of relationships.

Romance and Illusion in Present Day Culture

- Throughout history, sages of ancient times as well as master dramatists such as Shakespeare and performance artists such as the group *Main Ingredient*, have pointed out the folly of human emotion and irrationality as the cause of untold suffering and pain in life. The very popular song *Everybody plays the fool* presents a hauntingly real experience of losing touch with reality.

- Nevertheless, perhaps the most insidious aspect of the process of human delusion is that it is often known by a person but allowed because the person is incapable of stopping the process, due to having much invested in the desire and the unwillingness to face the apparent dire prospects of not pursuing the desire: loneliness, boredom, etc, i.e. facing reality. So to fill the time there needs to be parties, television, sports, family events or any activity that will distract the mind from reality. If those activities fail then there are always drugs.

- *Everybody Plays The Fool* - The Main Ingredient 1972

It may be factual it may be cruel cryin' cryin'
You say you're even thinking about dying?
Well before you do anything rash, dig this, baby listen to

Fallin' in love is such an easy thing to do
thing to do

Oh loving eyes they cannot see a certain person could never be
Love runs deeper than any ocean it clouds you're mind with emotion
There's no exception to the rule listen baby
It may be factual it may be cruel I ain't lying
Everybody plays the fool How can you help it when the music starts to play
And your ability to reason is swept away
Oh heaven on earth is all you see you're out of touch with reality
And now you cry but when you do next time around
someone cries for you How everybody plays the fool

They never tell you so in school I wanna say it again
Everybody plays the fool
Everybody plays the fool Everybody plays the fool sometime

Everybody plays the fool Every plays the fool sometime
There's no exception to the rule listen baby
It may be factual it may be cruel I wanna say it again
Everybody plays the fool

On then on the next slide, you have an example of that, a popular actress who's been married several times and she's trying to find her way, she's a beautiful person and an actress and she has everything going for her, and then in 2005, after years of smiling, you see the picture of her smiling with her husband, with her second husband I think it is, everything's wonderful. In 2005 she comes on the *Oprah* show, she's getting a divorce and she's saying that all those years that she was saying that she was happy, she was actually faking it. And so all those smiles that you see on her, on the camera, all the wonderful dresses and all the glitter, the fame and fortune, she's admitting that it was fake. Actually, it was the most miserable time in her life. During that time sh was also suffering spousal abuse.

The Poison in a Relationship: Self Delusion

- Berry's second marriage was to musician Eric Benét. They met in 1997 and married in early 2001 on a beach in Santa Barbara
- The couple separated in 2003.[58] After the separation, Berry stated, "I want love, and I will find it, hopefully."[65] While married to Benét, Berry adopted his daughter, India.[58] The divorce was finalized in January 2005.[66]
- Berry has been a victim of domestic violence, and now works to help other victims. In 2005, she said, "Domestic violence is something I've known about since I was a child.

"O fool, fool!, the pains which thou takest to hide what thou art, are far more than would make thee what thou wouldst seem; and the children of wisdom shall mock at thy cunning when, in the midst of security, thy disguise is stripped off, and the finger of derision shall point thee to scorn."
-Ancient Egyptian Proverb

It's like that whole parable of the thieves who go stealing things and they went to an old church building, an old temple building, the time before banks when people used to hide things in the wall, so they started breaking walls and sticking their hands in the walls to look for jewelry or hidden money or things like that, so one of the thieves puts his hand in, the chief thief, puts his hand in and he gets bitten by a scorpion and he doesn't tell anyone because he doesn't want to look weak or as if he's not living and enjoying his life the way he wants to and lose respect in their eyes. So, another thief asked him, "What happened? Is everything okay?" He said, "Yeah, everything is fine." And then that one puts his hand in and he gets stung and he doesn't say anything to anyone because he doesn't want to lose face with anyone either. And so on it goes and no one wants to face the truth, no one wants to face the pain of their dissatisfaction with life. And so from generation to generation, everybody's pushing the idea that you can be rich and famous and be happy, you can have a partner, a love affair, a mate, a soulmate, that you're going to be happy and no one ever finds this truth to be so but everyone keeps on pushing it, this very romantic idea, a very popular idea.

In the next slide, we see more of that. We just talked about Hollywood and on the bottom of the slide, you see many cheering people. They're not cheering at a church, they're not cheering at a temple. They're cheering at a football game. This is their religion. This is the way of escape. This is the way to do things, to lose your inhibitions, to paint your face and to scream and yell like a fool and it's because it's okay in that venue, to act like a fool and drink lots of beer and forget one's troubles, temporarily. Then you have governments and you have government leaders who are supposedly honest but everyone knows that they constantly lie, they constantly cheat and steal but everyone is, well, many people, most people are bent on believing them and sustaining them.

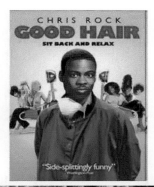

About the Chris Rock documentary, *Good Hair*, it's always interesting to me, especially in view of that documentary, the very stark reality that we have in society among many African and African American people who continue to straighten hair and or bleach their skins because I remember reading Malcolm X's autobiography where he was talking about having his hair done and having his hair straightened; so it goes back many decades. It applies to men and women. But it's interesting, that it seems like

African American men have moved away from the hair straightening but the women don't seem to have moved away from that. In fact, they have gotten into it more. Even though it may cost some thousands of dollars per month to maintain long hair or extensions or straightened hair or whatever it might be, they continue to do it and convince themselves that that's what they need to do to look good and also satisfy the deep-rooted aryu (unconscious tendencies). All I have to say about the issue is that, from a higher mystic standpoint, it's a ridiculous notion, an unnecessary expense and it's the sustaining of an unsustainable delusion about the body and the egoistic notions related to it that also drain resources and prevent one from accumulating resources to put towards a better life. But it goes along with many other aspects of life that turn towards a detrimental and even poisonous aspect of life including eating the pesticide laden processed foods and calling that soul food, watching degraded programs on television, needing to be constantly entertained and being unable to face and handle responsibilities from the job to effective political organization and civic actions, getting fat, obese, and overweight. It goes with the whole delusion of life that promotes a lifestyle of degradation, insanity, and diseases of the body and heart. These degradations are what human beings need to move away from if they intend to have a proper and fruitful relationship. Because those delusions lead them to have strife, frustrations and sufferings, the troubles in life.

So now, moving on to the next section of today's lecture which is dealing with conflict. On the next slide, we see some of the benefits of relationships. The impious soul screams, *"I burn; I am ablaze; I know not what to cry or do; wretched me, I am devoured by all the ills that encompass me about; alas, poor me, I neither see nor hear! This is the soul's chastisement of itself for the mind of the man imposes those on the soul."* This is to say that your sufferings, the sufferings of a human being, are created by themselves through their own mind, their own way of thinking, their own way of understanding. So, therefore, if your sorrows and pains are caused by your mind, your happiness can also be caused or generated by your mind, by the way, you think, the way you understand things. And so, the right way of thinking is a primary aspect of wellbeing, a feeling of wellbeing, a feeling of happiness, a feeling of living by truth.

Benefits of Relationships

- "The impious Soul screams: I burn; I am ablaze; I know not what to cry or do; wretched me, I am devoured by all the ills that compass me about; alas, poor me, I neither see nor hear! This is the Soul's chastisement of itself. For the Mind of the man imposes these on the Soul."

- "To suffer, is a necessity entailed upon your nature, would you prefer that miracles should protect you from its lessons or shalt you repine, because it happened unto you, when lo it happened unto all? Suffering is the golden cross upon which the rose of the Soul unfolds."

- -Ancient Egyptian Proverbs

This proverb above is talking about the necessity to have sufferings. You should not desire to have your ordinate sufferings removed. You should not desire to have an easy life without anything going wrong or any trouble in it. This is not to say that you should look for trouble. You should not look for trouble but the trouble that does come to you, that is divinely ordained through your *Aryu* {Ancient Egyptian concept similar to Indian Karma} to help you to progress in your spiritual evolution, should be faced.

And there's a saying in spiritual circles that if you want to grow spiritually, that you should not get married, but if you really want to grow spiritually you should get married. Obviously because your relationships in a myriad situation or a committed relationship without marriage, those relationships are most intense because of the intensity of the contact, the intimacy of the contact with the other person, both physically and mentally, psychologically, and so, therefore, if that is the case, then one should take great care with whom one enters into a marriage or close relationship with because that will either help to promote spiritual evolution and life enrichment or can degrade life and promote spiritual degradation and suffering. In a higher spiritual sense it helps either way actually, but the think about the context I'm talking about now, it helps you to evolve spiritually or it helps you to experience more pain and suffering. Now if your *Aryu* determines that you need more pain, then that's the kind of relationship that you're going to develop. And in a way, that is a help to you in the long run for your spiritual evolution as it will bring to you challenges and sufferings you need to overcome in order to move forward in your spiritual life. However, if you are not needing or desirous of those experiences because you have a higher understanding or have evolved beyond an interest in those experiences, then that kind of challenge and the sorrows it entails, along with the distractions, and divergences away from the direct spiritual path will be unnecessary.

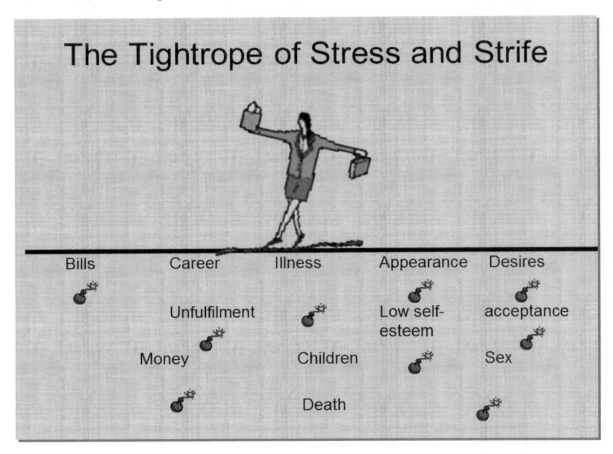

The Tightrope of Stress and Strife

Bills   Career   Illness   Appearance   Desires

Unfulfilment   Low self-esteem   acceptance

Money   Children   Sex

Death

Depth of ariu and the minefield of delusion due to Spiritual Ignorance

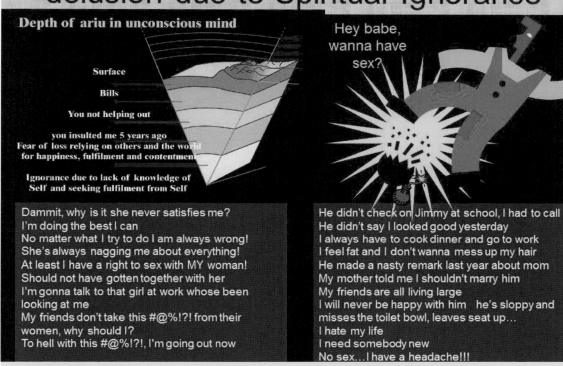

Depth of ariu in unconscious mind

Surface

Bills

You not helping out

you insulted me 5 years ago
Fear of loss relying on others and the world
for happiness, fulfilment and contentment

Ignorance due to lack of knowledge of
Self and seeking fulfilment from Self

Hey babe, wanna have sex?

Dammit, why is it she never satisfies me?
I'm doing the best I can
No matter what I try to do I am always wrong!
She's always nagging me about everything!
At least I have a right to sex with MY woman!
Should not have gotten together with her
I'm gonna talk to that girl at work whose been
looking at me
My friends don't take this #@%!?! from their
women, why should I?
To hell with this #@%!?!, I'm going out now

He didn't check on Jimmy at school, I had to call
He didn't say I looked good yesterday
I always have to cook dinner and go to work
I feel fat and I don't wanna mess up my hair
He made a nasty remark last year about mom
My mother told me I shouldn't marry him
My friends are all living large
I will never be happy with him   he's sloppy and
misses the toilet bowl, leaves seat up...
I hate my life
I need somebody new
No sex...I have a headache!!!

**MALES BECOME
FLEERS/WITHDRAWERS**
Why can't you shut up and leave me
alone...

**FEMALES BECOME
PURSUERS**
Why can't you do so and so...

Patterns of Strife and the Illusoriness of Worldly Love

**FROM HERE THE RELATIONSHIP DESCENDS INTO DISLIKE
AND THEN HATRED DUE TO CONSTANT ARGUMENT AND STRIFE
WHAT WAS CALLED LOVE IS LOST SO WHY CONTINUE THE RELATIONSHIP?
If there was love before but now there is no love, what does that say about the love that was supposedly there before, in the beginning?**

MALES BECOME FLEERS/WITHDRAWERS
Why can't you shut up and leave me alone…

FEMALES BECOME PURSUERS
Why can't you do so and so…

Dammit, why is it she never satisfies me? I'm doing the best I can No matter what I try to do I am always wrong! She's always nagging me about everything! At least I have a right to sex with MY woman! Should not have gotten together with her I'm gonna talk to that girl at work whose been looking at me My friends don't take this #@%!?! from their women, why should I? To hell with this #@%!?!, I'm going out now	He didn't check on Jimmy at school, I had to call He didn't say I looked good yesterday I always have to cook dinner and go to work I feel fat and I don't wanna mess up my hair He made a nasty remark last year about mom My mother told me I shouldn't marry him My friends are all living large I will never be happy with him, he's sloppy and misses the toilet bowl, leaves seat up… I hate my life I need somebody new No sex I have a headache!!!

I have talked, in other lectures, about the pitfalls of relationships, we talked about the minefield relationships, we talked about the tightrope of relationships, wherein people bury issues not dealt with and walk on egg shells around each other to avoid hitting touchy subjects and starting fights. I also talked about how the communication breaks down because one person (usually female) becomes a pursuer and another person (usually male) becomes a withdrawer. And communication should not be seen as a panacea but communication should be seen as an important aspect of a healthy relationship.   Communication doesn't solve all the problems.   Being a great communicator alone is not going to make your marriage survive any and all adversities and so it should not be thought of in that way but it is necessary to have good communication or to have a working relationship and avoid most struggles, especially unnecessary struggles of life. This is so because, due to the aryu in the personality, no matter how hard people may try to change, there remain powerful unconscious impressions of the past, putting pressure on the personality to feel, think and act in certain ways. Those egoistic imperfections, even if they are subtle, can produce adversities in life, from minor issues to great troubles. If powerful enough they are also immune to rational or logical arguments or intellectual explanations, no matter how truthful the arguments may be. Somone may want to contradict negative thought but cannot stop thinking negative thoughts. Another example is one may want to explain to another person the dangers of smoking but the other person does not want to listen and even if they listen to and understand the evidence of cancer causing nature of smoking, they cannot stop smoking anyway, because of the pressure from the aryu they have developed related to smoking. This theme will be explored further throughout this volume. On the next slide is the subject of the stresses of life that affect people's relationship with themselves and in turn with others.

An important aspect of relationships is stress. There are financial stresses. There are stresses related to people's inordinate and irrational expectations about life-based on their ignorant notions of reality and about themselves. There are issues related to raising children, and of sex. These are all areas of stress or the main areas of stress that people experience. In order to work through those, proper communication is needed. However, as you see in the next slide when proper communication cannot occur, then you have people who become adversaries and so shields go up and walls are created because people react with a defense mechanism. For men, they don't want to deal with it, and women, they want to deal with it more but after a while when people find that they're not able to deal with it (problem), because they 1- cannot get over their internal egoistic issues related to the 2- external problem stimulating the current strife, they build those walls; and even though they may come out under a flag of truce and may even have intimate relations sometimes, there are also bitter fights that all serve to reinforce feelings and thoughts of frustration, anger, uselessness, and pointlessness leading to the outcome of divorce.

Constant Fighting-No Joy in Relationship

So, you can see in the next slide, they turn away from each other and they start looking and acting and operating as if they're traveling separate roads. So, on the next slide, we see how does one get help with communication? We're talking here about people who are not schooled in Kemetic relationship philosophy, realizing that schools, high schools, colleges, etc., do not teach you about such things, they do not teach anything about relationships or communication issues and the culture itself is anti-social and pro individualism, pleasure-seeking and getting rich at the expense of others. If people had a background in the kind of mate that they should be looking for and the will to follow that wisdom, a lot of these problems would be resolved. But coming from a perspective where people have not been schooled in these teachings, counseling definitely can be of help if the current relationship has not been soured to a certain extent. And that, what I just said, should give us pause also; if a relationship can be soured, if you can fall out of love with a person or out of favor with the person, be it because of stresses, or because of money issues or sex or children or whatever, what does that say about your undying love? What does that say about "love" in general? It means that romantic, sentimental love is illusory.

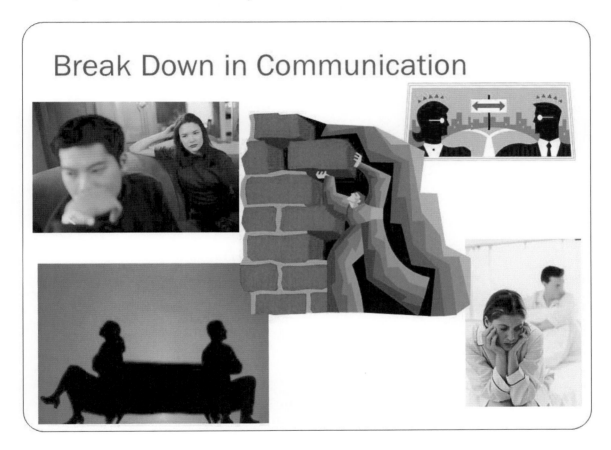

Everyone who gets involved in a relationship has an expectation that the love affair will be true and lasting and also bring happiness. No one really can have that kind of love because you can't have that kind of love in the realm of illusion, in the fleeting and changeable world of time and space. So, whatever you think that you can have, whatever you think that you can do eternally or in this kind of romantic way that you wanted, to stand with someone forever, all those kinds of things, you must realize, if you want to follow a Kemetic understanding, an initiatic path even, you must understand the delusion that you're following and how to break out of it.

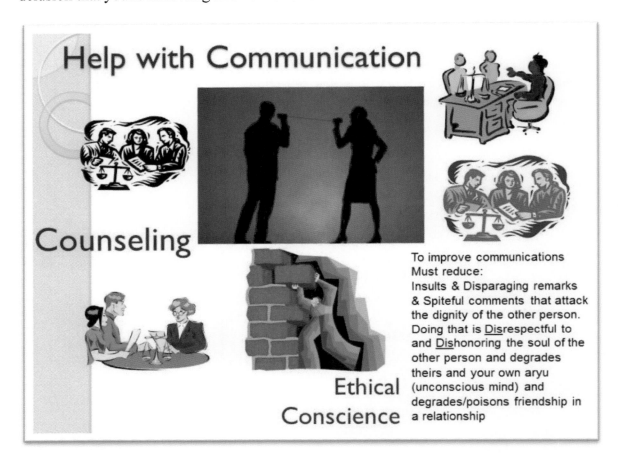

So, on the next slide we have the proverb, if you are a judge, don't stop a person from telling you everything they want to tell you. A person in distress wants to pour out their heart even more than they want their case to be won. If you stop the person who is pleading, that person will say, why does this judge reject my plea? Of course, not all that one pleads can be granted but a good hearing soothes the heart. The means for getting a true and clear explanation is to listen with kindness. A good counselor knows how to listen and partners in a relationship should also and not cut off each other's capacity for expression. This important teaching gives you the understanding that many times just listening is enough, you don't have to have any resolution or big brainstorming, but you can do that as part of a solution, working through to discover a solution, but sometimes only listening to a problem or discussing it soothes the soul, it alleviates the problem. And so, men can work on being willing to listen and discuss issues and women can work on being willing to apply less pressure in pushing issues. It is also important to realize that while this book is being written from an experience and wisdom related to western relationships, there are elements that apply to relationships in all countries. So, though there are specific nuances there are also universal principles as well.

a good hearing soothes the heart

- "If you are a judge, don't stop a person from telling you everything they want to tell you. A person in distress wants to pour out their heart even more than they want their case to be won. If you stop the person who is pleading, that person will say "why does this judge reject my plea?" Of course, not all that one pleads can be granted, but a good hearing soothes the heart. The means for getting a true and clear explanation is to listen with kindness." Ancient Egyptian Proverb

- Sometimes the resolution is just listening

- Listening goes beyond hearing, it is a genuine maatian concern for the concerns, feelings and needs of others.

We'll talk about that a little bit further on, that men tend to discount women as being emotional or as being nagging and women tend to discount men as being uncaring because they seem to be detached and don't seem to value their values in the same way, and so both of those problems need to be put aside because in the end all souls are of the selfsame nature and so, therefore, the hatred they may have or the anger they may have is out of delusion and not out of truth. And so, persons who can separate themselves from their emotionality, from their misunderstanding, can look beyond the outer expressions of themselves and of others. That's not easy. It takes practice, and you have to work on it sometimes for a long time in order to make that work.

Listening should go beyond just hearing. Sometimes people hear others but they're not really listening. They hear what others are saying but they're only just really thinking about what they want to say in response. That's not really listening with the idea of understanding the other before responding. Good listening is listening with a genuine concern for the feelings and needs of the other person. As the proverb says, not every request can be granted but a good hearing soothes the heart. And a good hearing also means trying to see what the true needs are, not necessarily the wants because wants can be expressions of egoism including many things that are outlandish or beyond the scope of truth, but seeing how the needs can be met or making an attempt towards that is necessary and beneficial.

On the next slide, we have improving communications. These are important points based on the Kemetic philosophy in order to improve communication. One of them is having reasonable expectations. Another one is breaking the cycle of fighting by scheduling your discussions. In order to avoid the minefield of topics that are problems in a relationship, you try to schedule your discussions at a particular time every week and that way you can be relaxed and you can have fun and you can enjoy each other's company the rest of the time and deal with issues at appointed times. You're not to be worried about every single minute that you're going to step on something and start a fight. Instead, you can rest assured that any issues will be discussed at a set appointed time so it does not have to be discussed now and disrupt the present day or the rest of the week.

Having reasonable expectations is not having the romantic delusions essentially, that the other person is going to make me happy or the other person doesn't do this and do that that makes me unhappy or whatever, leaning on the other person for your happiness, as a sole means for your happiness and so on. So realize that in this delusion you are leaning on the other person who's an illusory, changeable[4] object, for your fulfillment. This is what you're basing your happiness on. That's an unreasonable expectation.

---

[4] The other person has moods, opinions, physical needs, etc., that always change and will not always allow them to care for another person's feelings, wellbeing or happiness.

Improving Communication

- Have reasonable expectations
- Break the cycle of fighting by Scheduling discussions
- Brainstorming
- Solutions
- Have concern beyond the utilitarian perspective, care for the soul of your partner.

Part of problem-solving, when you have good communication, is that you can sit down and discuss the issues so the other person knows what is on your mind and so on. If it goes beyond that, you can just sit down, discuss some solutions, you can start brainstorming some ideas just freely, without criticism, and then discuss solutions that are best for everyone. And thus the key is again to have a discussion that honors the concerns of both parties and not just of one, because if you think that you have the right solution and the other person doesn't see it or they don't necessarily agree, if you try to impose yourself or if you assign the label of the other person as uncaring or as unfeeling or as irrational even, one person might say "he's silly or she's dumb, she doesn't understand what I'm thinking or what I want" or etc., and these are all forms of delusion, that other people should know what you think or what you want or what you like or what you think is correct and they immediately follow. The world can't work like that because everyone has a different *Aryu* and therefore since the world is fleeting and everything is changeable, you or your partner may feel different ways on a different given day.

It brings up another subject that is important to understand, that both men and women should try to, through this process of Maat and order in their life, they should also work on balancing emotions, balancing feelings. Well, the Maatian program of life will tend to balance feelings, and the balanced feelings will tend to bring forth balanced emotions.

You've probably have experienced in your life, that sometimes when you're with someone who is moody there are some variations on when and how they can be approached. An example is, perhaps, while growing up with your parents, for example, you asked your father for something and then he says "ask your mother", but then he tells you, "but right now is not a good time to ask anything. Just leave her alone until she feels better". Of course, this can operate in reverse with the emotional or stressed male parent and also, of course, that should not be that way. Ideally, you should not be allowing yourself to be controlled by your moods, by your feelings or stresses. You should be striving to have an intellectual capacity and will to be able to handle stresses and override your feelings and emotions in order to act based on truth and balance regardless of your feelings. This is the ideal whether you're feeling angry, whether you're feeling sorrow or whatever it is. You should be able to act on reason and that is called living by truth. That is the highest way of life. When the decision is arrived at with reason then you can allow your emotions to support that decision, not the other way around because then feelings would corrupt and distort the reasoning capacity. This ideal is achieved by living a life that avoids undue stresses and engages in right thinking and feeling about things, which is guided by living a Maatian lifestyle.

And you should have a concern for the other person and this is also part of the features or the qualities of an ideal partner for a Kemetic relationship. You should have a concern beyond the utilitarian perspective, there should be a genuine caring for the soul of the partner. This goes back to the, "What have you done for me lately?" concept or the idea. As I said before, most men are looking for a woman who will not nag and who will have sex at any given time of the day etc. Women may want a man who will bring in income to support the household and perfectly do whatever they want them to do, be it from taking out the garbage, to fixing the car, painting the house, having sex whenever they want also which may be less often than men or only to procreate so she can become a mother. Other desires may be fulfilling household or family duties like taking the kids or doing the dishes, whatever it might be, whenever desired, for one person's comfort. This is the utilitarian perspective, that the other person is there to do things for you and to satisfy your desires, and to that extent that they're useful, that they are okay to have around. If they are not useful then they are bad or lazy or selfish or stupid, less than or unworthy, etc. That's the utilitarian perspective. This way of carrying on relations, of course, tends to degrade a relationship and degrades spiritual caring towards a more material value of relationships that constitutes devolution. And since no one can serve another perfectly at all times, even if they were slaves, that incapacity is bound to cause disappointment and anguish in the relationship anyway.

And this is what we see on the next slide where you see the result of that. This is a funny thing that is around, they make T-shirts of it, of a woman who's sitting on a park bench so long that she turns into a skeleton due to waiting for the perfect man. And one can laugh at this but one should realize that men are in a terrible position also. Most men who have not been able to sublimate or to advance in their will aspect and their intellectual aspect, who are controlled by their lower nature, their lower energies, are in a terrible position because it's like females in the wild, in many animal species, they're going into heat at particular times of the month or the year or whatever and most men are in heat all the time, so they're constantly thinking about sex -- well, I mean constantly as intermittently like throughout the day several times or whenever they see a woman and the thoughts are triggered. And so, a person who is caught up, a man who is caught up in that way is extremely degraded and has an extremely tough time of it. And again, this is a way of delusion that you should be plunging yourself into sex and that's why they call men dogs or wolves etc.

The Problem of Irrational Desires or Unreasonable Expectations

𓀀𓏏𓆓 *aba* --passions and desires

- *"Passions and irrational desires are ills exceedingly great; and over these GOD hath set up the Mind to play the part of judge and executioner."*

- *"It is very hard, to leave the things we have grown used to, which meet our gaze on every side. Appearances delight us, whereas things which appear not, make their believing hard. Evils are the more apparent things, whereas the Good can never show Itself unto the eyes, for It hath neither form nor figure." –Ancient Egyptian Proverb*

It's a form of delusion of course and it is an aspect that sometimes women learn to manipulate. They calculate about it, about how they can control men by withholding or by giving sex etc. If they strain that too much, then men go outside to seek other ways of satisfying their sexual desires. On the other hand, men also calculate to see how much they can push women also. If they're paying bills, how much will women allow them to have affairs on the side and things like that? How many times they can get away with saying that they're sorry or they didn't mean it or they're just being a man, boys will be boys, etc. And of course, from the perspective of the worldly, that is all correct and true. From a perspective of a higher order of being, all this is degraded and animalistic and not to be accepted.

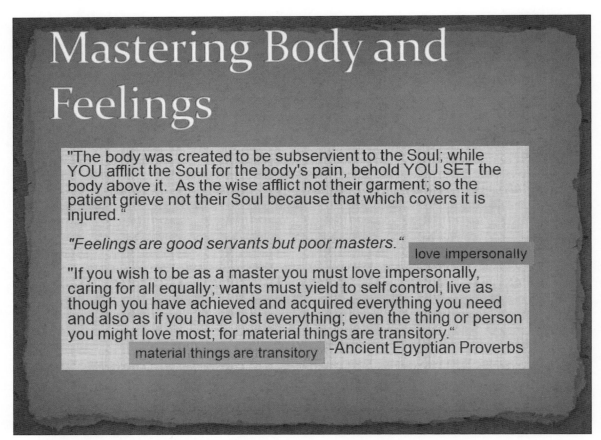

Mastering Body and Feelings

"The body was created to be subservient to the Soul; while YOU afflict the Soul for the body's pain, behold YOU SET the body above it. As the wise afflict not their garment; so the patient grieve not their Soul because that which covers it is injured."

"Feelings are good servants but poor masters."

love impersonally

"If you wish to be as a master you must love impersonally, caring for all equally; wants must yield to self control, live as though you have achieved and acquired everything you need and also as if you have lost everything; even the thing or person you might love most; for material things are transitory."

material things are transitory   -Ancient Egyptian Proverbs

So, one must strive to master the body and the feelings. The body was created to be subservient to the soul, not the other way around. While you afflict the soul for the body's pain, behold you set the body above it, as the wise afflict not their garment, so the patient grief, not their soul because that which covers it is injured. Our feelings are good servants and poor masters.

And I think an important key is in the next proverb, *"If you wish to be a master, you must love impersonally, caring for all equally. Wants must yield to self-control. Live as though you have achieved and acquired everything you need and also as if you have lost everything, even the thing or person you might love most, for material things are transitory."* So, loving impersonally and material things are transitory. Loving impersonally in this context means loving without attachment, loving without the egoistic notion, such as: "this is my woman" or "this is my man" and "you belong to me and I belong to you" and you're going to take care of your family and to hell with everyone else, all those kinds of thoughts are egoistic thoughts, possessive thoughts, exclusive thoughts. And again, since all things are transitory, all things are illusory, whatever you think that you're holding onto, even though you may hug a person or you may be having sex and part of your body is inside another person's body, that you think that you're so close, that actually doesn't mean anything as far as your closeness, it's just a closeness of the body. In fact, if you study modern physics, it is clear that nothing touches anything else in Creation; it only appears to, even at the physical level. The touching sensations are owed to the electromagnetic forces between atoms on skin that react to other atoms, which we may refer to as friction but that friction is not from actual contact since the atoms do not touch other atoms. This scientific perspective may help promote dispassion if it is thought of but in the heat of passions, it is ineffectual since the person is caught up in the delusion of physicality.

The body is an aggregate of physical elements, earth, water, air, fire, which is constituted by molecules, atoms, electrons, etc. The closeness of the body has nothing to do with the soul and so, therefore, that closeness since it's illusory, only an intermittent perception, cannot satisfy the needs of the soul. So, therefore, you have to constantly seek to have sex, you have to constantly seek to be in communication, constantly seek to be touching or seeking the company of others, which is all actually illusory. In actuality, you are as far away from the other person as if they were on the other side of the universe but your soul is as close as if it was in the very same spot because it is!

The next slide presents the concept or the idea to understand that if you're selecting a person to be in a relationship with, you should be trying to select a partner and not a mate. You should not be trying to find a soulmate or trying to find someone to "complete you" and following those kinds of illusory ideals. Again, because the soul cannot be completed, in other words, fulfilled through the activities or existence of mortal, ephemeral bodies, what you're really searching for is the satisfaction of knowing yourself, of knowing the truth of your existence, which can be helped by relationships but not derived from them. A relationship can work to help that process along if it is carried out in a correct way such that it helps a person learn about themselves and their spiritual nature. So, among the important aspects to be looking for in another person, the most important one is ethical conscience, and that is the most important because that is going to be a framework for your experiences with that person throughout the relationship period and during that time the experiences serve to enlighten or help produce more entanglements and delusions. If handled properly, with the appropriate partner, experiences with that other person, in areas such as, in raising a child or your finances or your sexual life or different aspects of your relationship that you engage in may allow you to discover things about yourself that otherwise would not be possible if you lived alone or not in such a relationship. On the other hand, a negative relationship can produce negative experiences and produce ignorance that would not otherwise be experienced.

Selecting a Partner, not a Mate

- Ethical Conscience
- Common life purpose
- Compatible Spiritual Paths
- Companionship and Understanding
- Facilitation
- Person to dialogue with on philosophical issues

- "Take a wife while you are young, that she may make a son for you while you are youthful..." (Instructions of Ani)

- "When thou find sensibility of heart, joined with softness of manners, an accomplished mind, with a form agreeable to thy fancy, take her home to thy house; she is worthy to be thy friend, thy companion in life, the wife of thy bosom."

- "Remember thou art man's reasonable companion, not the slave of his passion; the end of thy being is not merely to gratify his loose desire, but to assist him in the toils of life, to soothe him with thy tenderness, and recompense his care and like treatment with soft endearments."

- "When you prosper and establish your home, love your wife with ardor. Then fill her belly and clothe her back. Caress her. Give her ointments to soothe her body. Fulfill her wishes for as long as you live. She is a fertile field for her husband. Do not be brutal. Good manners will influence her better than force. Do not contend with her in the courts. Keep her from the need to resort to outside powers. Her eye is her storm when she gazes. It is by such treatment that she will be compelled to stay in your house."

If you're going into a partnership in a business, you don't want to go into partnership with people who are unethical, people who are going to steal from you, such as liars, thieves, embezzlers and so on. In the same way, you want to find someone who is ethically conscious, someone who's aware of the Maatian ideals and who agrees with them and is trying to live them. That person who has a common life purpose, to attain enlightenment, that is the highest purpose and the ideal of life.

Another aspect is spirituality. Maat philosophy has a secular component and a spiritual component. If the spiritual aspect is relevant for you then it relates to Ancient Egyptian religion. The person who is following a compatible spiritual path is, therefore, more ideal. A compatible spiritual path means if you are following the Kemetic religious path and the other person is following Christianity, you're eventually going to have problems with that person over religion. So, it's not recommended that you should enter into a relationship with such a person.

On the other hand, if you're partnering with a person who, say, follows Buddhism or Hinduism, we have talked about the factor that those religions have more philosophical and ethical compatibilities and there is, therefore, more possibility for harmonious and perhaps even complementary interactions. Or if you find another person following Native American, or African religion and not Africanized Western religion but authentic African religion, you'll find more compatibility there as well. You'll save yourself a lot of trouble, a lot of sorrow, unless that is what you want or unless that is what your path, your *Aryu* is dictating for you.

If you discount these things that I was talking about now, if you say, well, the person is following a different religion, the person follows Christianity or if they're secular and they agree with secular ideals, secular meaning the secular ideals of this culture, the pursuit of happiness and the making money in the corporation regardless of if you hurt other people, this is all covered in and prohibited by the ethical conscience wisdom of Maat Philosophy. If you say that it's okay for you to go into a relationship with a person with such beliefs and you're going to make it work somehow and the other person is going to change, or love conquers all, etc. etc., you must realize that you're following an illusion and you are opening yourself up for a fall and you have only yourself, like the proverb said, yourself to blame because you are participating in unrighteousness that imbalances the personality, that brings turmoil and strife to life; you are causing the suffering that your soul is going to experience.

You should be looking for someone who can provide companionship and understanding; Understanding of your spiritual path, understanding of your needs and vice versa. Again, not to say that everything can be satisfied by the other person but you want at least someone who has understanding of the spiritual practices and their requirements, someone you can have discussions with, like say if you have kids, if you want to meditate, the other person understands and they'll take the kids while you're meditating and you can take them while they're meditating, things like that. The righteous and non-egoistic utilitarian aspects of relationships are helpful also. It is beneficial to have a person to have a dialogue on the philosophy and share spiritual insights that lead to peace, understanding and spiritual independence instead of getting into a relationship to support codependent psychological weaknesses and spiritual ignorance.

Satisfying the soul

- I Feel The Earth Move Lyrics
  Artist(Band):Carole King

  Oh, darling, when you're near me
  And you tenderly call my name
  I know that my emotions
  Are something that I just can't tame
  I've just got to have you, baby

  I feel the earth move under my feet
  I feel the sky tumbling down, tumbling down
  I feel the earth move under my feet
  I feel the sky tumbling down, tumbling down

  I just lose control
  Down to my very soul
  I get hot and cold all over

  I feel the earth move under my feet
  I feel the sky tumbling down
  Tumbling down
  Tumbling down
  Tumbling down

- **Lose control – lose inhibitions like a drug addict**

- **Really want to lose bondage to the body and to the world**

- Body to Earth, Soul to Heaven

- "There is no happiness for the soul in the external worlds since these are perishable, true happiness lies in that which is eternal, within us."

- "The wise person feeds the KA with what endures, so that it is happy with that person on earth.

In the next slide, there is the issue of satisfying the soul. There's a song, from modern culture, that reminded me of some of the Ancient Egyptian poetry, a song by Carole King. It goes: *"I feel the earth move under my feet. I feel the sky tumbling down. I feel the earth move under my feet. I feel the sky tumbling down. I just lose control down to my very soul. I get hot and cold all over. I feel the earth move under my feet."* And many times what is going on in people's minds is that they're searching for an experience of being excited and overwhelmed, so much so that they should become elated and in so doing forget about the ordinary cares of life and thereby experience a higher form of being. That is an understandable and positive desire but the method and venue of seeking for that are flawed. This is the romantic and deluded vision of "falling in love". Again, something that is temporary and non-fulfilling. They are really searching for spiritual fulfillment, for the satisfaction of the soul but they ignorantly think they're going to find that by losing themselves in the arms of someone else or by losing themselves through falling in love with someone else and it's kind of like a drug addiction. They want to lose their inhibitions, lose their ordinary consciousness and be, as if, overwhelmed in happiness. What human beings really want is to relax and they want to have freedom. They want to have full openness. They really want freedom from the ego and body and the want freedom from the inhibitions of time and space.

As the Ancient Egyptian Proverb goes, the body belongs to the earth, the soul belongs to the heaven, and this is why the soul will never be satisfied with anything that you can do with the body. No matter how much pleasure it can experience, no matter how many drugs it can do, no matter how much sex it's going to have, no matter how much money it can have, it'll never be enough. And the other proverb says there is no happiness for the soul in the external world since these are perishable. True happiness lies in that which is eternal. The wise person feeds the Ka with what endures so that it is happy with that person on earth.

Your soul through your Ka (mind) needs to be fed with things that are of its kind, things that are real, things that are eternal and not fleeting or limited. Just like your body, if I say to you your body should be sustained with the eternal spirit of the universe, what does that mean? If you don't go to the grocery store or farm for your food and you say, "Oh, I can actually live off the spirit," what's going to happen to your body? Of course, it's not going to survive. Now on the other hand, if we say that your soul should live off the eternal spirit, then that's something else, quite different.

What you're trying to do is to feed the soul with things that are transitory, things that are illusory, and that's why the soul is restless, the soul is wandering, because you're living a lie, you're living a delusion, and the only way to satisfy that is to feed it things that are of its kind and as the soul is eternal, you have to feed it eternal things. Absolute truth is an eternal thing and the meditative experience of the soul in itself is an eternal thing. What you're trying to do is to clear out the delusions so that the soul can see through the body in time and space a reflection of itself and that will make a satisfied soul and that is what we call enlightenment or Nehast, when you can see the eternity in the world of time and space in yourself and in your partner and in the tree in front of your house and the metal that composes the cars and vastness of the sky, the clouds, the sun, the space in-between these, everything. If that perspective was to dawn on a human being, then they would not have any need for satisfying desires through fleeting worldly activities like eating ice cream or chocolates or sex or having the person do things for you or traveling or being rich or any of those things because the satisfaction will be of the selfsame nature coming from itself and that is why the happiness is within yourself and not in relationships.

There has been a question about a marriage agreement that involved compensation with silver, about whether or not the usage of silver as compensation in a divorce is appropriate. This question arises from one of the sample Kemetic marital contracts. While silver may have been used, there may have been gold, there may have been cattle, there may have been other forms of wealth that were used also. The idea here as you have stated in your question, is that the goal was to protect the rights of the other person and to create an amicable kind of separation if there was going to be a separation, and also there is sometimes a little bit of a bias against the person who is doing the break up, meaning that if you enter into partnership with someone and you want to dissolve the partnership because you don't want to do it anymore for whatever reason, it's your responsibility so you may have to pay a little bit of an addition so that the other person can be better taken care of because you are the one who is initiating it; you are the one who is adding any additional expenses related to it. But the use of silver is not a particular, shall we say, an aspect of compensation and it does not imply a commodification of the relationship but simply a matter of practicality in recognizing that in the world of time and space it is necessary to eat to survive and that requires a certain amount of wealth. Silver was one of the items used to store wealth as it is today so silver was just the wealth instrument used in that particular instance. Theoretically, it could be anything else of value in the society. But really, the idea and the concept is more important than the actual objects of compensation.

This concludes the discourse on Major Themes and Issues in Marriages and Solutions through Kemetic Marriage Philosophy.

HETEP-Peace

Chapter 2: Maat Philosophy in the Context of Kemetic Relationships and Creating a Kemetic Marriage Contract

Goddess Maat at far left, presiding over the Balance Scales judging the Heart of a person

The relationship and marital contract guide reflect actual Ancient Egyptian Principles for Kemetic Marriage as they are to be applied for our times. The marital contract allows people to have a framework with which to face the challenges of marital relations instead of relying on hopes or romantic dreams that everything will work out somehow; in other words, in contradiction with the famous song, love is not all you need. The latter is not an evolved, mature way of handling one of the most important aspects of human life. Therefore, it behooves anyone who wishes to enter into a marriage to first explore the issues of ethics in relationships, express their needs and seek to avoid costly mistakes, and resolve conflicts in the normal course of life or make sure that their rights and dignity will be protected if any eventuality should occur.

Marital relations in Ancient Egypt were not like those in other countries of the time and not like those of present day countries. Maat is the Ancient Egyptian goddess of truth, order, righteousness, and balance as well as the philosophy represented by those principles. Maat Philosophy has two major components relating to secular and non-secular life. The extreme longevity of Ancient Egyptian society, founded in Maat philosophy, allowed the social development of marriage to evolve and progress to a high level of order and balance. Maat represents truth, righteousness, justice, and harmony in life. Not a subjective truth but universal truth. This meant that the marital partner's rights were to be protected with equal standing before the law. So there was no disparity between rights of men or rights of women. Therefore, anyone who wants to enter into a marriage based on Kemetic principles must first and foremost adhere to this standard of equality of the rights of men and women.

This guide demonstrates procedures for following the Ancient Egyptian practice of formalizing marriage with a contract that spells out the important concerns of each partner in the marital relationship, based on Maatian principles [of righteousness, truth, harmony, and justice] so that the rights and needs of each partner may be protected within the marriage. It also allows the partners to think about issues that arise out of the marital relations so that they may have a foundation to fall back on in the event that those or other unforeseen issues arise and cause conflict in the relationship. By having a document of expressed concerns, needs and steps to be taken to address them, it is less likely that issues which affect the relationship in a negative way will arise, and when they do, they will be better handled, in a more balanced, just and amicable way.

The Egyptians appear to have reversed the ordinary practices of mankind.
Women attend markets and are employed in trade, while men stay at home
and do the weaving! Men in Egypt carry loads on their head, women on
their shoulder. Women pass water standing up, men sitting down. To ease
themselves, they go indoors but eat outside on the streets, on the theory
that what is unseemly, but necessary, should be done in private, and what
is not unseemly should be done openly.

(Herodotus II: 33-37)

Introduction to Maat Philosophy

Since Maat Philosophy is a cornerstone of the Kemetic Marital Agreement, it has been thought appropriate to include a brief introduction to Maat Philosophy here. For a more comprehensive study of Maat Philosophy, read the book *Introduction to Maat Philosophy* by Dr. Muata Ashby.

I am pure. I am pure. I am Pure.
I have washed my front parts with the waters of libations,
I have cleansed my hinder parts with drugs which make wholly clean,
and my inward parts have been washed in the liquor of Maat.

The Scribe Nu

Above: The Feather of Maat
Symbol of Truth, Righteousness, Justice and Social Order

PROVERBS ON MAAT PHILOSOPHY

"When opulence and extravagance are a necessity instead of righteousness and truth,
society will be governed by greed and injustice."

"When emotions are societies objective, tyranny will govern regardless of the ruling class."

"MAAT is great and its effectiveness lasting; it has not been disturbed since the time of Osiris. There is punishment for those who pass over it's laws,
but this is unfamiliar to the covetous one....When the end is nigh, *MAAT* lasts."

"Those who live today will die tomorrow, those who die tomorrow will be born again;
Those who live MAAT will not die."

"No one reaches the beneficent West (heaven) unless their heart is righteous by doing *MAAT*. There is no distinction made between the inferior and the superior person;
it only matters that one is found faultless
when the balances and the two weights stand before the Lord of Eternity.
No one is free from the reckoning. Thoth, a baboon,
holds the balances to count each one according to what they have done upon earth."

"The sky is at peace, the earth is in joy, for they have heard that the King will set right the place of disorder. Tutankhamun drove out disorder from the Two Lands, and *MAAT* is firmly established in its place; he made lying an abomination, and the land is as it was at the first time."

"Speak *MAAT*; do *MAAT*."

"They who revere *MAAT* are *long lived*; they who are covetous have no tomb."

"Do *MAAT* for the King, for *MAAT* is that which God loves!
Speak *MAAT* to the King for that which the King loves is *MAAT!*"

Doing Maat is breath to the nose.

The following is a compilation of the 42 laws or precepts of Maat and the corresponding principles which they represent. Maat philosophy was the basis of ancient Egyptian society and government as well as the heart of Ancient Egyptian myth and spirituality. Maat is at once a goddess, a cosmic force and a living social doctrine which promotes social harmony and thereby paves the way for spiritual evolution in all levels of society. In the absence of a social philosophy which promotes justice, peace and the sublime goals of life, a society cannot function equitably or survive the passage of time.

Other similar social philosophies have developed in other cultures. In India, the philosophy of Dharma, or righteous action, developed. In China, Confucianism served the same purpose. In Christianity, the Beatitudes and the new commandments of Jesus serve the same purpose. However, if moral injections are simply memorized but never applied, not understanding their deeper spiritual implications they will not be practiced correctly or at all. Thus the moral character of society declines and strife develops in society.

In reference to society, the follower of Maat would be innocent before the courts and society. In reference to the Temple, the injunctions of Maat were statements composed by the Ancient Egyptian Sages and recorded in temple walls and papyrus scrolls. They were to be used by spiritual initiates for the purpose of cleansing their personalities and making themselves pure vessels in order to promote spiritual self-discovery. These teachings came to be known as the *Book of the Dead*. The correct name is *Prt m Hru* or *Pert Em Heru* meaning "Utterances for coming into the light" or "Sayings for becoming Enlightened."

The True Name of The "Book of The Dead"

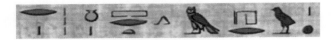

Rau nu pert m heru

=

The

"Chapters of going as light"

Or

The

"Book of Becoming Light"

Or

The

"Book of Enlightenment"

The teachings of *Pert em Heru* are related to the Yoga of Righteous Action. The word Yoga originates in the Indian Sanskrit, meaning the union of the lower self (mortal personality) with the higher (immortal spiritual Self). In Ancient Egypt the word for Yoga was *Smai.*[5] Yoga is the practice of spiritual disciplines which lead to positive spiritual evolution. There are four major aspects of Yoga: The Yoga of Wisdom, The Yoga of Devotion, The Yoga of Meditation and the Yoga of Righteous Action.

The teachings of righteous action originated in the early history of Ancient Egypt with the writings of the Ancient Egyptian Sages, known as the "Wisdom Texts." There were many Sages in Ancient Egypt, however, only a relatively small number of their writings have survived. Nevertheless, these are enough to provide a viable understanding of the Ancient Egyptian wisdom teachings and these writings reveal the source of the Maatian precepts and philosophy contained in the *Pert em Heru*. Therefore, as we study the precepts of Maat, along with the Wisdom Texts, we will obtain a deeper insight into the profound nature of the precepts.

The 42 precepts may be classified into six major principles, and within these three more can be subdivided. The six principles are Truthfulness, Non-violence, Right Action, Right Thinking, Non-stealing and Sex Sublimation. The subdivisions are under Right Action. They are Selfless Service to Humanity, Right Speech and Right Worship of the Divine or Correct Spiritual Practice.

---

[5] See the book *Egyptian Yoga The Philosophy of Enlightenment* by Muata Ashby

The number to the left of each precept denotes the order in which it appears in the *Papyrus of Ani* or *Pert em Heru* of Ani. Since there are various *Pert em Heru* texts that have been discovered and no two have the same exact wording, variants will also be included to elucidate on the expanded meanings accorded to the precepts by different Sages.

Truth (1), (6), (7), (9), (24)

Non-violence (2), (3), (5), (12), (25), (26), (28), (30), (34)

Self-Control-Right Action (Living in accordance with the teachings of Maat)
(15), (20), (22), (36)

   Selfless Service, (29)

   Right Speech (11), (17), (23), (33), (35), (37)

   Right Worship (13), (21), (32), (38), (42)

Balance of Mind - Reason - Right Thinking (14), (16), (18), (31), (39), (41)

Not-stealing (4), (8), (10)

Sex-Sublimation (19), (27)

What is Virtue?

The American Heritage Dictionary defines *Virtue* as:

"Moral excellence and righteousness; goodness."

What is virtue and where does it come from? Is it something which may be purchased? Is it something that can be cultivated? A person may be ordered to be obedient, to follow rules, etc. Is this virtue? If the ten commandments and so many other laws are established in society, why then is there increased crime and increasing strife among people? Why is there enmity in the world? Why is there a desire to hurt others? Why is there a desire to mistreat others and misappropriate the property of others?

Anger and hatred cannot be stopped by simply telling someone to be good, loving, forgiving and so on. One cannot become righteous by being ordered to or forced to, no more than a plant can be forced to grow, bear fruit or flowers through a command by the farmer. One can be compelled to follow rules but this does not mean that one is necessarily a virtuous person. Many people do not commit crimes and yet they are not virtuous because they are harboring negative thoughts (violence, hatred, greed, lust, etc.) in their hearts. Virtue is a profound quality which every human being has a potential to discover. However, this requires effort on the part of the individual as well as the correct guidance. Virtue is like a flower which can grow and become beautiful for the whole world to see. However, just as a plant must receive the proper nutrients (soil, water, sunlight, etc.) so too the human heart must receive the proper caring and nurturing in the form of love, wisdom, proper diet, meditation, and good will.

Many people are law abiding and peaceful under normal conditions, but if provoked or presented with an opportunity, they will engage in the unrighteous activity. Under pressure, they may be pushed into stealing, violence or other vices. This is not virtue. The development of virtue in a human being implies that sinful behavior will not be possible even if there is an opportunity for it. True virtue implies a profound understanding of the nature of creation and the heart which will make it impossible to commit crimes or to consider sinful thoughts; as we discover the teachings of Maat, the reasons for this will become clear.

Virtue is the quality which implies harmony with the universe. Virtue is that which leads a human being to come into harmony with the Divine. From a mythological standpoint, sin is to be understood as the absence of wisdom which leads to righteousness and peace and the existence of ignorance which leads to mental unrest and the endless desires of the mind. Sin operates in human life as any movement which works against self-discovery, and virtue is any movement towards discovering the essential truth of the innermost heart. The state of ignorance will end only when the mind develops a higher vision. It must look beyond the illusions of human desire and begin to seek something more substantial and abiding. This is when the aspirant develops an interest in spirituality and the practice of order, correctness, self-improvement and intellectual development. In ancient Egyptian Mythology and mystical philosophy, these qualities are symbolized by the Divinities MA'AT (Themis) and Anpu (Anubis). Maat is the truth and Anubis is the symbol of the discerning intellect which can see right from wrong, good from evil, truth from untruth, etc.

It must be clearly understood that vicious behavior or behaviors that are based on pursuing vices, is/are a factor of spiritual immaturity. Every human being has the innate capacity to develop and experience a virtuous character. Therefore, if one wants to promote peace and non-violence in the world, one must seek to promote virtue in others. This means helping others to discover their inner potential for experiencing a higher state of connectedness to humanity and the universe and a deeper fulfillment in life. Anger and violence are the marks of immaturity. Those who seek to use violence to have their way, to control others, or to promote order in society are in reality expressing their own inability to control themselves. When there is true virtue there will be no desire to control others for egoistic purposes or through the use of violence. A person of strong virtuous character will be able to control himself/herself so as to exercise great care and patience with others. This virtuous development allows a human being to develop a strong will and exert a strong influence on others which can be used to direct them toward what is positive and good. This kind of spiritual power was demonstrated by great Sages and Saints throughout history (Imhotep, Ptahotep, Osiris, Isis, Buddha, Jesus, Krishna, etc.). All of the Sages and Saints just mentioned are no different than any other human being who ever existed, except in the lifestyle they chose to live. They chose to live in such a way that the negative in them was eradicated and the wisdom of self-discovery was allowed to blossom. This is the path of virtue wherein life is lived for purifying the mind and body so as to allow the Higher Self, the Spirit in the heart, to emerge and be discovered.

In order to gain this form of spiritual power and spiritual enlightenment, it is necessary to root out every bit of ignorance and negativity in one's entire being. This means that there must be a clear insight into the nature of one's own spiritual innermost nature. This also means that one's actions, thoughts, and words must be pure. When the path of virtue is perfected, the heights of spiritual wisdom illuminate the heart. This is the meaning of MAAT Philosophy, Spiritual Enlightenment through the path of Virtue. In the journey of discovering the path of Maat, it is necessary to understand the ancient Egyptian concept of the Judgment.

The Science Of Virtues

"The Soul is a Prisoner of its own ignorance. In this condition it is fettered with the chains of ignorance to an existence where it has no control over its fate in life. The Purpose of Each Virtue is to Remove One Fetter."

Ancient Egyptian Proverb

Virtues are practiced to promote peace of mind and body: *Hetep.* Peace of mind promotes the study and listening. Study and listening promote reflection. Reflection on life and the teachings allows the mind to be concentrated:

"making the mind and body still."

The concentration of mind allows meditation to occur. Meditation allows the experiencing of increasing levels of awareness beyond the regular state of waking consciousness, leading to the experiencing of cosmic consciousness: complete freedom.

Practicing the virtues and living a life of simplicity opens the way for spiritual growth by decreasing mental agitation from worries or inordinate worldly concerns. If one maintains balance in all conditions, there will be no situation that will interfere with one's intuition of truth and righteousness, or in achieving mental calmness for meditation. This is the way to the top of the Pyramid.

"Feelings, emotions and passions are good servants

Giving into hate and vengeance will lead to the undoing of the body and spirit. To control one's passions is to master one's own fate. Study the teachings and practice self-control, silence and meditation.

Never go to extremes with anything, for one extreme leads to another. Always strive for balance in all things. Moderation and equanimity in all events and situations are the deeper implications of the scales of *MAAT*. In this manner, the inner peace that allows for the quieting of the mind occurs. In this quiet, it is possible to discover your deeper Self. This is the meaning of the ancient Egyptian admonition:

> "Now, make thy body still.
> Meditate that you may know
> truth."

Maat Philosophy is encapsulated in the scales of Maat. The human heart, which symbolizes the mind and its intent as well as the person's actions are compared to the standard of Maat and the result of this comparison is what leads a person to their fate. The scales of Maat imply balance, but balance decreed by whom and for what reason?

From the one: Pure Consciousness, GOD, comes the other two, male and female, so now there can be an interaction between the three, which are really one manifesting as three. This principle of duality (male and female) is present throughout all manifestations in the phenomenal world (nature) including the human body. In each of us, there is a male and female aspect of consciousness.

Therefore, in order for creation to exist, the ONE TRUTH must appear to be more than one. Maat is therefore composed of two aspects or two truths, which are really two sides of the same reality. This concept is termed *"MAATI."*

The task of all religious or mystical systems is to BALANCE the interplay between Male and Female (considered together: MAATI), that is, to achieve an internal mode of consciousness which is rooted in the one instead of being caught in the interplay. In other words, *"To keep the balance."*

> "Harmony is the Union of Opposites."
> -Ancient Egyptian Proverb

From a deeper perspective, by having an intuitive understanding of the union underlying creation and of its appearance of duality, one can identify with the Union, the Oneness, and therefore cultivate this unity within one's self. This is the basis of Egyptian Tantra Yoga --- seeking union with GOD through the worship and understanding of Nature (Female) as a projection of GOD (Male).

> "As above, So Below."
> "We are created in the IMAGE of GOD."
> -Ancient Egyptian Proverbs

If we understand that which is below (the physical, manifesting world), then we will understand that which is above (the spiritual world: GOD, who causes the physical world to exist). If we understand the human constitution, we will understand the cosmic constitution, because the manifestation is an exact image of the source. For every function of an organ in the human body and in the objects of the universe, there are likewise cosmic organs and functions which cause them to manifest. Therefore, in order to pursue union with GOD, one must seek to uphold the Cosmic Laws with respect to the balance of the opposites in all areas, through perfect justice, righteousness and with the greatest wisdom which comes not from our mental process, but from our soul (BA). The wisdom of the BA can be accessed through seeking purity of heart and meditation. As we pursue *"the union of opposites"*, we will discover that there are no opposites, only the projected appearance of them. We will discover that underlying the names and forms projected by the Neters (causal powers from GOD), the only reality is GOD. The Cause is GOD, the Causing Neters are GOD, "We are God," All is God. Therefore, from an advanced standpoint, we begin to see that there is no cause for the creation of the world, there is no past and no future but only an eternal present. Living life according to the teachings of virtue engenders a movement within the human heart which allows spiritual sensitivity to develop. A person becomes sensitive to a transcendental reality which goes beyond ordinary human perception.

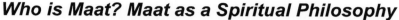

Who is Maat? Maat as a Spiritual Philosophy

MAAT is the *daughter of Ra (the Divine),* and she was with him on His celestial boat when he first emerged from the primeval waters along with His company of gods and goddesses. She is also known as the *eye of Ra, lady of heaven, queen of the earth, mistress of the Netherworld and the lady of the gods and goddesses.* MAAT also has a dual form or *MAATI.* In her *capacity* of God, MAAT is *Shes MAAT* which means *ceaseless-ness and regularity* of the course of the sun (i.e. the universe). In the form of MAATI, she represents the South and the North which symbolize Upper and Lower Egypt as well as the Higher and lower Self. MAAT is the personification of justice and righteousness upon which God has created the universe and MAAT is also the essence of God and creation. Therefore, it is MAAT who judges the soul when it arrives in the judgment hall of MAAT. Sometimes MAAT herself becomes the scales upon which the heart of the initiate is judged. MAAT judges the heart (unconscious mind) of the initiate in an attempt to determine to what extent the heart has lived in accordance with MAAT or truth, correctness, reality, genuineness, uprightness, righteousness, justice, steadfastness and the unalterable nature of creation.

The ancient Egyptian Goddess MAAT holds a papyrus reed scepter (See above). Papyrus is the ancient medium or writing upon which the teachings of wisdom are recorded. She is the symbolic embodiment of world order, justice, righteousness, correctness, harmony, and peace. She is also known by her headdress composed of a feather of truth. Her name is synonymous with mother since the syllable *"ma"* is a universal hekau or mantram signifying mother in many countries of the world. For example, mother in English, madre in Spanish, mata in Hindi all convey the same meaning. All of these arise from the root *Ma.* Thus, she is also known as *Ma* or *Maa* or the universal mother, the cosmic mother. She is a form of the Goddess Isis, *Aset,* who represents wisdom and spiritual awakening.

Figure 6: Goddess Maat

When Ra (the Divine Self, God) emerged in his Celestial Boat for the first time and creation came into being, he was standing on the pedestal of Maat. Thus the Creator, Ra, lives by Maat and has established Creation on Maat. Who is Maat? Maat represents the very order which constitutes creation. Therefore, it is said that Ra created the universe by putting Maat in the place of chaos. So creation itself is Maat. Creation without order is chaos. Maat is a profound teaching in reference to the nature of creation and the manner in which human conduct should be cultivated. It refers to a deep understanding of Divinity and the manner in which virtuous qualities can be developed in the human heart so as to come closer to the Divine.

Maat is a philosophy, a spiritual symbol as well as a cosmic energy or force which pervades the entire universe. She is the symbolic embodiment of world order, justice, righteousness, correctness, harmony, and peace. She is also known by her headdress composed of a feather of truth. She is a form of the Goddess Isis (Aset), who represents wisdom and spiritual awakening through balance and equanimity.

In ancient Egypt, the judges and all those connected with the judicial system were initiated into the teachings of MAAT. Thus, those who would discharge the laws and regulations of society were well trained in the ethical and spiritual-mystical values of life (presented in this volume), fairness, justice, and the responsibility to serve society in order to promote harmony in society and the possibility of spiritual development in an atmosphere of freedom and peace. For only when there is justice and fairness in society can there be an abiding harmony and peace. Harmony and peace are necessary for the pursuit of true happiness and inner fulfillment in life.

Along with her associates, the goddesses *Shai, Rennenet,* and *Meskhenet*, Maat encompass the teachings of Karma and Reincarnation or the destiny of every individual based on past actions, thoughts, and feelings. Thus, they have an important role to play in the Judgment scene of the *Pert Em Heru* or *Book of Coming Forth By Day*. Understanding their principles leads the aspirant to become free of the cycle of reincarnation and human suffering and to discover supreme bliss and immortality.

MAAT TEACHING #12: The Philosophy of Aryu

Figure 7: Judgment of the Heart in the Netherworld, detailing the philosophy of aryu (Karma) and Uhem ankh (reincarnation). Presented in the books: Egyptian Book of the Dead and the 2014 Neterian Conference presentation.

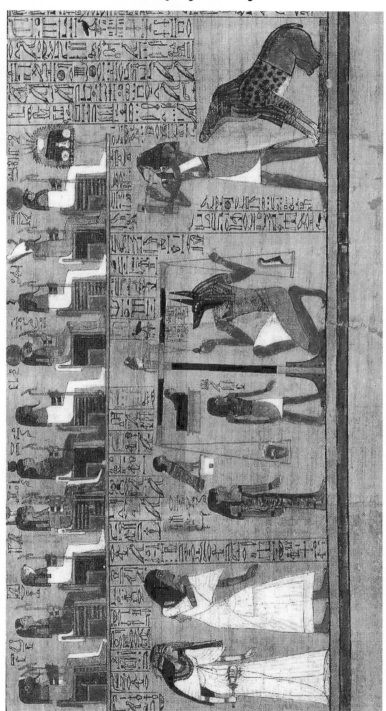

Figure 8: The characters in the Ancient Egyptian Judgement that work out the function of karma and reincarnation of the soul

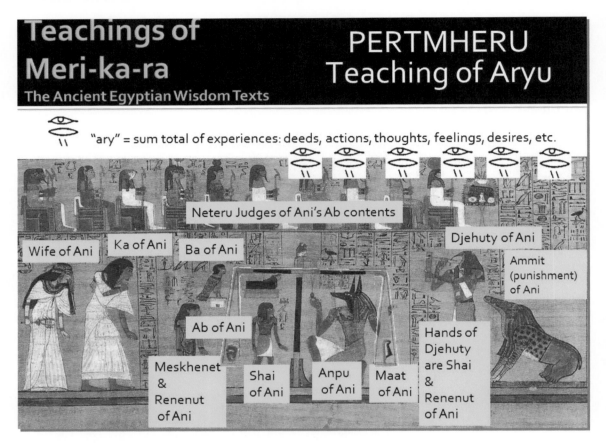

MAAT signifies *that which is straight*. Two of the symbols of MAAT are the ostrich feather (𓆄) and the pedestal (▱) upon which God stands. The Supreme Being, in the form of the God *Ptah,* is often depicted standing on the pedestal of Maat.

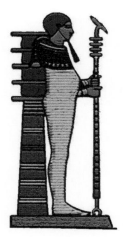

MAAT is the daughter of Ra, the high God, thus in a hymn to Ra we find:

The land of Manu (the West) receives thee with satisfaction, and the goddess MAAT embraces thee both at morn and at eve... the god Djehuty and the goddess MAAT have written down thy daily course for thee every day...

Another Hymn in the Papyrus of Qenna provides deeper insight into MAAT. Qenna says:

I have come to thee, O Lord of the Gods, Temu-Heru-khuti, whom MAAT directeth... Amen-Ra rests upon MAAT... Ra lives by MAAT... Osiris carries along the earth in His train by MAAT...

Who is MAATI?

In the segment above we introduced the idea of opposites in creation. The Hall of MAAT known as the hall of judgment for the heart is presided over by two goddesses known as *Maati*. The ancient Egyptian texts reveal that these two goddesses are none other than Aset (Isis) and Nebthet (Nephthys). They are complementary goddess principles which operate to manifest life-death-life or the cycle of birth-death-rebirth known as reincarnation.

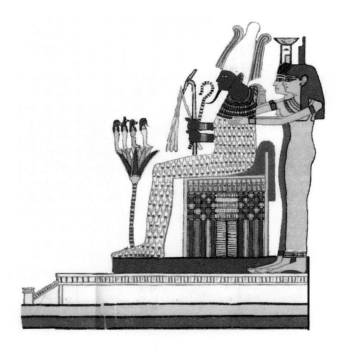

Aset (Isis) and Nebthet (Nephthys) are depicted as looking exactly alike, the only difference being in their head dresses: Aset ⬛, Nebthet ⬛ or ⬛. However, the symbols of these goddesses are in reality just inverted images of each other. The symbol of Aset is the symbol of Nebthet when inverted ⬛→⬛. Therefore, each is a reflection of the other, thus, it can be said that both life and death are aspects of the same principle.

The bodies and facial features of Aset (Isis) and Nebthet (Nephthys) are exactly alike. This likeness which Aset and Nebthet share is important when they are related to Asar (Osiris). As Asar (Osiris) sits on the throne, he is supported by the two goddesses, Aset and Nebthet. Symbolically, Asar represents the Supreme Soul, the all-encompassing Divinity which transcends time and space. Aset represents wisdom and enlightened consciousness. She is the knower of all words of power and has the power to resurrect Asar and Heru (Horus). Nebthet represents temporal consciousness or awareness of time and space. She is related to mortal life and mortal death. Thus, the state of spiritual Enlightenment is being referred to here as Isis, and it is this enlightened state of mind which the initiate in the Asarian (Osirian) Mysteries (*Asar Shetaiu*) has as the goal. The Enlightenment of Asar is the state of consciousness in which one is aware of the transient aspects of creation (Nebthet) as well as the transcendental (Aset). Aset represents the transcendental aspect of matter, that is, matter when seen through the eyes of wisdom rather than through the illusions produced by the ego which can only see Nebthet (gross nature and temporal existence). So, an enlightened personality is endowed with dual consciousness. To become one with Asar Higher Self-Supreme Spirit) means to attain the consciousness of Asar, to become aware of the transcendental, infinite and immortal nature (Aset) while also being aware of the temporal and fleeting human nature (Nebthet).

Aset and Nebthet are also known as *Rekhtti:* the two goddesses. They manifest in the Judgment hall of Maat in the *Egyptian Book of Coming Forth By Day* as *Maati* or the double Maat goddesses who watch over the weighing of the heart of the initiate (*The Asar {Osiris}*) in their name as *Rekhtti Merti neb-ti Maati*. Aset and Nebthet are the basis of the judgment of the soul and the criterion which decides its fate in life as well as after death.

What is True Virtue?

In order to understand what true virtue is and all of the elements that drive a human being and cause him or her to be the way he or she is, we must begin by understanding the teachings of karma and reincarnation. The human being is not simply a mind and body which will someday cease to exist. In fact, every human being's mind and body are in reality emanations or expressions of their eternal Soul. The mind and body are referred to as the ego-personality, and it is this ego-personality which is temporal and mortal. The Soul is immortal and perfect while the ego-personality is subject to error, confusion and the consequences of these. If a human being is aware of the deeper soul-reality, this state of being is known as the state of *Enlightenment.* However, if a human being does not have knowledge and experience of their Higher Self, then they exist in a condition of ignorance which will lead to sinful behavior, pain and sorrow in life.

The ego-personality is subject to the forces of time and space and will suffer the consequences of its actions. This is the basis for the teaching of Karma. When the physical body dies, the soul moves on. If the human being has discovered his/her Higher Self (purified the heart {mind and body}), then the soul moves forward to unite with the Supreme Self (God). If the ego in a person is fettered by ignorance, then the soul moves in an astral plane until it finds another ego-personality about to be born again in the world of time and space so that it may have an opportunity to have experiences that will lead it to discover its higher nature. This is the basis for the teaching of reincarnation.

"He delivers whom he pleases, even from the Duat (Netherworld)."
"He saves a man or woman from what is
His lot at the dictates of their heart."

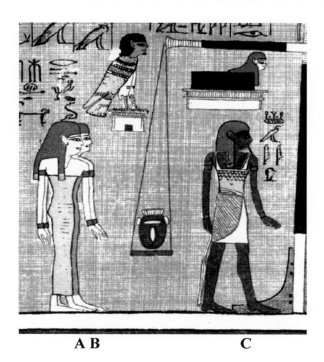

A B   C

The utterances above are directly referring to Meskhenet or karma. Many people believe that karma is equal to fate or destiny, however, this interpretation could not be further from the original understanding of the ancient Sages. The etymology of the word, karma, comes from the Sanskrit "karman" which means deed or action. In Yoga philosophy, karma also refers to one's actions and these same actions lead to certain experiences and consequences. In ancient Egyptian philosophy, the word Meskhenet comes from the goddess who goes by the same name. She presides over the birth circumstances and life experiences of every individual. She is the one who carries out the decree which has been ordained by Djehuty after the judgment of the heart in the hall of MAAT. It is Djehuty who records the deeds (actions) or karmas of every individual and then decrees what the Shai(C) and Rennenet(B) which are fitting for that particular individual. Then with the help of Shai and Rennenet, Meskhenet(A) causes the individual to experience the proper circumstances based on their previous deeds.

The ancient Egyptian hieroglyphic symbol of the heart is a heart shaped vase, ⏶. The vase is a container which may be used for water, beer, wine, milk, etc. Likewise, the human heart is seen as a vessel which contains thoughts, feelings, desires and unconscious memories. In mystical terms, the heart is a metaphor for the human mind including the conscious, subconscious and unconscious levels. The mind is the reservoir of all of your ideas, convictions, and feelings. Therefore, just as these factors direct the path of your life, so too they are the elements which are judged in the Hall of Maati by the two goddesses, Aset and Nebthet, along with Asar. The heart then is the sum total of your experiences, actions and aspirations, your conscience or karma, and these are judged in the balance against the feather of Maat.

ariu-(aryu) {actions, deeds}

The Ancient Egyptian word "*Ari*" [plural *Aryu*] means "action". It is akin to the Indian philosophy called Karma. Karma or *Aryu* should be thought of as the total effect of a person's actions and conduct during the successive phases of his/her existence through lifetimes. But how does this effect operate? How do the past actions affect the present and the future? Your experiences from the present life or from previous lifetimes cause unconscious impressions which stay with the Soul even after death. These unconscious impressions are what constitute the emerging thoughts, desires, and aspirations of every individual. These impressions are not exactly like memories, however, they work like memories. For example, if you had a fear, about something, in a previous lifetime or the childhood of your present lifetime, you may not remember the event that caused the fear, but you may experience certain phobias when you come into contact with certain objects or certain people. These feelings are caused by the unconscious impressions which are coming up to the surface of the conscious mind. It is this conglomerate of unconscious impressions which are "judged" in the Hall of MAAT and determine where the soul will go to next in the spiritual journey toward evolution or devolution, also known as the cycle of birth and death or reincarnation, as well as the experiences of heaven or hell. The following segment from the ancient Egyptian "Instruction to Mer-ka-Ra" explains this point.

"You know that they are not merciful the day when they judge the miserable one..... Do not count on the passage of the years; they consider a lifetime as but an hour. After death man remains in existence and His acts accumulate beside him. Life in the other world is eternal, but he who arrives without sin before the Judge of the Dead, he will be there as a Neter and he will walk freely as do the masters of eternity."

The reference above to "His acts accumulate beside him" alludes to the unconscious impressions which are formed as a result of one's actions while still alive. These impressions can be either positive or negative. Positive impressions are developed through positive actions by living a life of righteousness (MAAT) and virtue. This implies living according to the precepts of mystical wisdom or being a follower of Heru (*Shemsu Heru*) and Aset. These actions draw one closer to harmony and peace, thus paving the way to discover the Self within. The negative impressions are developed through sinful actions. They are related to mental agitation, disharmony, and restlessness. This implies acts based on anger, fear, desire, greed, depression, gloom, etc. These actions draw one into the outer world of human desires. They distract the mind and do not allow the intellect (Saa) to function. Thus, existence at this level is closer to an animal, being based on animal instincts and desires of the body (selfishness), rather than to a spiritually mature human being, being based on reason, selflessness, compassion, etc.

(Purification of the heart)

How then is it possible to eradicate negative karmic impressions and to develop positive ones? The answer lies in your understanding of the wisdom teachings and your practice of them. When you study the teachings and live according to them, your mind undergoes a transformation at all levels. This transformation is the "purification of heart" so often spoken about throughout the *Egyptian Book of Coming Forth By Day*. It signifies an eradication of negative impressions, which renders the mind pure and subtle. When the mind is rendered subtle, then spiritual realization is possible. This discipline of purifying the heart by living according to the teachings is known as the Yoga of Action or MAAT.

The philosophy of MAAT is a profound teaching which encompasses the fabric of creation as well as a highly effective system of spiritual discipline. In creation stories, God (Neter Neteru) is said to have established creation upon MAAT. Consequently, it follows that MAAT is the orderly flow of energy which maintains the universe. Further, MAAT is the regularity which governs the massive planetary and solar systems as well as the growth of a blade of grass and a human cell. This natural process represents the flow of creation wherein there is constant movement and a balancing of opposites (up-down, hot-cold, here-there, you-me, etc.).

Most people act out of the different forces which are coursing through them at the time. These may be hunger, lust, fear, hatred, anger, elation, etc. They have no control over these because they have not understood that their true essence is in reality separate from their thoughts and emotions. They have *identified* with their thoughts and therefore are led to the consequences of those thoughts and the deeds they engender. You, as an aspirant, having developed a higher level of spiritual sensitivity, are now aware that you have a choice in the thoughts you think and the actions you perform. You can choose whether to act in ways that are in harmony with MAAT or those that are disharmonious. You have now studied the words of wisdom and must now look beyond the level of ritual worship of the Divine to the realm of practice and experience of the Divine.

In ordinary human life, those who have not achieved the state of Enlightenment (the masses in society at large) perceive nature as a conglomeration of forces which are unpredictable and in need of control. However, as spiritual sensitivity matures, the aspirant realizes that what once appeared to be chaotic is, in reality, the Divine Plan of the Supreme Being in the process of unfoldment. When this state of consciousness is attained, the aspirant realizes that there is an underlying order in nature which can only be perceived with spiritual eyes.

The various injunctions of MAAT are for the purpose of keeping order in society among ordinary people, people without psychological maturity and, or spiritual sensitivity, meaning that they lack an awareness of spiritual principles and moral - ethical development. Also, they provide insight into the order of creation and a pathway or spiritual discipline, which when followed, will lead the aspirant to come into harmony with the cosmic order. When the individual attunes his or her own sense of order and balance with the cosmic order, a spontaneous unity occurs between the individual and the cosmos, and the principles of MAAT, rather than being a blind set of rules which we must strive to follow, become a part of one's inner character and proceed from one in a spontaneous manner.

This means that through the deeper understanding of cosmic order and by the practice of living in harmony with that order, the individual will lead him or herself to mental and spiritual peace and harmony. It is this peace and harmony which allows the lake of the mind to become a clear mirror in which the individual soul is able to realize its oneness with the Universal Soul.

Maat as a Legal Basis for Laws and Law Enforcement

Over the years I have lectured on the great ancient African philosophy known as *Maat,* the principle of righteousness, truth, justice, order, and harmony. It was in Ancient Egypt that this beatific vision for society was developed to a very high degree. It found expression through the spiritual researches of the ancient Egyptian sages and became the cornerstone upon which the entire civilization depended, beginning with the *Per-aah,* or Pharaoh. The Per-aah's (image right offering a statue of Maat) main duty was to see that the country was ordered by Maat, lest society be destroyed by the evil of greed, corruption, and lawlessness. This aspect of Ancient Egyptian culture is what allowed the creation of a well-ordered society that persisted for so many <u>thousands</u> of years. The Per-aah delegated the management of the laws of the country to the Vizier, who oversaw the judges and law enforcement officials of the country. Unlike the modern western system of justice, in

Ancient Egypt, there was no notion of an adversarial system. That is, there was an understanding that all parties should desire after truth and all advocates (lawyers) would be required to speak the truth.

The legal system of ancient Egypt was managed by the judges who were priests and priestesses of the goddess Maat and were expected to uphold very high standards of ethics in their judgments as well as their personal lives, lest they lose spiritual merit and be given over to the demoniac forces after death, due to their own unrighteousness. Laws were based on A- the teachings of the sages, B- decrees by the Per-aah as well as C- on previous court cases, which were recorded and kept in archives (previous case law).

Thus, Maat was not just a legal system but a philosophical way of life which promoted righteous dealing amongst human beings in order to promote social harmony and in turn this social harmony could then allow the entire society to turn towards spiritual pursuits. All members of society were expected to live by Maat, including especially the Per-aah and the Vizier. This factor is what allowed ancient Egyptian society to create such magnanimous monuments which still attest to their devotion to the Divine.

Grounded in spiritual principles, Maat Philosophy of Africa is in every way comparable to the *Dharma* of the Hindus and Buddhists. It can be taught in an ecumenical religious format or in a secular format. It is based on the teachings of the Ancient Egyptian sages such as Sage Ptahotep, Sage Ani, Sage Amenemope, Sage Kaqemna and many others (this is covered in *The 42 Principles of Maat and the Philosophy of Righteous Action* book).

Aside from the precepts listed in the *Pert M Heru* or *Ancient Egyptian Book of Coming Forth By Day,* and the writings of the Sages (Known as the *Wisdom Texts*), containing precepts and expositions on righteous living, the laws were not codified in Ancient Egypt. This is because the law was something to be applied in principle and spirit in everyday life as opposed to following a strict regulation for the court and law enforcement system alone. Maat was seen as an integral aspect of life and it was to be practiced not just in the court room but in all areas of life. However, in the late period of Ancient Egyptian history when the Persians temporarily conquered the country, a law code was written based on the preexisting statutes of Ancient Egypt. Emperor Darius commanded that the laws be written. This writing was set down in Aramaic, (the original language of parts of the Old Testament. After the Babylonian captivity, it was the common written and spoken language of the Middle East until replaced by Arabic and Demotic (late ancient Egyptian script).

It is appropriate to include here that ancient Greek ethics and spiritual culture were also an outgrowth of Kemetic (Ancient Egyptian) culture and religion and this all served as a basis for Western culture (see my books: *Egyptian Yoga Volume I* and *From Egypt To Greece*). Thus, the study and application of the timeless principles of Maat Philosophy have wide ranging implications for society, law enforcement officials, the clergy and for individuals who want to evolve spiritually. It can benefit society as a whole, the African community in general and individual practitioners in their specific spiritual pursuits, for, spiritual evolution cannot occur in unrighteous personalities and societies whose basis is unrighteousness, greed, and unfairness. Such societies will promote discontent and frustration in people, obstructing their spiritual lives. According to the Ancient Egyptian teachings, this type of society will ultimately experience unrest, disintegration, and collapse.

MAAT as the Spiritual Path of Righteous Action

MAAT is equivalent to the Chinese concept of the *Tao* or *"The Way"* of nature. This *"Way"* of nature, from the *Tao-te-Ching*, the main text of Taoism, represents the harmony of human and Divine (universal) consciousness. And as previously discussed, MAAT may be likened with the Indian idea of *Dharma* or the ethical values of life and the teachings related to *Karma Yoga,* the yogic spiritual discipline which emphasizes selfless service and the attitude that actions are being performed by God who is working through you instead of your personal ego-self. God is working through you to serve humanity, which is also essentially God. All Buddhist Monks utter the prayer *I go to the Buddha for refuge. I go to the Dharma for refuge. I go to the monastic order for refuge.*

Above: Ra, the father of Maat, traverses in his boat and she sits in the bow of the boat making order so that the boat may sail. This symbolizes the need to have order before spirituality can unfold.

The Buddhist aspirant is admonished to take refuge in the *Buddha* (one's innate *Buddha Consciousness*), the *Dharma*, and the *Sanga* (company of enlightened personalities). The following statement from chapter 9 of the Bhagavad Gita shows how Lord Krishna admonished his followers to seek sanctuary in him as Jesus did hundreds of years later.

32. O Arjuna, those who take refuge in Me

Jesus also exhorted his followers to bring him their troubles "and He will give them rest". Dharma is understood as the spiritual discipline based on righteousness, order, and truth which sustains the universe. In the same way, the ancient Egyptian Initiate was to lean upon MAAT in order to purify his or her heart so as to uncover the virtuous character which leads to Divine awareness.

"There are two roads traveled by humankind, those who seek to live MAAT, and those who seek to satisfy their animal passions."

Ancient Egyptian Proverb

It is important here to gain a deeper understanding of what is meant by *action.* In primeval times, before creation, the primordial ocean existed in complete peace and rest. When that ocean was agitated with the first thought of God, the first *act* was performed. Through the subsequent *acts of mind* or *efforts of divine thought,* creation unfolded in the form of the various gods and goddesses who form the "companies of Gods". They represent the qualities of nature (hot-cold, wet-dry, etc.) in the form of pairs of opposites. When the first primeval thought emerged from the primeval ocean of pure potentiality, immediately there was something other than the single primordial essence. Now there is a being who is looking and perceiving the rest of the primordial essence. This is the origin of duality in the world of time and space and the triad of human consciousness. Instead of there being one entity, there appears to be two. The perception instrument, the mind, and senses, is the third factor which comprises the triad. Therefore, while you consider yourself to be an individual, you are in reality one element in a triad which altogether comprise the content of your human experiences. There is a perceiver (the real you), that which is being perceived (the object) and the act of perception itself (through the mind and senses).

With this first primordial act, God set into motion events which operate according to regular and ceaseless motion or action. This is the foundation upon which the universe is created and it emerges from the mind of God. Therefore, if one is able to think and act according to the way in which God thinks and acts, then there will be oneness with God. Human beings are like sparks of divine consciousness, and as such, are endowed with free will to act in any given way. This free will, when dictated by the egoism of the individual mind, causes individual human beings to feel separate from God. This delusion of the mind leads it to develop ideas related to its own feelings and desires. These egoistic feelings and desires lead to the performance of egoistic acts in an effort to satisfy those perceived needs and desires. This pursuit of fulfillment of desires in the relative world of the mind and senses leads the soul to experience pain, sorrow, and frustration because these can never be 100% satisfied. Frustration leads to more actions in search of fulfillment.

The fleeting feelings which most people have associated with happiness and passion are only ephemeral glimpses of the true happiness and peace which can be experienced if the source of true fulfillment within you was to be discovered. MAAT shows a way out of the pain and sorrow of human existence and leads you to discover Osiris within you, the source of eternal bliss and supreme peace. If you choose to act according to your own will (ego), then you will be in contradiction with MAAT. This means that you are contradicting your own conscience, creating negative impressions which will become lodged in the heart (unconscious mind) and will cause continuous mental agitation while you are alive and hellish experiences for yourself after death. The negative impressions rise up at given times in the form of uncontrolled desires, cravings, unrest, and the other forms of self-torment with which human life abounds.

It is important to understand that when the soul is attuned to a physical body, mind, and senses, the experiences occur through these. Thus, the experiences of pleasure and pain are regulated by how much the body, mind, and senses can take. If there is too much pain the body faints. When there is too much pleasure the mind and senses become weakened and mind swoons into unconsciousness or sleep. If there is too much pleasure, there develops elation and the soul is carried off with the illusion of pleasure, which creates a longing and craving for more and more in an endless search for fulfillment.

However, after death, there is no safety valve as it were. Under these conditions, the soul will have the possibility of experiencing boundless amounts of pleasure or pain according to its karmic basis. This is what is called heaven and hell, respectively. Therefore, if you have lived a balanced life (MAAT), then you will not have the possibility of experiencing heaven or hell. Rather, you will retain the presence of mind and will not fall into the delusion of ignorance. Therefore, the rewards of developing a balanced mind during life continue after death. This mental equanimity allows you to see the difference between the truth and the illusions of the mind and senses, in life as well as in death.

Thus, if you choose to act in accordance with MAAT, you will be in a position to transcend the egoistic illusions of the mind and thereby become free from the vicious cycle of actions which keep the mind tied to its illusory feelings and desires. When the mind is freed from the "vicious cycle", the soul's bondage to the world of time and space is dissolved because it is not being controlled by the mind but has become the controller of the mind. When the practice of MAAT is perfected, the mind becomes calm. When this occurs, the ocean of consciousness which was buffeted by the stormy winds of thoughts, anxieties, worries, and desires, becomes calm. This calmness allows the soul to cease its identification with the thoughts of the mind and to behold its true nature as a separate entity from the mind, senses, feelings, and thoughts of the ego-self. The soul is now free to expand its vision beyond the constrictive pettiness of human desires and mental agitation, in order to behold the expansion of the inner Self.

Actions are the basis upon which the Cosmic Plan of creation unfolds. In human life, it is the present action which leads to the results that follow at some point in the future, in this life or in another lifetime. Therefore, if you are in a prosperous situation today or an adverse one, it is because of actions you performed in the past. Thus, both situations, good or bad, should be endured with a sense of personal responsibility and equanimity of mind (MAAT). From a transcendental point of view, the Soul looks at all situations equally. This is because the Soul knows itself to be immortal and eternal, and untouched by the events of human existence which it has witnessed for countless lifetimes. It is the ego, which is transient, that looks on life situations as pressing and real and therefore either tries to hold onto situations which it considers to be "good" or to get away from or eradicate situations which it considers to be "bad". All situations, whether they are considered to be good or bad by the ego, will eventually pass on, so we should try to view them as clouds which inevitably pass on, no matter how terrible or how wonderful they may seem to be. When life is lived in this manner, the mind develops a stream of peace which rises above elation and depression, prosperity and adversity. By looking at situations with equal vision and doing your best regardless of the circumstances, you are able to discover an unalterable balance within yourself. This is MAAT, the underlying order, and truth behind the apparent chaos and disorder in the phenomenal world. In doing this, you are able to attune your mind to the cosmic mind of the innermost Self which exists at that transcendental level of peace all the time.

This means that if you are, deep down, indeed the Universal Self, one with God, and if you have come to your current situation in life of bondage to the world of time and space due to your own state of mental ignorance, then it follows that if you undertake certain disciplines of knowledge (studying the teachings) and daily practice (following the teachings), those same actions will lead you to liberation from the state of bondage. Ignorance of your true Self is the root cause of your bondage to the karmic cycle of life-death-reincarnation-life-death-reincarnation, etc.

Actions must be performed by everyone. Even breathing is an action. Therefore, nobody can escape actions. No one can say: "I will go far away from civilization and escape all actions and then my actions will not lead me to a state of ignorance about my true Self". This form of thinking is a fallacy because, as just discussed, breathing, eating, drinking, sleeping, sitting, and walking are actions. The process of liberation requires more than just removing yourself from the field of physical actions. You could go to a quiet cave, temple or church and you would still be plagued by the unruly thoughts of the mind which cause distraction from the Self. Thoughts are subtle forms of actions. Therefore, an action performed in thought can be equally significant and cause as much karmic entanglement as an action performed with the body. An action first originates in the mental field (astral plane) of consciousness which is stirred by desires rising from the unconscious mind. This agitation prompts the mind toward thoughts and actions in an attempt to fulfill the desires of the unconscious, but those actions and thoughts create more desires and more future agitation. This is the state of bondage which is experienced by most people and it continues for lifetimes without end. This cycle continues until there is a discovery that desires cannot be fulfilled in this manner. Therefore, the root of desire, ignorance, must be eradicated in order to end the desires of the mind and achieve true peace and balance.

You need to develop subtlety of intellect and profound insight into the nature of the universe and of your innermost Self. The best way to achieve this goal is to practice a blending of wisdom and action in your personal spiritual discipline in order to harmonize your mental and physical qualities.

In this process, you must understand that the ancient Sages have given guidelines for which thoughts and actions are in line with the scales of MAAT, and which actions and thoughts are not. The 42 precepts of MAAT constitute the focus of the Egyptian Book of Coming Forth By Day, however, throughout the book, many injunctions are given. Their purpose is to cleanse the heart of the aspirant.

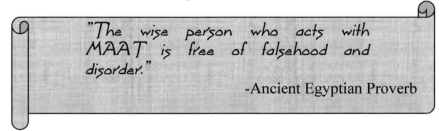

"The wise person who acts with MAAT is free of falsehood and disorder."

-Ancient Egyptian Proverb

The practice of MAAT signifies *wisdom in action*. This is to say that the teachings are to be practiced in ordinary day to day situations, and when the deeper implications of this practice are understood, one will be led to purity in action and thought.

In order to become one with the Divine, you must become the Divine in thought and deed. This means that you must spiritualize your actions and your thoughts at all times and under all conditions. Actions which present themselves to you in the normal course of the day, as well as those actions which you have planned for the future, should be evaluated by your growing intellectual discriminative quality (Anubis and Saa), and then performed to your best capacity in a selfless manner.

MAAT and Yoga Philosophy

Yoga is the practice of mental, physical and spiritual disciplines which lead to self-control and self-discovery by purifying the mind, body, and spirit so as to discover the deeper spiritual essence which lies within every human being and every object in the universe. In essence, the object of yoga practices is to unite or *Yoke* individual consciousness with universal or cosmic consciousness. Therefore, ancient Egyptian religious practice, especially in terms of the rituals and other practices of the ancient Egyptian temple known as *Shetaut Neter* (the way of the hidden Supreme Being), may be termed as a system yoga, *Egyptian Yoga*. In this sense, religion is a form of yoga system which seeks to reunite people with their true and original source.

The disciplines of Yoga fall under five major categories, these are *Yoga of Wisdom, Yoga of Devotional Love, Yoga of Meditation, Tantric Yoga* and *Yoga of Selfless Action*. Within these categories, there are subsidiary forms which are part of the main disciplines. The emphasis, in the Osirian Myth, is on the Yoga of Wisdom, Yoga of Devotional Love and the Yoga of Selfless Action. The important point to remember is that all aspects of yoga can and should be used in an integral fashion to effect an efficient and harmonized, spiritual movement in the practitioner. Therefore, while there may be an area of special emphasis, other elements are bound to become part of the yoga program as needed. For example, while a yogin may place emphasis on the yoga of wisdom, they may also practice devotional yoga and meditation yoga along with the wisdom studies.

So the practice of any disciplines that lead to oneness with Supreme Consciousness is called yoga. If you study, rationalize and reflect upon the teachings you are practicing *Yoga of Wisdom*. If you meditate upon the teachings and your Higher Self you are practicing *Yoga of Meditation*. If you practice rituals which identify you with your spiritual nature you are practicing *Yoga of Ritual Identification* (which is part of the yoga of wisdom and the yoga of devotional love of the Divine). If you develop your physical nature and psychic energy centers you are practicing *Serpent Power* (*Kundalini or Uraeus*) *Yoga* (which is part of Tantric Yoga). If you practice living according to the teachings of ethical behavior and selflessness you are practicing *Yoga of Action* (Maat) in daily life. If you practice turning your attention toward the Divine by developing a love for the Divine then it is called *Devotional Yoga* or *Yoga of Divine Love*. The practitioner of yoga is called a yogin (male practitioner) or yogini (female practitioner) and one who has attained the culmination of yoga (union with the Divine) is also called a yogi. In this manner, yoga has been developed into many disciplines which may be used in an integral fashion to achieve the same goal: Enlightenment. Therefore, the aspirant should learn about all of the paths of yoga and choose those elements which best suit his/her personality or practice them all in an integral, balanced way.

The Significance of The Precepts of Maat

At the time of death or prior to death, the heart (consciousness, Ab) of the human being is weighed against truth, symbolized by the feather of Maat. Here our divine faculties of reason and moral rectitude and our ability to practice the precepts while on earth are judged. Below: The Scales of Maat in the Ancient Egyptian Judgment scene from the *Book of Coming Forth By Day* (Book of the Dead).

Below: The Scales of Maat from the Qenna (Kenna) Papyrus.

In the Hall of Maati, the heart and internal organs of the deceased are judged by the 42 judges (gods and goddesses) who are each in charge of one regulation. All 42 regulations or virtuous guidelines for righteous living make up the basis for the 42 "negative confessions." If one lives righteously, one will be able to say that one has <u>NOT</u>

committed any offense. Upon uttering these words, the deceased takes on a new name. For example, instead of Lisa Williams, it is now Asar Lisa Williams.

The objective of life is to become "light of heart." That is to say, one should live a life that is free of stress and which promotes mental peace. When this is possible, the mind relaxes and reveals the divine nature of the soul. If the heart is weighed down by egoism due to a life of worry, lies, frustration, and desire, the heart will be judged as heavier than the feather. Instead of moving forward to join with Asar (God), the deceased, in this case, Asar Lisa Williams, is sent back to the world in the form of an animal if her acts were very sinful or she will undergo reincarnation into a human form to again try to become "light of heart."

If the heart of Asar Lisa Williams is found to be lighter than the feather or of equal weight, it signifies that she has led a virtuous life and has mastered the *knowledge and wisdom of every god* (all of which are aspects of the one God, meaning she has mastered all 42 precepts) and that she is fit for a new life. Asar Lisa Williams is ready to transcend this world onto the next realm of existence. She is ready to journey back to meet Cosmic Asar, who represents Cosmic Consciousness, her own Higher Self (God).

Asar Lisa Williams, through her own virtuous life, is allowed to take or fashion a new, glorious body, to live in eternity as one with Asar (God). Thus, Asar Lisa Williams, the individual human soul, meets and joins with Asar (God), the Supreme Being. This is the attainment of Enlightenment or the Kingdom of Heaven. This signifies that our own nature is that of universal consciousness. What was separated only by ignorance is now re-united, re-membered. It is only due to ignorance and to distraction in the world of seemingly desirable objects that we think we are individual human beings with bodies which are mortal. In reality, we are immortal and eternal beings who are one with the universe and each other. Through ignorance, fueled by egoistic desire, we have come to believe that the human existence is all there is. Through the process of living the teachings of Maat, the mind can be lightened to such a degree that it allows the soul to behold its true nature unclouded by the passions and desires of the mind.

The objective of all mystical religions and philosophies is to achieve this realization before the time of death. To realize this even before death, it is necessary to live in a virtuous manner, learning the lessons of human existence and uncovering the veil of ignorance which blinds us from the realization of our essential nature. We must, therefore, master the knowledge and wisdom of every "god," every precept.

Anubis (god of discernment between reality and illusion) and Djehuty (god of reason and truth) oversee the scales of Maat. They judge the condition of the Heart (Ab) and determine its level of spiritual achievement. This is also symbolized by the Ammit monster, devourer of hearts, who, according to the Ancient Egyptian *Kenna* papyrus, determines those who are the advanced spirits and worthy of salvation (those who have developed their higher consciousness centers: selflessness, peacefulness, universal love, etc.), symbolized by the fourth through seventh rings or levels of consciousness, and those who have not progressed beyond their base animal natures (lower consciousness centers: fear, attachments, egoistic desires, anger, hatred, etc.), symbolized by the lower three rings. The unrighteous are symbolically devoured by the Ammit monsters (demon).

As in the *Kundalini Chakra* system of India, those who achieve no higher than the level of the third Energy Center or Chakra are considered to be people on the same level of consciousness as animals. They are mostly concerned with satisfying the pleasures and desires of the senses (food, sex, controlling other people) and, therefore, will have to reincarnate in order to further evolve beyond this stage. Upon reincarnating, they will once again have the possibility of confronting situations which will afford them the opportunity to perform a corrective action and thus, to change. Correct action leads to correct feeling and thinking. Correct feeling and correct thinking lead to a state of consciousness which is unburdened. This is the goal— to unburden the mind so that consciousness, the soul, may be revealed in its true appearance. When this occurs the soul is discovered to be one with God and not individual and separate. One realizes that the Kingdom of Heaven is within oneself. This is the highest realization of all mysteries, yogas and religious systems.

The Egyptian *Book of Coming Forth By Day* is a text of wisdom about the true nature of reality and also of *Hekau* (chants, words of power, utterances [Indian *mantra*) to assist the initiate in making that reality evident. These chants are in reality wisdom affirmations which the initiate is to recite in order to assist him or her in changing the consciousness level of the mind. The hekau themselves may have no special power except in their assistance to the mind to change its perception through repetition with understanding and feeling in order to transform the mind into a still and centered state. Through these affirmations, the initiate is able to change his/her consciousness from body consciousness ("I am a body") to Cosmic Consciousness ("I am God"). This form of affirmatory (using affirmation in the first person) spiritual discipline is recognized by Indian Gurus as the most intense form of spiritual discipline. However, there must be clear and profound understanding of the teachings before the affirmations can have the intended result. It is also to be found in the Bible and in the Gnostic Gospels as we will see. Compare the preceding statements in the Indian Upanishads and the Christian Bible to the following Ancient Egyptian scriptures (*Metu Neter,* Sacred Speech) taken from the *Egyptian Book of Coming Forth By Day* (c. 10,000-5,000 B.C.E.) and other hieroglyphic texts:

From Indian Yoga wisdom:	From the Bible:	From Ancient Egypt:
"Aham brahma asmi" - I Am the Absolute	On the name of GOD: *"I Am That I Am."*(The Bible, Exodus 3:14)	*Nuk Pu Nuk. ("I Am That I Am.")*
	Jesus speaks of his own origin and identity: *"I and the Father (GOD) are ONE."* John 10:30	In reference to the relationship between GOD and Mankind: *Ntef änuk, änuk Ntef. ("He is I and I am He.")*

The 42 declarations of purity have profound implications for the spiritual development of the individual as well as for society. They may be grouped under three basic ethical teachings, *Truth, Non-violence,* and *Self-Control.* Under the heading of self-control, three subheadings may be added, *Balance of Mind or Right Thinking Based on Reason, Non-stealing,* and *Sex-Sublimation.* The principles of Maat may be compared to the principles of Dharma of India.

The Ancient Egyptians included elaborate scrolls with the mummies of the dead. These were known as the Books of the Dead. The early Coptic Christians also included a Book of the Dead and mummified their dead in keeping with the Ancient Egyptian traditions. The book consisted of sheets of papyrus inscribed with Gnostic Christian texts such as the gospels. Many of these Books of the Dead can be found in the British Museum. One of the surviving books, (Oriental #4919 (2), contains a copy of the Apocryphal letter of King Abgar to Christ and the first words of each of the four Gospels.

Maat Principles of Ethical Conduct	Hindu Dharma Principles of Ethical Conduct (From the *Manu Smriti*)
• **Truth** (1), (6), (7), (9), (24) • **Non-violence** (2), (3), (5), (12), (25), (26), (28), (30), (34) • **Right Action- Self-Control (Living in accordance with the teachings of Maat)** (15), (20), (22), (36) • **Right Speech** (11), (17), (23), (33), (35), (37) • **Right Worship** (13), (21), (32), (38), (42) • **Selfless Service** (29) • **Balance of Mind - Reason – Right Thinking** (14), (16), (18), (31), (39) • **Not-stealing** (4), (8), (10), (41) • **Sex-Sublimation** (19), (27)	• Firmness. • Forgiveness, forbearance. • Control of Senses. • Non Stealing. • Purity of body and mind. • Control of mind. • Purity of Intellect. • Knowledge. • Truthfulness. • Absence of anger.

There is one more important factor, which is inherent in the Precepts of Maat that must receive special mention. Generally, when people are ignorant of the greater spiritual realities and caught up in the emotionality of human life, they tend to look for something to blame for their miseries. They want to find a cause for the troubles of life and the easiest way to do this is to look around into the world and point to those factors around them, which seem to affect them, be they people, situations or objects. In Chapter 125 of the *Book of Coming Forth By Day,* the use of the word *nuk* ("I") is emphasized with a special connotation. The spiritual aspirant says continually "I have..." He or she does not say "You have allowed me" or "The devil made me do it" or "I wanted to, but I couldn't" etc.

There is a process of responsibility wherein the spiritual aspirant recognizes that he or she has the obligation to act righteously and, in so doing, to purify their own heart. Spiritual practice can succeed only when you assume responsibility for your actions, thoughts, words, and feelings. If you constantly blame your adversities on others or on situations, etc., you will be living life according to ignorance and weakness. True spiritual strength comes from leaning upon the Self within for spiritual support and wellbeing, rather than upon external situations, people or objects, even though the help itself may come in the form of external situations, people or objects.

Thus, within the teachings of Maat can be found all of the important injunctions for living a life, which promotes purity, harmony, and sanctity. While these may be found in other spiritual traditions from around the world, seldom is the emphasis on non-violence and ethics to be found. In Christianity, Jesus emphasized non-violence and in Hinduism and Buddhism, the discipline of *Dharma*, composed of *Yamas and Nyamas*, which are moral (righteous) observances and restraints for spiritual living, emphasizes non-violence. These are the restraints *(Yamas)*: Non-violence, Abstinence from falsehood (Truthfulness), Non-stealing, and Abstinence from sex-pleasure. These are the ethical observances *(Nyamas)*: Purity, Contentment, Austerity, Study of scriptures (and - repetition of *Mantra*- chanting*)*, and Surrender to God.

The Ancient Egyptian, Hindu, and Buddhist traditions were the first to recognize the power of non-violence to heal the anger and hatred within the aggressor as well as the victim. When this spiritual force is developed it is more formidable than any kind of physical violence. Therefore, anyone who wishes to promote peace and harmony in the world must begin by purifying every bit of negativity within themselves. This is the only way to promote harmony and peace in others. Conversely, if there is anger within you, you are indeed promoting anger outside of yourself and your efforts will be unsuccessful in the end.

The following is a composite summary of "negative confessions" from several Ancient Egyptian *Books of Coming Forth by Day*. They are often referred to as "Negative Confessions" since the person uttering them is affirming what moral principles they have not transgressed. In this respect, they are similar to the Yamas or ethical restraints of India. While all of these books include 42 precepts, some specific precepts varied according to the specific initiate for which they were prepared and the priests who compiled them. Therefore, I have included more than one precept per line where I felt it was appropriate to show that there were slight variations in the precepts and to more accurately reflect the broader view of the original texts.

(1) "I have not done iniquity." Variant: Acting with falsehood.
(2) "I have not robbed with violence."
(3) "I have not done violence (To anyone or anything)." Variant: Rapacious (Taking by force; plundering.)
(4) "I have not committed theft." Variant: Coveted.

(5) "I have not murdered man or woman." <u>Variant: Or ordered someone else to commit murder.</u>

(6) "I have not defrauded offerings." <u>Variant: or destroyed food supplies or increased or decreased the measures to profit.</u>

(7) "I have not acted deceitfully." <u>Variant: With crookedness.</u>

(8) "I have not robbed the things that belong to God."

(9) "I have told no lies."

(10) "I have not snatched away food."

(11) "I have not uttered evil words." <u>Variant: Or allowed myself to become sullen, to sulk or become depressed.</u>

(12) "I have attacked no one."

(13) "I have not slaughtered the cattle that are set apart for the Gods." <u>Variant: The Sacred bull – (Apis)</u>

(14) "I have not eaten my heart" (overcome with anguish and distraught). <u>Variant: Committed perjury.</u>

(15) "I have not laid waste the plowed lands."

(16) "I have not been an eavesdropper or pried into matters to make mischief." <u>Variant: Spy.</u>

(17) "I have not spoken against anyone." <u>Variant: Babbled, gossiped.</u>

(18) "I have not allowed myself to become angry without cause."

(19) "I have not committed adultery."

(20) "I have not committed any sin against my own purity."

(21) "I have not violated sacred times and seasons."

(22) "I have not done that which is abominable."

(23) "I have not uttered fiery words. I have not been a man or woman of anger."

(24) "I have not stopped my ears against the words of right and wrong (Maat)."

(25) "I have not stirred up strife (disturbance)." "I have not caused terror." "I have not struck fear into any man."

(26) "I have not caused any one to weep." <u>Variant: Hoodwinked.</u>

(27) "I have not lusted or committed neither fornication nor excessive ejaculation."

(28) "I have not avenged myself." <u>Variant: Resentment.</u>

(29) "I have not worked grief, I have not abused anyone." <u>Variant: Quarrelsome nature.</u>

(30) "I have not acted insolently or with violence."

(31) "I have not judged hastily." <u>Variant: or been impatient.</u>

(32) "I have not transgressed or angered God."

(33) "I have not multiplied my speech overmuch (talk too much)."

(34) "I have not done harm or evil." <u>Variant: Thought evil.</u>

(35) "I have not worked treason or curses on the King."

(36) "I have never befouled the water." <u>Variant: held back the water from flowing in its season.</u>

(37) "I have not spoken scornfully." <u>Variant: Or yelled unnecessarily or raised my voice.</u>

(38) "I have not cursed The God."

(39) "I have not behaved with arrogance." <u>Variant: Boastful.</u>

(40) "I have not been overwhelmingly proud or sought for distinctions for myself (Selfishness)."

(41) "I have never magnified my condition beyond what was fitting or increased my wealth, except with such things as are (justly) mine own possessions by means of Maat." <u>Variant: I have not disputed over possessions except when they concern my own rightful possessions. Variant: I have not desired more than what is rightfully mine.</u>

(42) "I have never thought evil (blasphemed) or slighted The God in my native town."

More Detailed Books of MAAT Philosophy

By

Dr. Muata Ashby

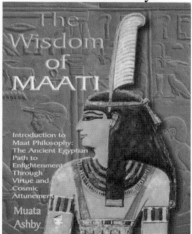

INTRODUCTION TO MAAT PHILOSOPHY: Spiritual Enlightenment Through the Path of Virtue Known commonly as Karma in India, the teachings of MAAT contain an extensive philosophy based on aryu (deeds) and their fructification in the form of Shai and Renenet (fortune and destiny, leading to Meskhenet (fate in a future birth) for living virtuously and with orderly wisdom are explained and the student is to begin practicing the precepts of Maat in daily life so as to promote the process of purification of the heart in preparation for the judgment of the soul. This judgment will be understood not as an event that will occur at the time of death but as an event that occurs continuously, at every moment in the life of the individual. The student will learn how to become allied with the forces of the Higher Self and to thereby begin cleansing the mind (heart) of impurities so as to attain a higher vision of reality. ISBN 1-884564-20-8

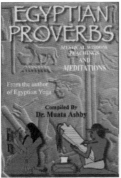

EGYPTIAN PROVERBS: A collection of —Ancient Egyptian Proverbs and Wisdom Teachings -How to live according to MAAT Philosophy. Beginning Meditation. All proverbs are indexed for easy searches. For the first time in one volume, ——Ancient Egyptian Proverbs, wisdom teachings and meditations, fully illustrated with hieroglyphic text and symbols. EGYPTIAN PROVERBS is a unique collection of knowledge and wisdom which you can put into practice today and transform your life. ISBN: 1-884564-00-3

HEALING THE CRIMINAL HEART. Introduction to Maat Philosophy, Yoga, and Spiritual Redemption Through the Path of Virtue   Who is a criminal? Is there such a thing as a criminal heart? What is the source of evil and sinfulness and is there any way to rise above it? Is there redemption for those who have committed sins, even the worst crimes?   Ancient Egyptian mystical psychology holds important answers to these questions. Over ten thousand years ago mystical psychologists, the Sages of Ancient Egypt, studied and charted the human mind and spirit and laid out a path which will lead to spiritual redemption, prosperity, and Enlightenment.   This introductory volume brings forth the teachings of the Asarian Resurrection, the most important myth of Ancient Egypt, with relation to the faults of human existence: anger, hatred, greed, lust, animosity, discontent, ignorance, egoism jealousy, bitterness, and a myriad of psycho-spiritual ailments which keep a human being in a state of negativity and adversity   ISBN: 1-884564-17-8

50- <u>Growing Beyond Hate: Keys to Freedom from Discord, Racism, Sexism, Political Conflict, Class Warfare, Violence, and How to Achieve Peace and Enlightenment</u>---INTRODUCTION: WHY DO WE HATE? Hatred is one of the fundamental motivating aspects of human life; the other is desire. Desire can be of a worldly nature or of a spiritual, elevating nature. Worldly desire and hatred are like two sides of the same coin in that human life is usually swaying from one to the other, but the question is why? And is there a way to satisfy the desiring or hating mind in such a way as to find peace in life? Why do human beings go to war? Why do human beings perpetrate violence against one another? And is there a way not just to understand the phenomena but to resolve the issues that plague humanity and could lead to a more harmonious society? Hatred is perhaps the greatest scourge of humanity in that it leads to misunderstanding, conflict and untold miseries of life and clashes between individuals, societies, and nations. Therefore, the riddle of Hatred, that is, understanding the sources of it and how to confront, reduce and even eradicate it so as to bring forth the fulfillment in life and peace for society, should be a top priority for social scientists, spiritualists, and philosophers. This book is written from the perspective of spiritual philosophy based on the mystical wisdom and sema or yoga philosophy of the Ancient Egyptians. This philosophy, originated and based on the wisdom of Shetaut Neter, the Egyptian Mysteries, and Maat, ethical way of life in society and in spirit, contains Sema-Yogic wisdom and understanding of life's predicaments that can allow a human being of any ethnic group to understand and overcome the causes of hatred, racism, sexism, violence, and disharmony in life, that plague human society. ISBN: 1-884564-81-X

Chapter 3: Advanced Issues in Kemetic Relationships for Modern Times

As we continue with the studies on Kemetic relationships this section will proceed to discuss some expanded aspects of relationships that produce perhaps more intense negative issues in modern times as opposed to the ancient times. In previous lectures on the subject, I have previously discussed the complication of relations in the world of time and space. We were getting to the core of the issue of the problem of relationships, which essentially is the ignorance of the knowledge of Self or "Khemn", the Kemetic term for ignorance of knowledge of Self. That ignorance leads a person to a duality of experience of existence that gives rise to egoism. What that duality means is that you start to feel a two-fold experience of existence based on your individual perception of reality founded in your personality as an individual among other individuals and individual objects in Creation. This two-fold experience is actually a syndrome of human experience based on the duality of what is perceived as either good or bad for your own perceived vision of happiness or unhappiness. This syndrome of duality is characterized by two issues: desire and repudiation.

This duality syndrome means you are living in a duality. From within that duality, you start feeling that since you're experiencing a duality, that you are experiencing yourself as something separate from everything else. Since you don't experience yourself as a whole, you experience yourself as something wanting, as something that is incomplete. While being in the state of ignorance, you spend your life trying to fill the perceived void. The most accessible way to achieve that is thought to be by uniting oneself with other objects. The objects might be persons, inanimate objects, animals, land, a country, a job or ideas. Also, some people try to cleave themselves to an ideology or philosophy, to religion, mythologies or other belief systems, even atheism, to resolve the issues produced by the incompleteness. All this process necessarily involves externalizing oneself, which means getting more involved with the world and moving away from the internal essence which is actually the support and essence of experience itself, the transcendental consciousness, which leads to more ignorance, more feeling of separateness, unrest and delusion.

But essentially we are going to go into more detail into the scripture that I'm reserving for the end but essentially it explains that the problem of existence is not having entered into Higher Consciousness. Because of that, because of one's desire to remain in or ignorance about how to get out of a dualistic state, that maintains the state of unhappiness and un-fulfilment. Again, when we say dualistic state it means that you experience yourself as an individual, from other individuals and you're in a world of individuals where people are trying to find their way in individuality to satisfy themselves. We have discussed previously that that is impossible. You can never satisfy yourself with anything in time and space (Creation) because time and space is fleeting and changeable and therefore illusory. But because of the ignorance you carry on, you think that you are going to somehow, if you find somebody that you fall in love with and that goes badly, then you say, "Oh maybe if I find somebody else it will work" or "if only I could get a nice car I'll feel good"; or "maybe if I buy some land back in Africa or Hawaii on a beach or I'll be happy"; "maybe if I have a child, I don't need a spouse, maybe I'll just have a child and that will make me happy." Since all of those things change and all of those things have their own issues, and because each has their own aryu based on ignorance and desires. A process that is a futile effort.

Aryu is an important concept to understand. I gave some examples in previous lectures to understand how aryu works, that when you are young you used to like ice cream but now that you are an adult you don't eat it so much but whenever you hear the little ice cream truck passing by or you drive by an ice cream shop or something like that you think about it and an urge emerges in the personality. If you think about it enough, one day you say, "Oh let me stop and get some ice cream. I deserve it." You start rationalizing that you deserve it even though you may be overweight. You may say: "I can get some, I've been good all week". Or "I worked hard in my job, I deserve it" and you start rationalizing in that way so it ends up with you getting what the desire is pushing you towards. The same thing, you can rationalize with everything else. The important thing to understand is that the rationalization occurs as a response to the urge and that urge is based on previous experiences in your past of things you either desired because they gave you pleasure or repudiated because they brought pain or discomfort.

Another example is when you know a person that you shouldn't be hanging out with but you say, "Oh they look good to me and it would be nice to be with that person so I deserve it, or why not?" The rationalization is driven by the desire to feel the perceived pleasure or happiness that the relationship will bring; though actually, this is an illusion based on overwhelming the wisdom that is known with the force of desires right or wrong. Then you push out the wisdom. So the desire and ignorance cripple your intellect in other words. This is the process of what the scripture calls "Mer hena medjet" which means "Loving and hating things". Because of your love or hatred, it means you are attaching yourself to desiring something or you are repudiating something else. This is the rollercoaster of life, caused by aryu composed of past experiences of desire and repudiation. When caught up in that syndrome you are either clinging and desiring or running away from things and then, of course, the attachment to things leads to hatred because if you cleave to something, that something is not going to satisfy you always. If you have a love affair, your lover is not going to always satisfy you or make you happy and you will hate that situation when it happens and it will taint the relations when it is not happening since the memory and anticipation of when it will happen again, are still there in your unconscious. Then you'll start hating them, you will have love and hate feelings for them too. If you get what you desire, you are going to be stressed because you are going to be trying to hold onto it and hating situations and people that try to take it away from you and so on. So the scripture says that for those people, those of you who are on earth, in the land of the living and who experience love and hate because of your desire to stay on earth as a human being, what should you do? We'll leave it there for now and come back to this theme.

The Issue of Undue Dependencies

An important problem that exists in modern society is undue dependency which may also be termed "codependency", which is born of insufficient self-esteem/self-worth and insufficient self-confidence due to degraded aspiration and self-discovery both professional and inner spiritual. This personality deficiency causes a myriad of personality disorders and imbalances as well as conflicts with relationships. So if you are codependent you will cause untold difficulties and miseries for yourself and your partner and likewise. This leads to manipulative behaviors to get the other person to do what you want so you can be happy. It might manifest as the other person emotionally blackmailing you or threatening withholding sex or comfort until you give up your desire and adopt theirs and many other permutations of the syndrome. A society that promotes individualism as opposed to a culture of caring and community exacerbates the issue. A society wherein people are allowed to grow up with psychological deficiencies such as poverty, missing parents, unresolved fears or traumas in youth, etc. all contribute to the syndromes. Obviously, a person who sees such issues in the personality, often characterized as "drama" one should seek to avoid as opposed to ignoring or embracing them.

A codependent person may manifest behavior like having to be connected to social media a significant portion of the time and basing their self-worth on their interactions there. They may be looking to be liked by others and experiences self-loathing if they are not liked or do not get a sufficient number of lies or complementary messages from others. It may manifest as having to constantly update their pages on what they are doing so that others can see and approve or be awed by what they see and thereby this type of person seeks validation since they do not know or understand how to provide for their own self-worth or self-esteem. This personality may manifest as loathing to be alone, needing to be in communication constantly, never wanting to be out of a relationship, loathing the idea of being quiet with their thoughts and worse the practice of meditation. And yes, those who practice meditation and yoga can have calm sides to the personality and yet harbor feelings and desires for companionship and relationship since they are not fully satisfied by their yogic practices. Their yogic practices delude them into believing that they can have "spiritual relationships" with others of like mind and eventually they are led to relations with others who are as flawed and needy as themselves so their dependency, which is, in reality, suppressed worldly desires, affects their relations negatively. This latter group can possibly grow out of the lower dependencies if 1-guided by competent counselors or 2- taught by the school of hard knocks that is a life of mixed spiritual thoughts and feelings commingling with issues and experiences of worldly relations which is a longer road and less certain.

So the question arises, how to abate and resolve the issue of *undue dependency*. The problem becomes possible when a soul separates itself (psychologically) from transcendental consciousness and it becomes individual (psychologically in perception, not in reality) or aware of its own ego only as being a subject in an ocean of other egos. Then the creation of duality in the mind wherein the ego sees itself as being a pole in a field of opposites and everything other than self is the opposite in the dualistic perception of life comes into being. The essential cause of egoism and duality is ignorance of the knowledge of self and the efficient cause, or vehicle through which the egoistic duality manifests and is constructed is attachment and hatred.

The syndrome of attachment and hatred operates when you move towards some things and you repudiate others. Usually, it's based on the pleasure of the ego or what the ego thinks is true based on its *Aryu*. *Aryu*, of course, is the sum total remnant or impression of the result of feelings, desires, fears, successes, etc. of past experiences that resides in the mind. So if you have learned that a certain type of people are fearful or there are objects to be feared, then that *Aryu* is going to come out in the form of repudiation when those people or objects are perceived since when they appear, your perception resonates with your past experiences of them and thereby a reaction is triggered of love or hate. If you think that some kinds of people are lovable then you are going to try to attach yourself to them based on your *Aryu*. *Aryu* (the result of past dualistic experiences) is sustained by your egoism, meaning your idea of yourself as an individual; and all of this is possible because of the absence of knowledge of Self, which means that you are spiritually ignorant in the parlance of the spiritual teaching.

If you are knowledgeable about the Essence of Self, then you are referred to as an "Enlightened Being". You are referred to as a "Wise Soul"; all of these terminologies, such as *Nehast* or Spiritually Awakened in Ancient Egypt, *Moksha* or Liberation in India, *Nirvana* in Buddhism, etc. all refer to the same idea. Now, this issue of duality leads to undue dependency on the world and its objects for one's self-satisfaction, reduction of stress and self-fulfillment. Undue dependency means that you have to depend on the world for certain things; you have to depend on the sun shining, the world for air to breathe. If you are going on a bus or a train or plane you depend on the pilot or driver to take you there safely. So there are things, you naturally must depend on, like your mother or your parents when you come into the world as a baby, to feed, clothe and wipe your behind, show you the ropes of the world and things like that. That is normal dependency.

Now if you develop *undue dependency* it means that you are leaning/craving/longing for/depending on those forms of relation as sources for your satisfaction, happiness, fulfilment, etc. and that becomes synonymous with your self-identity, self-esteem, happiness, etc. as an unhealthy, shaky foundations for your idea of self-worth, even as concerns you as a person who deserves to exist, who is worthy of respect, let alone a person with capacity for greatness; Since you unduly depend on those as sources for your ability to exist as well-adjusted human being, to that extent you are not able to discover and self-actualize yourself, meaning to discover truly all you can be, not in the army sense but truly all you can be as a human being without being defined by other people or dependent on their opinions, feelings or desires. Self-Actualization means being able to explore all of the gifts that you have and discovering the greatness that is within you without being hampered by the "denigrate" or limiting thoughts or feelings of others. All of that is suppressed when you have egoism, duality when you have an undue dependency on the world, its limitations, and ignorant people because you are depending on other people to tell you if you are worthy or if you are a good person, capable or lovable. With that dependency, you are also depending on them for saying positive or negative things about you. If you depend on that you come to believe it, you come to accept it and you come to base your life on it and act on it and this issue or personality disorder can roll on from life to life. This can lead to relationships in which you start to relate to other people in that way and of course it is a roller coaster of negative feelings, resentments, anger, frustrations and life dramas. You hate others since they do not approve of you but you depend on them so you keep listening to them. Or you might love those who tell you what your ego wants to hear and not the truth. Or since you do not have self-esteem for yourself you disagree and fight with those who tell you that you are lovable and good and since they are also co-dependent they stay with you even when you give them drama and start fights just to prove them wrong. If not resolved, these psychological issues and immaturities as a human and spiritual being can persist from life to life. Also, it could have originated by something that happened in a previous life when you experience degradation or that you were mistreated when you were a child and then you developed maladapted ways of handling the world that deepened, intensified and went on even up to the time of death and were unresolved.

One example is when they were a child growing up, the nanny was there but the parent was never there so the person felt unloved, unworthy and so they tried to grow up and have a relationship with a spouse since they were constantly looking for validation and if they don't get it constantly, there will be a fight, a big upset and all kinds of ramifications to this. How can you love a person who, due to "issues", does not know how to love themselves? How can a person who does not have self-esteem accept compliments or accept affection? How will you react when that person rejects your attempts to be affectionate or show caring? So we are just mentioning a few of the ramifications of this issue; there is a myriad of manifestations which can be given varied psychological terms, yet that is what referred to in the spiritual field as "egoism". These problems cause turbulence in relationships because even if one partner is relatively balanced the one who is unbalanced will produce disharmony, unrest and utilitarian caring (caring only when getting their way) in the relations. An example of how such imbalances may manifest is, when the balanced person tries to show affection the unbalanced person will rebuff the attempts due to seeing them perhaps as advanced that might lead to their own stirring of feelings of self-hate so they may resist those advanced or perhaps start a fight to deflect the interest or perhaps accuse the person of not caring for them, indeed, the very same thing they are actually doing, caring, so as to start a fight that will stop the actions of the balanced person that they cannot accept due to not knowing how or because it might stir up unwanted feelings they do not know how to handle. Perhaps they cannot handle it because they feel inadequate, unworthy, gross or bad over something they regret or feel remorse about, from the past, or fears of what might happen in the future if they allow themselves to receive the love or caring that they feel they are not worthy of, etc., etc. There are many ramifications to these psychological problems that can stem from childhood traumas or psychological traumas from past lives that have not been resolved up to the present. A different problem in coping is that a person may feel trapped in their life; trapped with responsibilities to others that their ethical conscience will not allow them to release even if those responsibilities are killing them, literally, which by definition would not be in accordance with the teachings of Maat. The caring advances of the other person may be seen as a possibility of stirring up feelings of desire to be free which they cannot allow themselves to experience for thinking those are wrong or unrighteous. Perhaps they do not want others to care since that might relieve the burden which they feel they deserve since they are not worthy and should be made to suffer. Or perhaps they may feel life is horrible and this is proof and if someone comes along to help they may have to think otherwise, that life is not all horrible; and that would force them to change their perspectives but their self-hate does not allow them to allow the help or caring to assist so they can maintain the self-hate and the gloomy perspective on the world. Still another possibility is the idea that life always ends in disaster or death and all good things go away, which is true; so then they go about making sure that every and all situations they engage in never lead to any happy moments or happy times or times of fulfillment or times of peace. Therefore all situations must end in gloom, pessimism, a fight, depression, anger, etc., to prove and uphold the moroseness of feeling and thinking. In this latter form or way of being as was stated, life situations end in death but that way of being alone does not lead to lucid dispassion about the world but instead rather, it leads to a morbid and dull sense of egoism. If this flaw in life, that it ends ultimately in death and loss, were to be followed with wisdom and introspection about the nature of self then it would lead rightly to turning away from worldly ideals, which are illusory, and towards spiritual ideals that are uplifting and enlightening, which is another truth of life. Therefore, when seeking a partner with which to have relations, these "syndromes" of which only a few have been mentioned, should be reviewed within oneself and then also about others before entering into relations so as to lead to a more harmonious and enlighteningly fruitful relationship. These themes will be reviewed in more detail later in this volume.

In psychology circles, it can be referred to as "issues". That is a popular term. Another popular term is "dysfunctional" or "dysfunctionality". Another popular term in the last 20 years is "co-dependency". In terms of Kemetic psychology, we are using the term "undue dependency". All of these terms refer to symptoms and problems that originate in egoism. In order to practice the spiritual teaching truthfully, the wisdom teaching has to be applied honestly and faithfully and persistently to resolve this egoism and that is actually what we are talking about and what it means to understand the teaching, the philosophy and what it all means in reference to handling and dealing with and resolving the issues of the ego. This of course also means enlightenment or becoming an enlightened being. That brings us to facing and dealing with the issue of undue dependency. If it is not faced it means that as individuals, people's egos are not healthy and human beings in this unhealthy, weak state, are not operating under *personal sovereignty* but rather subservient to desires, which will make them compromise their ideals to have a relationship that will likely be wrong for them and in which they will suffer a myriad frustrations and disappointments even while sentimentally holding on so as not to lose the relationship. An extreme example of this degradation is a slave fighting to protect the slave master despite the degradation and tortures experienced in the slavery relationship; this kind of psychological issue has been termed "Stockholm Syndrome."

One area that researchers have found is that these issues are perpetuated since people are not facing them, so the first thing is to face that you have an issue, acknowledge it, say: "yes I have it". You don't have to say it to the world but you have to say it to yourself. Then realize that is a limitation, or dysfunction or whatever you want to call it and work on how to handle it and resolve it. One of the ways is to learn about it, the way we've talked about it and some other practical ways are to look for it and recognize its manifestations. Another technique to handle these issues might be looking for or making boundaries for yourself so as not to overstep yourself getting into situations where you should not become involved with other people's issues and theirs in your life and self-esteem. But it is important to understand that boundaries are not just physical boundaries.

You have three main aspects or planes that the personality exists in: one is the Physical plane; one is the Astral plane and the other one is the Causal plane. So you have an unconscious reality and that is where your *Aryu* (impressions from past thoughts, feelings and actions of the past that drive feelings, thoughts, and desires in the present) are lodged, in the Causal. You have a mental reality in the Astral and you have a physical reality in the Physical plane. From a disciplinary perspective sometimes it is necessary to make physical boundaries. Like people invading your physical space or touching you in an unwanted way, things of that nature. Or people taking liberties with you, taking you for granted and things like that. So you have to say, "Ok stop, I don't feel comfortable, I don't think that is correct" and you want to assert your self-worth/self-esteem and integrity. Somebody hitting you or beating you is also an invasion of your physical boundary. Someone denigrating you or trying to emotionally blackmail you so as to make you back down and do what they want instead of following your conscience etc. is another example. If you allow that it is because you don't have the self-worth and you are codependent. You don't love yourself enough to stand up for your principles and integrity as a human being, deserving and worthy to be loved and respected. You don't regard yourself sufficiently and others more. You may even agree with the beater, like the lady in India that we talked about who took the husband to court because he stopped beating her since she saw that type of interaction as proof of his love!

Now, psychological abuse is also another area of denigration; getting into another person's mental space and the physical and the mental aspects are areas that I have talked about before, that create new *Aryu* in the personality that shapes desires and feelings in life going forward. Through your experiences in these areas, the abuse in the physical and the mental plane, you create new *Aryu* through those and that goes into your unconscious mind, shapes your present perceptions and future desires and ways of perceiving future events and relations. That is the entrance way and so if you protect your physical and astral aspects of your being (physical body and conscious waking reality) then you are at the same time protecting your unconscious mind also. If you do this you are going to prevent it from being degraded either by internal issues such as feelings of self-deprecation (due to misunderstandings, embarrassments, errors of the past, etc.) or external forces such as physical or mental/psychological abuse by other people. You are going to promote the cleansing of your personality as well as its strengthening. This is the wisdom subject of developing a healthy mind that can be a gatekeeper for not allowing negative *Aryu* to come into the unconscious mind and instead being able to produce positive *Aryu* and allow that to go into your personality and unconscious. From a mental perspective, you set the boundaries there, based on the wisdom of Maat ethical conscience which rejects unrighteous statements (statements that are nonfactual or based on emotional attacks due to the other person feeling hurt or caught in the throes of emotional negativity such as anger, despair, stress or other delusions projected on others). Thus, to uphold the boundary you need to say something like, "ok you said something to me that is denigrating and I don't appreciate that, I don't accept it, I would like you to stop. If that is not possible then I will leave until we can have a civil conversation;" If that is sufficient, then fine; If not then remove yourself physically from that environment. If you are being physically or mentally hurt or threatened then there is no question, just leave and seek safety immediately and do not return until the abuser has been restrained and has received psychological counseling and has been cleared for re-engaging a relationship on more ethical grounds. If that does not resolve the issue then leave permanently and go on with your life. Life is not for producing, giving or receiving pain and abuse in relationships unless you feel you deserve it due to your degraded state of mind. Also realizing that if you have the self-worth and the maturity, you would not allow yourself to come into that kind of relationship or situation, to begin with; But nevertheless, part of growing as a human being not just a spiritual being is to mature and to develop understanding of what is correct and what is not for you and living true to your Self and developing your self-worth if that is lacking; and then making adjustments as you discover higher truths and develop will power to live by that higher truth. So if you find yourself in such a situation, do what is recommended by Maat wisdom, realize the error and extricate from the situation or relationship and move on to a better life and do not accept your degradation or the negative words of others telling you deserve what you get.

A few other ideas on handling such situations, when dealing with anger or hatred from other people, as told to initiates, is working on being non-resentful when experiencing wrong and to breathe and to remember the teaching whenever in a negative situation or a situation is perceived by you as negative. Then that bringing yourself into the present allows you to have clarity of mind, instead of allowing the agitation of mind through attachment and hatred, through the swinging thoughts of attachment and hatred to guide your actions towards emotionally charged behaviors you will regret later. The human mind in general and you, in particular, can have attachment and hatred for the same object at the same time. You can love somebody and desire them and also hate aspects of them too because your *Aryu*, in your unconscious mind, is layered and those aspects can be triggered, at the same time, by your present experiences. Example, a person you have had a relationship and intimacies with caused you joy several times and at other times yells at you, calls you names and insults you which causes pain. The impressions of the joy and pain become aryu in your unconscious mind and when you interact with the person both feelings are rising in your personality at the same time so you may be standoffish even while making love or feeling conflicted and lost even while feeling attached. This is the predicament of the complexed human mind that living by Maat wisdom will straighten out and it's the purpose of this volume as well as one of the main messaged being conveyed.

Therefore, Love *Aryu* and also Hate *Aryu* can exist in the unconscious at the same time and they can be triggered simultaneously. So that is something to keep in mind. By triggered we mean that it is stimulated by an outside object or situation that resonates with the *Aryu* in your unconscious mind and that resonance stimulates those unconscious impressions to bubble up to the surface like we discussed before. Then how you handle that, when it comes up, that is also an aspect of dealing. If you allow them to fully express and agree with them then you are going reinforce and support the present negative condition of the unconscious mind and you are also going to set up more of the dysfunction, more of the pain and sorrow of life, or the entanglements, and more of the undue dependency.

Now, we touched on hurtful aspects of the current life and of the previous lives. We've tried to use the teaching to have an understanding of those and also an understanding of the illusoriness of those issues. But having said that, the Wisdom Teaching and this is where a lot of aspirants fail and that is the reason for this series, the working out or the applying of the teaching has been deficient in this area. People can have very advanced understandings of the philosophy but also at the same time hold onto and carry on the mental issues. Then they may wonder why they are successful in intellectually understanding the spiritual teaching and in the performance of some practices such as the yoga postures, but then they have disharmony and or fights with their mate or they sabotage their relationships. Again, we've discussed the area of sabotage previously. Perhaps your mother had a negative relationship with your father and the father left so you didn't grow up knowing what it was to have a legitimate father or someone to love you from a fatherly perspective. Since you didn't know that, you grew up, but you may develop issues with your perspective mate, you don't know why but you sabotage your relationship because you don't know what it is to be loved or how to accept love since you were unloved as a child and grew up with the idea that you are unlovable or do not deserve to be loved, or some such combination of mental complex issues. The relationship may seem to go well but at some point then for some reason, you have to leave or you start fights with them purposely to sow disharmony because you can't handle the closeness and the contradiction internally. What do you imagine we would see when people with insecurities engage in relationships? We see the results all over every day in the doubts, angst, frustrations, and fears of being in, seeking, leaving, fighting and sabotaging but also having children when the parents themselves are immature or acting out pursuit and withdrawal in relationships. You can't love someone truly if you do not love yourself just as you can't love someone who does not love themselves; another way to think about this is you cannot have a sane and productive relationship with another person if either they or you are suffering from psychological issues related to self-esteem balance. Self-esteem in balance means having healthy self-regard, neither deprecating yourself but also not being narcissistic, neither overinflated ego or having undue dependencies. This is referred to as a healthy or well-adjusted ego.

So due to this reason, this issue of relations it goes deeply into the philosophy as we discussed before and I'm coining a new phrase today, the term is **"Relationing"**, meaning the manner of relating yourself to the objects of the world and time and space. Just to clarify, when we say "objects of the world and time and space" that also refers to your ego and the egos of others. Your ego is an object that you are relating yourself to, your Higher Self is relating to it and through it to the world of time and space with other egos which are relating with their souls and so on. Of course the problem of relating is that most people do not have direct awareness and contact with their soul so the ego, for the most part, acts independently, ignorantly, emotionally and failing, stumbling through life to generate and suffer through insecurities, frustrations, and delusions to cope with the miseries and disappointments in life rather than facing the truth which Maat wisdom presents. Psychological studies have demonstrated that most people operate on "automatic conscience" meaning they do not actively or consciously think and make decisions at least 95% of the time. This is like when you are driving or walking and all of a sudden you realize you drove or walked some distance but were not concentrating on that; the mind was elsewhere but the unconscious handled the driving or walking. The mind might have been imagining something, remembering a past event or thinking about the future and not the present. So the thought and decision-making process is handled 95% of the time by the bubbling thoughts coming from the unconscious mind based on the unconscious impressions, i.e. the aryu (the basis of the ego). When you don't have awareness of your Higher Self, your ego operates based on its own storehouse of knowledge, *Aryu*, (feelings based on ignorance and delusions of the past) with some impetus from Spirit but since you are ignorant and your ego is so encrusted you are not able to see that, not able to feel that, and you don't have the will to follow higher ethical, moral or spiritual insights that might come from deep within your personality. You are leaning on your ego, on how your body looks to other people, on how you feel about yourself, how other people think about you, or how others appear to you, how you like them, or what you think about the world and about life, having a career, etc.; all of these kinds of things are based ultimately on the ego (aryu) depending on how much they are or are not infused with ethical, moral and spiritual values. Therefore, ultimately they (aryu) are directing the personality to positive and elevating experiences or to limited and or failed experiences through life including failed relationships.

We've also discussed, in previous classes, that the ego itself is illusory. If you were to cleanse out your unconscious mind and the erroneous notions that you've developed (the basis of the ego) to discover your true self you would realize that all these things, so many issues, so many dysfunctions or co-dependencies or whatever you want to call them, is based on erroneous duality thinking and dualistic self-concept, as we discussed last time and that is what the Maat text is also saying. Of course then, therefore, if you were to eradicate that error you would also eradicate the problems because they are ramifications of that fundamental error. First of all, you have to know that that has to be done and how to do it. Those are the first two steps and then thirdly, to go ahead and do it, all of which is what we've been discussing.

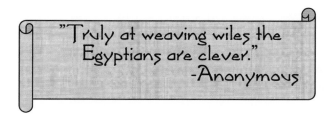

"Truly at weaving wiles the Egyptians are clever."
-Anonymous

One more point is that we started discussing some of the techniques last time of working on yourself within your boundaries because the problem with boundaries also is that oneself does the breaking of those boundaries and opening up to things that should not be opened up to. We discussed previously, that there is an interesting proverb about Ancient Egyptians that they were very wily and reserved. This is one of the Greek proverbs talking about the Egyptians. One of the issues that a person who has not bounded themselves (to the boundaries suggested by the teaching) is that when communicating with others they are always seeking approval, being externalized and allowing their self-worth to be determined by outside factors instead of internal self-awareness and self-regard as a worthy entity with right to and deserving of existence with a valuable contribution to offer to humanity. By living a life that is constantly seeking approval from what the other person thinks or even someone on the street, then the person will adjust their self-worth opinions based on the opinions of others. This is one of the big problems in politics. We have lots of people who listen to Fox News or who listen to right-wing radio or left-wing radio or TV but they don't have any boundaries and are thus controlled and robotically caused to spout the TV rhetoric or espouse the radio opinions as their own, a pathetic situation that has led to leaders who lead by creating and maintaining a weak and co-dependent population to do their bidding on command. That degraded population is rendered completely open to anger, hatred, and denigration of others. Obviously what we are saying is that they feel that, within themselves, they don't have the self-worth, the validation that they can offer something independently, positively and ethically valuable to others. There are those people, who are on the radio, who also feel that and also experience that and they take advantage of that. So it is a very negative cycle of low self-esteem and self-hate in the degraded population that can be manipulated by TV and Radio or Church or Government leaders that can be directed outside for satisfaction to hate the other, (whoever is a minority, or whoever is of a different "race"[6], or different class or whatever). In order to overcome this problem, these issues are to be reflected upon and thought about deeply, about what your opinions are,

---

[6] There are no different "races"- there is only one human race.

about yourself; where they arose from and what is your legitimacy, what is your standing in your own eyes and what is the opinion of others. This is to be done, ideally, before interactions though also later as evaluation afterward so that you can have a conversation and not be unduly contaminated with other people's thoughts which can be ignorant or can be based on their own issues. So speaking truth is bound by the truth. What we're talking about "with the truth" is the teachings of Maat. Maat means Truth; of course that means a vision or understanding of reality that evolves or that develops, progresses based on your knowledge of self, based on your ethical conscience. Also, this does not mean do not listen to the opinions of others but that needs to be evaluated with the filter of Maat Wisdom before it can be allowed to influence one's personality and have possibly deleterious effects.

NOTE: It is important to understand that the deficiencies in the personality caused by negative aryu that lead a person to behave and live in a state of undue dependency whereby they accept everything, in relationships, from minor discourtesies to major "inconsiderations" and disrespect is not only due to external reasons, coming from other people. So, one is complicit with the world to the extent that the person is dependent on it; therefore, in allowing self to be trained to accept that disrespect and or degradation one's very self-has had a role in the degradation and allowing the dependencies to develop that degrade the personality. This training effect of negative interactions in the world is to be confronted with ethical wisdom as well as spiritual practices that purify the ego and bolster the psycho-spiritual personality in order to not only resist such inordinate dependencies and degradations but to also train the world in reverse, to force the world to treat one with honor and respect by discovering internal dignity and self-respect and demanding the same from worldly interactions and relationships.

The Kemetic Ideal of Friendship

Now, I would like to discuss an aspect of Kemetic relationship that relates to friendship. I would like to begin this teaching by reading an article about friendship that I think is very compatible with the Maat Philosophy or relationships. This is from an article called, **"Happiness in this World, Reflections from a Buddhist Position" by Alex Lickerman and the "True Meaning of Friendship, What is it that Makes a True Friend?"** *"The Japanese have a term, "kenzoku" which translated literally means family. The connotation suggests a bond between people who've made a similar commitment and who possibly, therefore, share a similar destiny. It implies the presence of the deepest connection of friendship, of lives lived as comrades from the distant past. Many of us have people in our lives with whom we feel the bond described by the kenzoku. They may be family members, a mother, a brother, a daughter, a cousin. Or a* *friend from grammar school with whom we haven't talked in decades. Time and distance do nothing to diminish the bond we have with these kinds of friends. The question then arises: why do we have the kind of chemistry encapsulated by the word kenzoku with only a few people we know and not scores of others? The closer we look for the answer the more elusive it becomes. It may not, in fact, be possible to know but characteristics that define kenzoku relationship most certainly are.*

WHAT DRAWS PEOPLE TOGETHER AS FRIENDS?

1. ***Common interests.*** *This probably ties us closer to our friends than many would like to admit. When our interest diverge and we can find nothing to enjoy jointly, time spent together tends to rapidly diminish. Not that we can't still care deeply about friends with whom we no longer share common interests, but it's probably uncommon for such friends to interact on a regular basis.*

2. ***History.*** *Nothing ties people together, even people with little in common, than having gone through the same difficult experience. As the sole glue to keep friendships whole in the long run, however, it often dries, cracks, and ultimately fails.*

3. ***Common values.*** *Though not necessarily enough to create a friendship, if values are too divergent, it's difficult for a friendship to thrive.*

4. ***Equality.*** *If one friend needs the support of the other on a consistent basis such that the person depended upon receives no benefit other than the opportunity to support and encourage, while the relationship may be significant and valuable, it can't be said to define a true friendship.*

WHAT MAKES A FRIEND WORTHY OF THE NAME?

1. ***A commitment to your happiness****. A true friend is consistently willing to put your happiness before your friendship. It's said that "good advice grates on the ear," but a true friend won't refrain from telling you something you don't want to hear, something may even risk fracturing the friendship if hearing it lies in your best interest. A true friend will not lack the mercy to correct you when you're wrong. A true friend will confront you with your drinking problem as quickly as inform you about a malignant-looking skin lesion on your back that you can't see yourself.*

2. ***Not asking you to place the friendship before your principles.*** *A true friend won't ask you to compromise your principles in the name of your friendship or anything else. Ever.*

3. ***A good influence.*** *A true friend inspires you to live up to your best potential, not to indulge your basest drives.*

Of course, we may have friends who fit all these criteria and still don't quite feel kenzoku. There still seems to be an extra factor, an attraction similar to that which draws people together romantically, that cements friends together irrevocably, often immediately, for no reason either person can identify. But when you find these people, the kenzoku, they're like priceless gems. They like finding home."

================================

Muata Ashby - I found this essay to be very much in harmony with the Maatian teaching of what friendship is supposed to be according to Kemetic Maatian principles. This physician, who penned this essay, is a practicing Buddhist. As you know I consider Buddhism as a distant cousin of Neterianism (Ancient Egyptian Religion) because the early Buddhists visited ancient Kemet at an early period in the development of Buddhism. As we demonstrated in the books: *Ancient Egyptian Buddha* and *African Origins Vol. 3 Egypt and India*, there was a connection especially between early Buddhism and the Ancient Egyptian city called Memphis, which was the seat of the teaching of the religion of the Ancient Egyptian god Ptah whose religious tradition (a denomination of Ancient Egyptian Religion) was called Memphite theology. I'd like to read a couple more Ancient Egyptian proverbs on friendship to better see the synergy of the teaching and help guide our discussion further; then I want to go directly into the higher aspects of friendships, relations, and boundaries.

ANCIENT EGYPTIAN PROVERBS ON FRIENDSHIP:

"Are not the enemies made by truth, better than the friends obtained by flattery?" -AEP

Of course, we can easily see the wisdom of this statement. This is what I've been talking about, related to having friends because one feels low self-esteem as opposed to having friends because you are so comfortable and aware of your capacities that you want to have friends to share and contribute with on the journey of life, to help and be helped to become better and stronger as a human being and as a spiritual being, to explore and discover each other's gifts and make the world a better place by expressing the benefits each can bring to each other, the community and the world. In a state of degradation and self-deprecation, you want to be friends with whoever it is no matter how negative the person is because you are so degraded you need constant validation or being in situations that will not be challenging or questioning your ethics, morality or capacities. From the perspective of sanity, healthy self-esteem and evolving personal sovereignty and spiritual emancipation, it would be better to have friends that are based in truth, who care so much as to tell it like it is and who see one's spiritual essence and worldly potential and want to see the higher manifestation instead of a partner to wallow in the miseries and dramas of lower living, like animals following instinctual drives and urges. It is better to have friends that are not going to be based on flattery for yourself or for agitated worldly living for the sake of living a life being distracted with meaningless activities and pursuits like the animals who do not have the capacity to exercise intellect and only have instincts, animalistic urges and emotional reactions to live by.

> "If you examine the character of a friend don't ask other people. Deal with them alone so as to not to suffer from their anger. You may argue with them after a little while. You may test their heart in conversation. If what they have seen escapes them, if they do something that annoys you, stay friendly with them and do not attack. Be restrained and don't answer them with hostility. Do not leave them and do not attack them. Their time will not fail to come. They cannot escape their fate." -AEP

The proverb is saying yes, if you have to tell people what you have to tell them, try to do it in private. Try to do it in a way that does not stir up anger but yes you have to tell them. If they attack you, don't attack them back but don't break the friendship. Let them come down from their anger or the emotional feeling of being hurt by your words and let them be. Let them re-establish the friendship when they take the time to see your words were not meant to hurt but to help. In a case where a person cannot realize that then you don't need that kind of friendship. That is what I was talking about before.

> "Indulge not thyself in the passion of Anger; it is whetting a sword to wound thine own breast, or murder thy friend." -AEP

This is one of the big detriments of worldly living. If you were to lead a life that is based on truth, you will be much farther away from anger. You develop anger because you can't have what you desire, which is usually something unrighteous or based on delusion. You live a life of desire because as we explained before, you are living your life of attachment and hatred, of duality. When you have attachment and hatred naturally you are going to be angry when you can't get what you want or what you have is taken, if you lose it. You are going to be angry at whatever it is you perceive is not allowing you to be happy when you really should be angry with your own ego. You should be directing your wrath at your ego for putting you in that position of dependency and degradation. If you learn to do this discipline you are going to destroy your ego eventually by its own actions. Train yourself to be angry with your ego whenever you have pain or sorrow and you will see what happens to your ego, you'll see how small it gets very quickly.

> *"Avoid conversing with many on your knowledge. Do not keep it selfishly but do not seem ridiculous unto the multitude. The like's acceptable to the like."* -AEP

This proverb relates to people who like to hear their own voices and like to show how knowledgeable they are and in so doing often put off others with their egoism and arrogance. That is not being a true friend and neither is the opposite, cutting people off when they are speaking because you cannot handle what they are saying or because you are so caught up in your life that it's all about you. In the last line, the unlike develops in a lopsided way so it is difficult to have relations with people who are not alike or do not have commonalities and similar levels of intellectual and emotional development. Many people try to do that, having relations with others with whom they are in reality not compatible with because their self-esteem compels them; they want to be friends with someone they can control, someone that they can denigrate and put down to make themselves feel good and that is dysfunctional. Or the other way, they want to be in relations with someone who will abuse them because they feel degraded and weak and deserving of denigration. Those are some of the issues we have discussed in this volume, the issues of co-dependencies, etc. So those are negative kinds of friendships.

On Self Love and Self Hate

"Those who have learned to know themselves, have reached that state which does transcend any abundance of physical existence; but they who through a love that leads astray, expend their love upon their body, they stay in darkness, wandering and suffering through their senses, things of anxiety, unrest and Death." -AEP

Elsewhere in this volume has been discussed the issue of how *Aryu* operates at different levels of the unconscious and also at same levels even when of opposing nature, such that you can love somebody and hate them at the same time. You can also love and hate yourself at the same time based on different impressions of self-esteem and self-loathing lodged in your own unconscious. The *Aryu* in your unconscious mind works that way with everything. You can love something and yet sabotage yourself with it. You can and we see this happen often, where people sabotage relationships with people that are seemingly good for them; additionally, you can unwittingly sabotage yourself when attaining your goals of life. This means that consciously you may truly want something and somehow screw up your opportunities.

This is not a mystery; the aryu in your unconscious mind must be agreeable to what you want consciously. Otherwise, what you want consciously will be thwarted by your unconscious negative "issues" and psychological contradictory complexes. You might say consciously, "I really want to do this, I can do this. I can become a doctor or lawyer". However, since you have a lot of negative *Aryu* that's operating against you, then you will thwart yourself when you try to attain your goal. You may really want a job but when the time comes to go for the interview you overslept, you did not wake up even though the alarm sounded, because your unconscious prevented it [perhaps out of fear or insecurity, etc.] and so you missed the interview and someone else got it. You get upset and say "how could that have happened? How could I have done that? If your unconscious is not in line with the conscious then you will find some way to thwart yourself n matter how much you consciously desire what you desire. This flies in the face of such new-age teachings as "the secret" or the "laws of attraction". You can succeed only when the unconscious is cleansed, purified and made powerful with positive impressions and freed from negative egoistic complexes.

Another example is you want to go to college real bad but somehow you delay in sending in the application to the school and the enrollment period passes. You will not put in the application, because deep down (not consciously) there is a conversation going on in the unconscious that is asserting: "Oh, I can't study that, I can't understand this, I can't do this or that or the other thing, I'm going to make a fool of myself; I'm stupid and if I get into college I have to go away and leave my girlfriend and my parents, I'm afraid." With that chatter and the energy behind it in your unconscious mind, that negative aryu compels you to be forgetful, dismissive or dull when it comes to applying or thinking of yourself as a successful student. And then even if you get admitted the aryu may stop you from being a diligent student and cause failure there too. So you don't apply and you don't attend because you have impure aryu and are not working to cleansing your *Aryu* by living the philosophy of Maat. So what I'm leading you to understand is that in order to have proper friendships and proper relationships it is important to start creating positive *Aryu* and to stop the negative *Aryu* from forming in your personality which will create a negative situations in your life and obstruct your capacity to live life successfully and also attain the spiritual goals of life.

Other examples of complexes formed in the personality due to and sustained by aryu in the unconscious mind, formed through lifetimes of socialization/conditioning through family, friends, schools, government, religious customs and norms and beliefs inculcated since birth may manifest in varied ways and here are just a few examples: Maybe the person grew up poor so could not keep up with friends and other peers in school or neighborhood so developed low self-esteem. Perhaps you grew up with parents who constantly told you that you were not good enough because you did not get as good grades as your sibling and now in your relations you have trouble accepting compliments or praises for your work since internally you still carry the aryu of feeling inadequate or "less than" others; so you throw compliments back in people's faces or feel embarrassed and uncomfortable and display inappropriate emotions, gestures, like smiling or grinning or crying, to mask or display the feelings evoked that cannot be suppressed. Maybe the person was made to feel insecure and feels everyone watching them and disapproving all the times so even in their private bedroom they cannot feel free to be intimate, so is inhibited with the partner; maybe it's a boy that felt picked on and ridiculed so he gets a pit bull dog to compensate for feeling inferior and insecure. Another boy grows up and can't wait to get a muscle car to impress his friends and girls since he feels inadequate without such compensation. Maybe it might manifest as a person who grew up with overbearing parent(s) that constantly nitpicked everything and nothing was ever perfect so now in the relations after growing up that person constantly nitpicks everything about their partner and how it's never perfect or acceptable and therefore never good enough so the person and their actions are never good enough and the partner is therefore never respected or appreciated for anything they do and whatever they do has to be approved by the fastidious nitpicked grown up partner, causing constant strife, insecurity and resentment in both since the other partner does not always agree but the nitpicker feels they are always right and thus also disrespected. Maybe it's a person that is so insecure and maladapted they constantly threaten to get a divorce or not go on vacation or withhold sex until they blackmail their partner to get what they want which is to have the partner dominated so they can feel secure in themselves even if it means constant arguments and fighting. There can never be amicable disagreement since disobeying the one who is supposedly "correct" is not tolerated. Maybe it manifests as that person's partner who puts up with the emotional blackmailing due to their own insecurities and fear of moving on and finding someone else. Maybe it's a man that feels the burden of providing for the family and insecure about his abilities or the prospects and choices made, so he works constantly so as to not think about the fears but not taking care of himself goes to an early grave; maybe it's a woman that feels caught by the society and obligated to take care of others and not herself even if it kills her. Maybe it might manifest as moodiness followed by depression and then up to elation and apparent happiness that internally causes angst since the person is dreading the inevitable come down, even during the times of smiles and apparent fun and good times, that fool their gullible friends who have their own complexes, in a roller coaster ride of emotions based on feelings coming from maladapted unconscious impressions from past experiences (aryu) that have produced a conflicted and troubled personality (ego).

Compounding these mental and emotional complexes are external factors such as chemicals in food and in the environment, and drugs. Compounding issues internally include the factor of the force (sekhem) of the aryu whereby even when a person comes to understand that their actions are based on maladaptation, ignorance or delusion, they cannot stop themselves from acting out the negative behaviors since there is momentum built up over lifetimes, pushing those patterns and supporting the negative unconscious impressions. The recognition and acceptance of these issues and then working on the issues in a clinical therapy environment may be necessary while at the same time working to adopt the Maatian wisdom of life. Needless to say, all involved in such relations may need counseling therapy to overcome the maladaptations and distortions gained from past lifetimes and the present socializations/conditionings of the present lifetime. Then the adoption and practice of the Maatian philosophy will have a better chance of success.

So, how does one overcome these issues? One of the first things to do is to change your belief system from a worldly values perspective, from pleasure-seeking and belief in the goals and ideals of popular culture, government, and orthodox religious leaders or ignorant family and friends, to the wisdom of Maat Philosophy. You have to understand what life is supposed to be and what is happening in your unconscious mind. You also need to understand your stage in life and face your issues, your dysfunctions honestly and understand what is the correct way to act, think and feel in order to lead yourself to freedom, self-mastery, and spiritual emancipation? You have to understand that first which means changing your lifestyle to one that incorporates study and practice of the teachings. You have to change to a healthy lifestyle that affirms life and sanity instead of death and dullness of mind while at the same time associating with people who are also following that path and moving away from those who don't, those who are still caught in the matrix of degraded worldly life. If you used to smoke or you used to eat meat, you have to change that. Do it gradually if you need to but you have to do it. Then you have to live in a way, in a culture, a kind of environment of positive and righteous (followers of Maat) people, and of friends, that help towards that higher perspective. So if you can avoid it you should not live with thieves or thugs or with angry persons, or hateful persons etc. In the context, the best friends in the world that you can have are those who are advancing on this path. Also, you need to forge a friendship with yourself by not living sentimentally, not with your ego but with your higher self. So you live in an ethically conscious way. You live in a wise and an introspective way. So you want to find people who are like that also. So you want to develop right thinking for your mind and right acting for your physical existence that's called "Anpu" and for your intellect called "Djehuty" you want to have wisdom and you want to have the understanding of that right thinking of the teachings. That is going to lead you to develop "Aset" or "Intuitional Higher Consciousness."

I started talking about the boundaries and we have talked a lot about physical boundaries and communicating with others and keeping in mind how you think and feel about things before you communicate with others so you won't be mixing yourself in a negative way with other people's thoughts, other people's desires and recognizing when other people are trying to manipulate you or change your mind for whatever reason.

The next boundary is the boundary of Mind. The boundary of mind relates to your understanding of the philosophy, like we just said, but also of being a "gatekeeper" for what comes in. What does the President say is it nonsense, is it stupidity, is he trying to pull one over? Or a friend can do the same thing. Is your family member trying to do the same thing? Or are you yourself, your ego trying to do the same thing? Pull one over on you? You say, "Oh I haven't eaten any meat for a whole month, so I can have a hamburger with my friend now." That's your ego trying to pull one over on you. So you have to have boundaries to prevent the ego, other people, the world from coming in and defining you, your higher nature of who you are with corruptions or ignorance that will subvert your higher goals. You need to setup filters so that information is not just accepted and saved in the unconscious mind regardless of the source, veracity or quality. Information is to be judged with the knowledge and wisdom of Maat first. That is the discipline of the philosophy of mind and the discipline of Maat for your physical aspect. For your soul boundary to develop, for that you use meditation; you use the teaching and practice of meditation to start developing calmness and developing a feeling of joy in aloneness, in being by yourself. In being in a situation where you do not need other people to make yourself feel happy, or you don't need to do anything to make yourself feel happy or to feel that you are valuable as a human being, and not existing or having a right to exist because the people say that you are good or that you are ok or somebody loves you or and they hug you; if you live in this way you are defining yourself. So you practice these disciplines, the boundaries for your physical self, your mental self and your spiritual self. Ultimately if you become seated in that meditative experience, that aloneness, that oneness, all boundaries fall asunder. Meaning that if you discover your higher nature of who you truly are as "All-encompassing Divinity" then you are making the relationship with that which all relationships are fulfilled. So it means that what we call "Neberdjer" if you become seated and related to that as the higher truth of existence, then it doesn't matter what other relationships you have or don't have and all boundaries are torn asunder. They are unnecessary. But in a disciplinary way you have to develop those boundaries so that you can discover who and what you are in the world of time and space. Of course what relates to your personality and how other people see you and what you do for your life's work and all of that kind of thing, that is the what. The "who" is what you are, but transcending all limited, changeable and relative things. The part of you that was alive before you were born and is alive after your body dies, that is the who. The Who Am I is the ultimate self. That ultimate knowledge is what has been lost in this negative way of relating. That is what the *Aryu* is clouding. That is what the atrophied intellect doesn't allow you to see. If you practice these disciplines that have been discussed throughout this whole series and of course this series within a series on relationships, then you are going to discover and grow beyond dysfunction of relations or wrong "relationing", as we call it, and you are going to have the kind of relationships that Sages have. They can have relationships with all people and they are not affected by them and they are not dependent on it. That is why they are free and they can be a beacon of true wisdom because they don't have an ax to grind, they don't have a vested interest. If you have a vested interest in your relationship that is going to taint your capacity to relate because you want to be in a relationship more than you want to live by truth so you are going to accept things that are not in harmony with Maat. You are going to like the proverb said, you are going to eat your own heart, you are going to stab yourself, you're going to hurt yourself. Since Sages don't have that problem, they are not bothered by the world in that way, they are not troubled and they are not defined by the world. This is what it means to be free, this is what is called "Nehast" and the Buddhists called it "Enlightenment" the Hindu's call it "Moksha Liberation" and the mystic Christians may call it "Kingdom of Heaven"; all these are the same, this is what the wisdom is leading us to understand. But what I very much appreciate about the Kemetic teaching is that it gives you a road map, a specific teaching and philosophy, and discipline to reach that higher goal.

Figure 9: *From the 42 Precepts of Maat:*

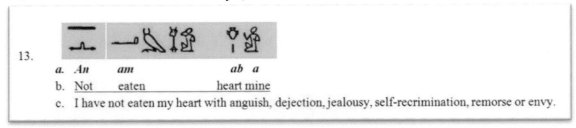

13.	*a. An*	*am*	*ab*	*a*
	b. Not	eaten	heart	mine
	c. I have not eaten my heart with anguish, dejection, jealousy, self-recrimination, remorse or envy.			

It is important to understand that what has been presented here as the Kemetic Philosophy of relationships is an ideal and no one is expected to practice this teaching fully just by listening or reading about the teaching. It takes time of reflection and time of actual practice in the world of time and space within your own relationships and also observing others; then also it is necessary to start working on changing the aryu. However, the first step is to at least know what the teaching and ideal are supposed to be so you can start recognizing the faults when they appear and then be able to work to correct them. You are living in a mirage and it is so compelling because of your past aryu. So it will take time for you to be able to live in the mirage and recognize it for what it is and also not get ensnared in its scintillating dreamlike traps of apparent reality and compelling events. The work you do to raise yourself to the standard presented by this teaching is the key to eventual success. So there is no need to feel despair or hopelessness or frustration about it; the key is to patiently allow yourself to grow with dispassion (Kemetic term khak-ab) and then be relentless in your efforts (Kemetic term antet-begag) and these will pave the way to success and the discovery of a heretofore unknown higher existence that is more glorious than you can imagine.

Here are some final Ancient Egyptian Proverbs relating to Friendship. First, Ancient Egyptian Proverbs on the Subject of Friendship:

"If you want friendship to endure in the house that you enter, the house of a master, of a brother or a friend, then in whatever place you enter beware of approaching the women there. Unhappy is the place where this is done. Unwelcome is he who intrudes on them. A thousand men are turned away from their good because of a short moment that is like a dream, and then that moment is followed by death that comes from having known that dream. Anyone who encourages you to take advantage of the situation gives you poor advice. When you go to do it your heart says no. If you are one who fails through the lust of women, then no affair of yours can prosper." -AEP

"Help your friends with the things that you have, for you have these things by the grace of God. If you fail to help your friends, one will say "you have a selfish KA". One plans for tomorrow, but you do not know what tomorrow will bring. The right Soul is the Soul by which one is sustained. If you do praiseworthy deeds your friends will say "welcome" in your time of need." -AEP

"Know your friends and then you prosper. Don't be mean to your friends. They are like a watered field and greater than any material riches that you may have, for what belongs to one belongs to another. The character of one who is well born should be a profit to him. Good nature is a memorial." -AEP

"Do not be greedy in the division of things. Do not covet more than your share. Don't be greedy toward your relatives. A mild person has a greater claim than a harsh one. Poor is the person who forgets their relatives; they are deprived of their company. Even a little bit of what is wanted will turn a quarreler into a friendly person." -AEP

Chapter 4: Questions and Answers About Relationships, and Friendships and Kemetic Relationships and Friendships

Question 1- Why are things still the same in my relationship as before I came into these teachings?

I've been in a relationship with a person and we have been reading your books and in Kemetic communities and we have tried to apply these principles of maat to relationships and even created a Kemetic marriage contract as you had in a previous book. Still, things are as before we came to these teachings and I don't understand why my boyfriend starts arguments and sometimes yells at me for no reason and some agreement vows are broken. We went to regular counseling and the therapist said we needed space and to work on communication. Still, nothing changed and he is sometimes moody and depressed and I go to him and he slams the door on me. Can maat help me?

ANSWER

Keep in mind that the effectiveness of Maat Philosophy in any relationship, romantic, coworker, parent, with nature, community, etc. is predicated on sanity, the balance of mind, and well-adjusted personality. If a person is off balance, disturbed, suffering paranoid delusions or psychotic issues or if they are sociopathic, etc., then the teachings will not be as helpful. There is a saying in spiritual circles that you must "Normalize before you Spiritualize." This means there needs to be as is discussed in the Kemetic Diet book, proper nutrition for body, mind, and soul. Also, there should be gradual and progressive and properly led spiritual practice so as to lead the personality to cleanse and purify body mind and soul. Otherwise, there can develop imbalances leading to abrupt changes in moods, reduced concentration ability and overall peace of mind, or even more serious mental pathologies, wherein relations will be rocky at best if possible at all, depending on the issues involved. Therefore, a person desiring to enter into a relationship with another person should first see if that person meets the basic standards of Maatian balance, sanity, and ethical conscience. If they do not meet those standards then it is best to hold on proceeding with such a relationship. If you are a person already in the relationship while only now realizing these issues in the light of Maatian Wisdom, then you need to choose how to proceed in terms of upholding the principles of maat that you want to grow into while determining if the situation can be improved and to what extent that will not violate your ethical principles and still honor your Maatian aspirations for life. So, if the person you want to relate to can be helped within these parameters and the relations can be improved to a beneficial degree for all involved you can consider proceeding. However if the prospects are not so good or the person refuses to acknowledge or seek assistance or if they themselves cannot see the issues that not only you but other qualified persons such as therapists, etc. can witness, then you also have a choice after reflecting about if such a relationship would be righteous and worthy to be continued.

Question 2: Is there any truth to women being from venus and men from mars?

ANSWER

There has been a theme for many years, running through popular culture that women and men are fundamentally different in terms of the manner in which the genders relate or are different fundamentally. This is a wide subject that in terms of this book has limited application since this treatise deals with the fundamental nature of humanity, which is that both personalities manifesting as male or female are innately one and the same essence and can reach the heights of personal, societal and spiritual experience through Maatian living. That said, the manifestation of that same essence, soul, via the vehicle of body and gender, is influenced by various factors including hormones and other physiological differences but also the manner in which the particular society socializes the genders and thereby the mannerisms and ways of communication and patterns of thought that may be engendered in them such that they may manifest in ways dictated or acceptable to the social norms while at the same time influenced by a person's own ego unconscious. This means that while fundamentally the soul of all human beings is the same the filter through which that consciousness manifests can redirect that in various ways and due to varied possible complexes that can cause individual as well as gender patterns that may be later confused with fundamental ways of being. Furthermore, the aforesaid is further compounded by the factor of socialization/conditioning in a diseased culture (Inc. conditioning from diseased religious institutions, parents, friends, government, schools, etc.), that exacerbates some or suppresses other patterns of behavior such as exaggerated sexuality, ideas of manhood tied to being a breadwinner or a woman as being a mother; and some others that may also become society-wide self-fulfilling biases like preventing a group from acquiring education and then later saying those people are genetically dumb or suppressing the rights and expression of another group and then later saying that group is emotional and not worthy of consideration, or giving the advantages of society to one group and when they are more successful than everyone else then saying those people are smarter and more deserving than everyone else, etc. Therefore, we must realize that as we are entertaining this subject of Kemetic Relationships it relates to Kemetic Relationships between Kemetic people and that ideally means people who have grown up in a sane society based on balance and truth, i.e. Maat Philosophy or who have at least adopted the righteous culture AND worked through the negative learned ignorance from previous lives or the socializations of the present lifetime. In such a world, the ways of relating would be influenced by that paradigm or social matrix instead of the one based on a culture of violence, sexism, egoism, crime, and corruption, etc. Therefore, the issue of mars and venus does not apply to our study as those distinctions relate to determinations arrived at by observers, who themselves may be tainted by the culture, looking at the gender interactions within that diseased culture and thus such reference, in this volume, to behaviors or patterns should be taken as a description for contrasts and comparison to the ideal proposed by Maat Philosophy and not taken as an assignation to a particular gender of a label or hard and fast finding, pegging one or the other gender as being definitely and unchangeably one way or another.

Finally, two points, gender is an external and ephemeral aspect of soul manifestation, therefore, regardless of the gender, Maat Law applies equally to both and both are charged with the duty of respect for the other, firstly just for existing, and thus being a manifestation of the Divine and then by extension also being respected in legal, family, government, economic, personal, etc., areas of human activity. Point two: The goal of the reader of this text ideally would be to work through their social and personal biases, maladaptations, mental complexes, and egoistic patterns to discover inner peace and the source of being that is beyond those limited and distorted manners of manifestation so as to discover the Higher Self that transcends them.

Question 3: Does this teaching mean that no relationship is a good relationship and that the best relationship is no relationship?

Figure 10: The African Monkey Trap

ANSWER: The answer is no and yes. No for the first part and yes for the second part. The first part is "no relationship is a good relationship," that is a no because there is a good relationship (discovering your true Higher Self as opposed to the little self, the limitations of your ego and the egos of others). The second part "the best relationship is no relationship "and that is true. True in the sense that you must realize that anything you relate to in the world of time and space if you have relativity in your relationship, your relationships are tainted. Relativity means that your relationship has the consciousness of being related to an "other", something other than self. If you see yourself as individual and you see yourself relating to other individuals then your relationship is doomed essentially. No matter how fun, or wonderful or how much passion you have or how great things are at the time. Conversely, if your relationship is the idea and the knowledge of "oneness" meaning that you are not relating yourself as an individual to another individual but you are recognizing your oneness with all then there are no individuals. There is no multiplicity and there is no relativity. There can be no disappointment, there can be no changes, no fleetingness in the relationship because it is constant, it is perennial, eternal. That is, of course, the higher goal to strive for in a relationship as opposed to having a relationship based on duality which is what most people accept and what they seek for in the world of time and space. So basically this issue of relativity in the personality due to the existence of "Khemn" or spiritual ignorance, composed of the duality of love and hate, otherwise termed, attachment and the repudiation, leads to the corruption of the heart, of feeling, because when you have relativity you are going to have corruption. When you have the opposite, nonduality or the vision of oneness, then you will have clarity, harmony, and peace as well as power and self-worth with self-will. Corruption in mind is the *"Indj Set"* –affliction of Set. "Inj" means afflictions and that constitutes "disease" that produces the *"Saiu Set"* or that which closes your mouth (metaphor of mind); it is a bandage, and metaphorically, it is that which obstructs your consciousness. In other words, it binds you and constricts your mind and makes you an egoistic being so that you cannot expand into full human freedom and higher consciousness, into Spirit or the *"Akhu"*, the experience of the One, the Higher Shining Spirit. So the lack of this experience leads us to the *"Khemn."* Khemn is the state of ignorance that supports the duality in the heart (mind), which leads to the loving and hating, that brings us to attachment and repudiation; and so the cycle goes until we die and then are reborn to do it over again until at some point the personality gets tired of the suffering cycle and determines to mature and become a fully human and spiritual being. That complexed mind caught up with affliction and ignorance leads to *"an-Maat"*. "An Maat" (not-truth) is that which is against Maat or that which is unrighteous. This is an unrighteous way of living, feeling, thinking and that taints the relationships and that feeds back into, like a feedback loop into the experiences of corruption in life. What I mean by corruption is that the actions and relations in life are perverted, because they are engaged by an afflicted, ignorant and unrighteous personality based on reflexive (have influence on the personality even without one knowing or noticing) desires and repudiations. They are not based on righteousness, order, truth, thoughtfulness, justice, and peace in mind.

As explained before when you go out on a date with someone or you want to get with someone romantically you bathe, you put on makeup, put on nice clothes, maybe a couple of tattoos so you can look cool, have a nice car and you are not presenting yourself as you really are. You are lying basically. So you end up caring about your appearance, caring about how people think about you so that they will like you and you can get what you perceive as something that will make you happy and or bring you pleasure. All this stress and strife, and the frustrations of life, people accept and suffer through, because they believe that it is the way to happiness and fulfillment even though they do not realize and do not want to listen to reason and accept that they cannot really get what they want through those means. So that leaves them in a kind of mental degradation which in modern parlance is termed as psychological complexes or as dysfunctions or as co-dependencies or as "issues" of which the essentially the essential source problem, the underlying illness is ignorance of the knowledge of Self that has led to a wrong understanding of what life is and to attachments to things that are fleeting, changeable and insufficient to meet the deeper needs of the soul. The answer to this problem is wisdom or *Rekh,* a wisdom that leads to a concept called *"Fek",* which in the Kemetic terminology means *"to loosen, to undress, to detach, to strip"* the veils of illusion so we can see the true naked form which of the universe, how the universe really looks – i.e. in a state of oneness and wholeness wherein there is no want causing desires or repudiations; a state that is fulfilled and at peace, without undue dependencies. So this is the process that needs to be undertaken, to "Fek" which means to loosen, to let go of your grip on the egoistic vision of life. It is like that African parable of the monkey. The monkey trappers used to trap monkeys by putting a tasty morsel, like a banana, inside a bottle that is big enough to stick their hand in but if they grab the banana and make a fist, they can't pull their hand out of the bottle which is tied say to a tree. When the monkey grabs he can't get his hand out and then the trappers come running out and then he is so flustered that he doesn't know what to do. In the stress of the time, he may even grasp more strongly and be trapped more securely. He doesn't realize that all he needs to do is to release his hand and pull his hand out of the bottle and run away. He is caught by his ignorance and the overwhelming stress of emotions of fear, desire, anxiety, etc. His intellect has been atrophied out of fear. That is what happens to human beings living in the world with ignorance desires and repudiations. The scripture of the Wisdom Texts (see below) talks about that, about how people have desire to stay on earth and they experience love and hate and not realizing that there is something better, something higher to experience. They are caught up because they are ignorantly lost in the experience of human life and clinging to that even though it is temporary and it has to end at some point and whatever is gained has to be let go. Yet they are still holding on to it. So that is what the teaching is all about for this particular question. The task next is how to get the mind straight so as to project Maat in the world and in the field of mind discover order, peace, truth, and spiritual emancipation, which is a main subject of this text and our other works as well.

Figure 11: Ancient Egyptian Stele of Abu Teaching: #4 –Life of Worldliness-Attachment & Hatred & Their Results

Verse 1.

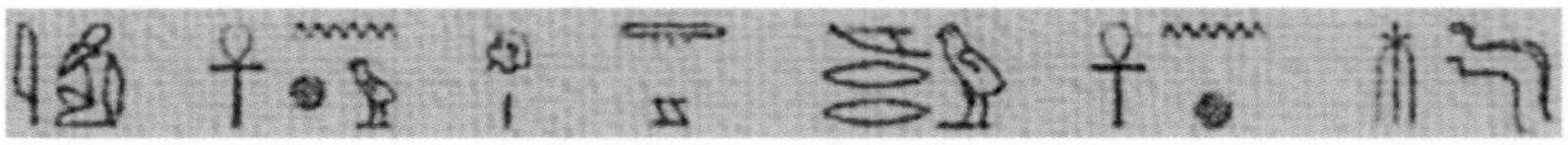

1.1.	A	ankh	dep	ta	merru	ankh	mesdjed
1.2.	Listen! Living		on	earth	loving	life	hating

1.3.   Now hear this, if you live your life while you are on the earth plane, the way most ignorant people do, by loving some things and feeling attached to them and then hating other things and trying to get away from them,

Verse 2.

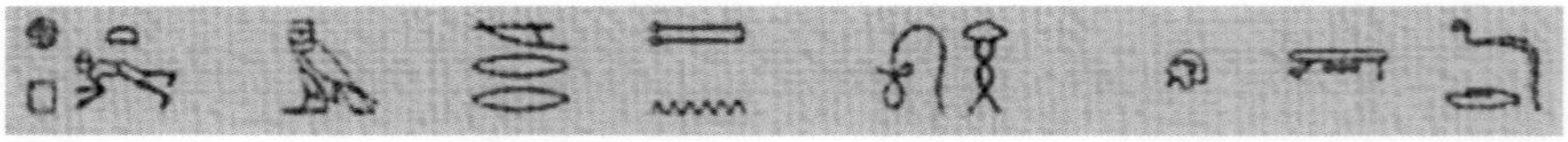

2.1.	chept	m	merr	tjen	oah	dep	ta	djed
2.2.	death	by	desire	that of	planting	on	earth.	I Say

2.3.   that kind of lifestyle is of death and not of life since if urges you to stay on earth to keep on experiencing the ups and downs of life in search of pleasure and avoiding pain followed by the grave. This is not a way to exist with true life but rather away to be dead to that higher part of your existence and turning attention to what is earthly and physical and ephemeral, constantly changeable.

Verse 3.

3.1.	ten	chat	ta	nu	n	amakhy abu	er	ra-per
3.2.	to you: thousands of loaves,		drink,		to revered bull		of	temples

3.3.   Therefore my advice to you is the following. Go to the temples of the gods and goddesses and make offerings to the sacred bull, symbol of the divine, thereby turning towards the divine to provide you with divine grace, to be free of the ignorance of love and hate and provided with the wisdom of spirit which is beyond that duality and ignorant human desires, engendered by loving and hating things.

Question 4- Can relations with friends contribute to Enlightenment or re relations with close family more important as related to Enlightenment?

ANSWER: All relations provide a contribution to one's capacity to be either peaceful or unstressed, which is necessary to attain enlightenment, or agitated and dull by your anguish, frustrations, and stress in a relationship. The issue comes in especially more acutely the more intimate the relationship is, whether it is with a friend, like with a spouse or with children, family, parents, friends, etc., The specific relation doesn't matter so much as the approach and the intimacy. What I mean by intimacy is how close are you to the person and how attached and entangled you are with them in an unrighteous (overly dependent) manner. That is the issue that contributes or detracts from your capacity to attain enlightenment from relations with friends and family. If you are very attached to someone, whoever it is, friend or family, in a wrong way, an ignorant, negative way, then that will be detrimental to your attaining enlightenment. That attachment causes negative *Aryu* of agitation and *Aryu* that clouds your intellect and clouds your capacity to see your Higher Self, like the monkey that became trapped and lost the vision of his freedom.

Question 5- What is the best form of relationship in a person's life and who is that with?

ANSWER: Clearly the best form of relationship is with yourself. If you are related to yourself, your ego, but in a healthy way, without egoism, then your human existence will be fruitful. If you are related to your Higher Self in a proper and full way you don't need any other relationships. So you will approach the worldly relations with freedom and peace instead of anxiety and frustrations through the futile efforts at trying to find desirable relations, keep them and draw happiness out of them. Your worldly relationships will be like having your cake with a cherry on top, they will be the cherry, they will be the flowers in your garden, but you don't need a garden with flowers. If you have a garden with flowers the more the better but the real benefit of a garden is the sustenance from the life essence that gives rise to and sustains all the plants and their fruits. So, your best relationship and most important relationship is with yourself.

Question 6- You spoke about boundaries. Once I had a best friend. Should I have kept within my boundaries and stayed silent? I still feel bad when I think about it

A great talk, this question is about boundaries. I once had a best friend and I thought he did something wrong and I felt sad about giving him my opinion. He yelled at me and we have not spoken for years. You spoke about boundaries. Should I have kept within my boundaries and stayed silent? I still feel bad when I think about it.

**ANSWER:** Before I say what I'm going to say about that, I'd like to see what Sage Amenemope says about that kind of situation. In **Chapter 9 of the Wisdom text of Amenemope verse 35,** he says, _"Do not befriend the heated man, nor approach him for conversation, avoid the scandal monger. His lips are dates (meaning that it is sweet) but his tongue is the deadly dagger and a blazing fire is within him. Avoid converse with evil men for that God hates. Make thy plans wisely. Keep dignified. Place thyself for safety in the hand of God. The liar is an abomination to Him." **Verse 40:** "Don't force yourself to greet the heated man. For then you injure your own heart. Do not say greetings to him falsely while there is terror in your belly." **Chapter 12 Verse 45:** "Do not converse with a heated man who has to befriend a hostile man."_ The point that I'm bringing out here is that you have a friend and the friend only likes you or can only take you when you do things that he likes. He can't take criticism; you know what kind of friend that is? You are asking about the boundaries, the boundaries are not from you exercising Maat, exercising truth or what you see as righteousness and order. If a person is doing something that you think is negative, it is your right and your duty as a friend to speak up and to face them. If they cannot take that, meaning that if you have to be tiptoeing around them or talk to them only when they are in a good mood, that is an immature person that will be a poor friend because of their incapacity to honestly look at their own ego and make the changes necessary to move it towards Maat (righteousness, order and truth); this is what it means to live by truth and not stop the ears from listening to truth. It would be unwise to be friends with such a person. If you are yourself weak and you desire the friendship and you are going to compromise yourself and accept their unrighteousness then you are in the same category with them, degraded and caught in the matrix of egoism, delusion, and ignorance that leads to pain, suffering and frustration throughout life. This is what Sage Amenemope meant about, that you are going to injure your own heart, this is what he says. This is so because you are doing something that you, yourself think is morally or ethically wrong, yet you are accepting within yourself, something that will injure you down the road by the feelings, thoughts, and actions that will in the future lead you to unrighteous, painful and frustrating situations. In reference to the issue of the boundaries that we're talking about. It relates to how you are allowing other people and the world to affect you and to warp your sense of reality about yourself and thereby cause you to act in ways that are against Maat that lead you on a road to perdition. As far as the issue of friendship, that is not what true friendship is. You should be able, to be honest with a true friend, and say what you need to and they may get a little upset at facing a truth they know deep down but may not have wanted to face; if they start attacking you then, again, you know what kind of friendship that is, which is really no kind of friend but rather a sentimental and immature attachment relationship. It is a dysfunctional relationship with a person who has issues and they're attacking you, potentially infecting you with the disease of egotism. If they can't come down from it and can't realize the wrong that they did and are trying to make you feel bad for not accepting their unrighteousness, that is a person you don't need to be friends with; you need to have better friends. Better friends will accept the friendly advice and work to better themselves and they will offer helpful insights to you as well and help you be a better person as well; they are going to help you attain enlightenment as you will help them and they are not going to keep you feeling bad about it. It is not something you should feel bad about. The other person should feel bad, it is their loss and you need to move on, otherwise, it will be your loss as well, unnecessarily commiserating in an endless ocean of delusion.

Question 7-How does aryu influence thoughts?

You have spoken about a concept called "aryu" as the total of the past thoughts, feelings and desires of the past residing in the unconscious, that influences us and directs our life. Can you explain how that influences our thoughts, feelings, and desires and how to overcome that?

ANSWER

Perhaps you have a predilection for people with a certain skin color or particular sex or of a particular ethnic group or who are young but not for people who are of another group or ethnicity, etc. It must be understood that any and all preferences are determined by the content of your aryu, the thoughts, desires, feelings, and experiences of the past that have left impressions in your unconscious mind and inform your opinions, desires and preferences at present. That is, even if you learn from others in your social group, your aryu determines if you will agree or disagree with those notions. If your aryu is of weakness and ignorance you will find yourself in the company of weak and ignorant people and believe as they do and act as they do, etc. Therefore, these impressions are filters through which ignorant human beings see the world not realizing they are being led along paths depending on the nature of their unconscious impressions. An enlightened person sees through the impressions just as a person who realizes he/she is looking at a mirage, can discount the mirage even if it is still visible as a mirage. The ignorant person believes the mirage is real so much that even when the knowledgeable person tells them it's a mirage, they cannot believe that and even fight against the person telling them the higher truth. In the same way, the wisdom teacher tries to impart the wisdom but it is up to the person's capacities of being strongly or more loosely held by their delusions, to listen and live in accordance with the higher truth so as to develop new and more powerful impressions that cleanse the mind and allow a person to see through the delusions of desires and repudiations in the mind. This is the process of moving towards enlightenment. Enlightenment is realizing that the deluded desires and hatreds of the mind are as illusory as a mirage.

Question 8-When I relate to others does the negative Aryu come from the interaction or the thoughts about relationships?

ANSWER: The interaction and the thoughts about a relationship both may be considered as one and the same since the sum total in your personality is one experience in your single personality. The negative *Aryu* comes from the interaction and your thoughts about that interaction. Meaning that when you have an interaction or experience you are developing a feeling related to that experience and thoughts related to it and if you do not consider those thoughts or feelings judiciously, whatever they are, they are going to leave a residue or impression that is going to be lodged in your unconscious mind. So it comes from the interaction that you perceive and your manner of processing of that in your personality determines its effect in your personality. Now, after the present experience is processed, then when you are confronted with the same kind of experience in the future, the feelings created then, in the future experience, will resonate with the past one and depending on that new interaction the past one will be evoked, and reinforced, or diffused and resolved.

Depending on how much residues you have in your unconscious mind, you will be either impelled or compelled to engage in that action. For example, if you have an experience in a relationship, you like someone but you broke up and you are not with them anymore, the feelings related to that relationship are still there unless you have dealt with them unless you have faced them and diffused them. If the feelings and urges related to the relationship of the past was not dealt with and yet even though you know it was a bad relationship, you may be compelled to enter into a new relationship with the same person again. If you may see someone else in the future that reminds you of that past relationship unconsciously it stirs up and resonates with those feelings from the previous relationship. So a different bad person can stir up the past feelings and compel you're getting into the new relationship with the same type of bad person. Then if you have not dealt with that previous relationship, which means you agreed with those past feelings and thoughts by affirming over the years to yourself, "Oh I wish I had that boyfriend/girlfriend I had years ago, Wow, we had some fights but, they were really good in bed"; the more you think about it and reinforce that thought the more you accumulate impressions and energies related to that impetus and the more you forget about the negative aspects and in an illusory way highlight the positives, strengthening the delusion (not seeking or perceiving truth).

In the state of delusion, you work to only remember the good aspects. So you reinforce the good aspects. Then you are confronted with another person, in the present, who has many features of that old relationship and since you have focused on the positive aspect of the past you are again blinded now, in the present, to the negative ones. Your intellect is atrophied; overwhelmed by delusions. You are going to have another dysfunctional relationship and since you are ignorant you are going to lodge those new impressions in the unconscious mind and you are going to amplify their power. You may say: "I don't know why I keep on falling for wrong guys" or "I don't know why I keep on falling for wrong girls". You are going to continue doing this on and on and you may be bound and you don't know why you can't leave the person; you don't know why you don't want to move on, or you move on and you find another dysfunctional person again and again. You may get to a point and say "I can't find any good relationships and all are bad so I'm going to give up on that and just have a baby without having a spouse, then the baby will love me and I can love them the way I can find a partner for."

Of course, this is just a different form of the same delusion, a way of compensating for one delusion by seeking satisfaction through another which one is immature and incapable of handling either. The child grows up in an imbalanced way, possibly due to the overcompensating or overbearing single parent and the relationship is strained as the child grows up without the balance of a second parent and or not knowing how to relate to the members of that gender since they only grew up interacting with the gender of one parent. These are just a few examples of a myriad of possible psychological complexes that canaries even when there are two parents, let alone one. This syndrome manifests in a man looking for the same kinds of women or women looking for the same kinds of men, bad boys or boys or men who cheat on them and things like that. You might say, "Oh why is this happening to me? Why can't I find a good man? Again, this originates from the issue of spiritual ignorance that causes men and women to lead their lives in such a way that they are distracted by desires and repudiations (egoism), they are constantly mentally agitated, never finding peace, thoughtfulness and wisdom and filling the minds with impressions of ignorance, desires and delusions. Told by the world that this is what relationships are, that you are to have a roller coaster and sometimes it is good and sometimes it is bad and that's just how it is, there is no other way it can be, it always was and will be this way, etc. so a human being grows up in a way conditioned by those thoughts and the impressions they and the actions based on them engender. Of course that's nonsense; the problem persists because your mind has agreed with and has accumulated the impressions (aryu) of that conditioned reality or way of viewing life, in the unconscious mind, and becomes a compelling way of feeling and thinking within you that shapes your behaviors, opinions and actions, essentially producing a self-fulfilling prophecy in life based on a mental content of the unconscious that you have allowed to develop and be sustained.

The wisdom of Maat affirms that it doesn't have to be that way; it wasn't always that way and it is not that way for everyone now and in the past of history either. Other countries have different ways of relationship. You should stop looking at things in the way that everybody has to look at it in your particular country, its media and customs and beliefs as if they should apply to everyone in the world generally; that is a myopic vision that constricts the mind and its capacity to learn and grow to a level of maturity necessary for having a viable, balanced and positive relationship. Everything has to be the way things are here in your country or according to your beliefs and no one can ever look at things the way they are elsewhere. This points to a weak and limited mind that leads to weak and limited relations. Limitation and weakness lead to degraded relationships and degraded life in general. An example of this issue is the healthcare issue; people in the United States of America can never look at how Europe does it or how Canada does it, it has to be a USA solution and that is propaganda to tap into national pride and the delusion of national exceptionalism but in reality it is a ploy to maneuver people into the policies that benefit the drug companies and insurance companies. The solution always has to be in favor of corporations and those are just more impressions foisted on people's minds to cause them to support causes that are good for other persons and not for themselves. That is also an example of how ignorance and mental limitation leads to being dominated, enslaved and exploited either by corporations or other people in relationships.

Question 9-Does the teaching of detachment mean feeling distinct in order to prevent dysfunction?

ANSWER: I would say that ultimately it does mean feeling distinct and separate at an ego level meaning your personality is separate from others; However, at an essential soul level it means feeling kinship and oneness. That is what the healthy boundaries are all about. The boundaries are so that at the ego and time and space level, you can start developing a feeling of distinction or being distinct from other people, their feelings, thoughts, opinions, and perspectives; Then you are able to discern what your deeper felt thoughts and feelings are and not get mixed up in the perceived positiveness or negativeness of others or of the world and thereby also not feel compelled to participate with others when the internal ethics tell you that you should not and thus have power and sovereignty over your life, a truly live and let live scenario instead of sentimental attachments and going along with things you don't want or don't believe in, causing yourself miseries and compromising your own principles and morals. This is being distinct from the world and actually leads to being distinct from your ego self so as to discover what there is beyond your unconscious impressions of the past, including the opinions, feelings, desires and other delusions in your own mind.

Wisdom of Personal Sovereignty

Finally, when you are able to discover true _personal sovereignty,_ meaning that you can know what you feel and think as opposed to being mixed up with or overly concerned about what others think, feel and desire, then you can truly discern what is your own deeper and honest feelings, thoughts, and desires and then be able to make the best decisions for yourself first and then in relation to others. This is the problem of the realm of relativity; being mixed up with others relative to yourself and seeing your life relative to that of others. Of course, there is a part of life that relates to others but that is not all of life. If that sovereign part were discovered it is a window and pathway to discover the part of yourself that transcends relativity and time and space itself even as you live in the world of time and space and relativity. When we speak of this concept of relativity it implies external issues, which were just mentioned, and also internal issues such as biological or gender urges and feelings. Therefore, that same transcendental part within that is to be discovered also allows one's deeper self to become sovereign and separate and powerful over the biological imperatives such as eating, desire for sex and feelings of being male or female as well (in other words being polarized in consciousness and identifying as a man or woman-instead of androgynous spirit beyond the dualities of time and space). This teaching certainly blows up the illusion that balance and harmony imply that in a relationship everyone is supposed to be on the same page and harmonious, believing the same things, desiring the same things all the time. It is possible to be on the same page in general areas of agreement but ultimately everyone has an individual life path so individuals can form long-term and or temporary partnerships through life. However, the idea of complete or absolute agreement or harmony in relationships, that is a delusion that often becomes a source of frustration and anguish that should be set aside on the quest for relationship freedom and spiritual emancipation.

Question 10-What happens when one or the other partner starts to develop, and one partner the person who is not developing?

Let me explain the question more. What happens when in the Kemetic, (this doesn't just happen in the Kemetic field, Shemsu (temple followers) and Asaru (temple initiates) and people who are aspirants, it happens in people who are in Indian Yoga, people who are in Buddhism, people in Hinduism or what not) when one or the other partner starts to develop, and one partner (and this can be male or female) develops and starts practicing more meditation, attending classes and starts developing a little more dispassion and detachment, the person who is not developing, who does not want to develop (let's say you have a wife and the husband and the husband starts being interested in Yoga and the Kemetic Wisdom, practicing meditation and developing a little dispassion, but then the wife doesn't like that necessarily so she doesn't go to classes, she doesn't really develop, she wants to be more in the world and then she starts developing a feeling that the husband is moving away and not taking care of her or attracted to her. So then she starts complaining and the husband is not having sex like he used to or that he doesn't buy her flowers or take her out to movies or whatever it is. It could happen the other way that the wife starts developing and the husband starts thinking, a. you're not having as much sex as you were and you are not spending time with me, so you don't love me. Because love is equated with gifts, sex or with physical contact which of course is illusory and fleeting. Then in either situation, the woman may want a divorce because of that or the man may start going around and cheating because he supposedly _has to_ get what he needs. This is what society says that men can't control themselves because of course, we know that men are more sexually active and interested and the libido is stronger. Women find it easier to withhold sex than men do. But my point is that the exacerbation of that due to society which promotes and pushes men, who already have a tendency of higher libido, to be more sexually aggressive and active, then this is going to cause problems in the relationship. So what is there to do? I've seen this happen several times over the years in our teaching that people come asking, "You know my husband is not interested in the teaching but I am and what should I do?" Or "My wife is not with it". So both ways.

ANSWER: Ultimately, you have to look at your life, as an individual, and think about how you are going to develop yourself, how you want to lead your life in the context of realizing that we came into the world alone and we leave alone also and that we have a purpose and goal in life beyond being in limited, strife stricken relations that do not uplift us but rather point us constantly to the dramas of human existence which, after being indulged in, end in death at the end of a lifetime; what would be the purpose of living life that way? If you want to continue with the relationship as you were in the beginning and not change or grow, meaning that maybe you got together in an ignorant way, in a worldly way, in a dependent way and want to stay that way, that is your choice. But you are supposed to grow up, both of you ideally but if not then individually; and when that happens it affects the person who does not seem to want to grow at the time, in ways that may help them in the future of this lifetime or the next; However your main responsibility is your life and you can urge others or try to help others but ultimately you have to let them take care of their life; you cannot live it for them, for if you do you lose the chance to live yours and achieve what you need to achieve in life. Ideally, the other partner would come along, and if they are not fully into it they would, at least, be participating in some functions and programs and they would be aware of some aspects of the teaching and they would be affected in a positive way by that relationship, albeit in a limited fashion. But in this society where there is so much distraction and so much worldliness, what usually happens is that that ideal does not occur since people believe in the worldly culture of being here not to grow spiritually but to have physical pleasures and physical family closeness and dependencies (even when they don't last forever) and eventually the partners go their separate ways. That is what usually happens. Now sometimes people can negotiate and the person who is developing higher aspiration, since they are doing that, they don't need as much physical sex to feel self-worth or to feel they have a loving relationship and so on so forth. However, they may need to, or they may want to negotiate with the person who is not developing to not give them necessarily everything they want but at least to give them something of their needs to be satisfied. Here is an Ancient Egyptian Proverb to conclude our discussion about these teachings.

Egyptian Proverb: "Do not be greedy in the division of things. Do not covet more than your share. Don't be greedy towards your relatives. A mild person has a greater claim than a harsh one. Poor is the person who forgets their relatives. They are deprived of their company. Even a little bit of what is wanted will turn a quarreler into a friendly person." -AEP

So the teaching is about balance, it is about Maat. Maat doesn't necessarily mean all or nothing. It means a balance and if you are going to be in a relationship, especially a marital relationship if you have children and things like that you may want to negotiate something that is beneficial to your spiritual practice and also does require you to fulfill some marital relationship duties so on and so forth. If you are going to be in that kind of relationship, that is up to you; if you are not then fine. But if you are and if you can negotiate, then that can be beneficial for everyone. What happens is that sometimes people don't want that, they want all or nothing. Speaking from the other side, the person who is not developing, they want all or nothing or they want things the way they were or they are afraid of what you are doing. So there are many other issues that are going on, to be considered and worked out but the ultimate goal of life, while being either in or out of a relationship, is to become an enlightened being. What I have to say to that is: this is your lifetime, this is your responsibility this is, after all, an illusory world of time and space and what you hold on to, that is what you take with you from the standpoint of your *Aryu*. What you let go that allows you to climb higher and reach the higher consciousness and to relinquish the pain and sorrow of time and space.

Question 11- Does the fact - that I still cry imply a certain level of egoism because I am certain that I will cry when my Mother, children or any of my loved ones die?

Greetings, I am still reflecting on your comments on how you did not cry when your father died and how you comforted your Mother. To me crying is a natural thing to do when sad - as events in time and space will sometimes be. Crying for me can be very therapeutic and can help to relieve stress that may be built up because of the situation. Does the fact - that I still cry implies a certain level of egoism because I am certain that I will cry when my Mother, children or any of my loved ones die. Please provide more information on this subject.

ANSWER:

THE IMPORTANCE OF THIS QUESTION

Thank you for asking this question and sharing your feelings on this issue and in this forum, which will help others, as it is a fundamental issue of the teaching, the incorrect understanding of which would lead to a stagnant or erroneous spiritual movement. Therefore I am pleased to spend the extended time to conduct an extensive discourse on this issue.

Firstly, you stated that you find crying as therapeutic and stress relieving. That may be true under the current paradigm of life the way it is being lived but may not be true for other ways of living. The question then is, is the stress that is causing the need for relieving stress legitimate? If you feel stress due to or caused by loved one or troubles in life are the troubles legitimate and is that a legitimate way of life, being ok sometimes and then at others being stressed out to the point of having to cry to relieve stress? Or is it possible that the troubles of life have become so normalized that the stress and crying seem to be normal human activities? If that is so then does everyone in the world carry on that way? If not then we are forced to consider that having to cry due to stress or due to actions or inactions of loved ones or due to relationships or due to gain and loss, or due to conditions in a particular country or community, etc. is conditional and therefore, relative and thus illusory.

Your question has several other components so we will deal with it in the following breakdown as separate questions.

Question 12- WHAT DOES THE TEACHING SAY ABOUT THE ISSUE OF FEELINGS FOR FAMILY OR OTHER PERSONS YOU ARE ENGAGED IN RELATIONSHIPS WITH?

ANSWER

There are several areas of the teaching that we can consult for answers about this issue. We will explore some relevant teachings and then we will determine their specific application to the question at hand. This question also implies other questions such as what is the origin of sorrow, of feelings in general? what is their purpose and value, if any? How should feelings and emotions be handled? Is there a difference between feelings and emotions? We are told by the teaching itself:

Figure 12: From the 42 Precepts of Maat:

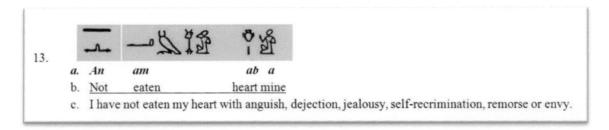

13.
a. An   am   ab   a
b. Not   eaten   heart mine
c. I have not eaten my heart with anguish, dejection, jealousy, self-recrimination, remorse or envy.

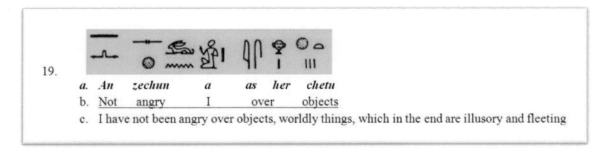

19.
a. An   zechun   a   as   her   chetu
b. Not   angry   I   over   objects
c. I have not been angry over objects, worldly things, which in the end are illusory and fleeting

While it is permissible, to some degree, for ordinary people to grieve and feel as well as express sorrow (eat their heart) over loss it is so because those persons are feeling out of an erroneous notion about the nature of life and the reality of human existence and have led themselves to a condition wherein the feelings born of ignorance and delusion currently hold sway over the personality. Allowances need to be made for those persons because otherwise making demands of them or holding them to requirements they are not ready to uphold would be detrimental to their psychological health and to the overall health of society in general; but this allowance is not made because it is normal or natural for human beings to require the allowance but rather because the degradation, the mental illness, requires that allowance in order to be able to work through the issues and process the psychological complexes that have been built up over lifetimes. So, the problems did develop over a period of time and consequently, they will take some time to be resolved. However, the time for resolution will be less than the time of the development of the illness; yet the time is indeterminate, depending on the level of devotion and study of the wisdom teaching, and the intensity of the shedy practice. So for them, it is natural and expected. However, for someone who has a different insight and sensibility about life, for them, it would not be natural to feel sorrow. For them, it would be possible to recognize and sympathize with the sorrow being experienced by others just as a parent recognizes and sympathizes with a son that fell down and hurt their leg. They recognize what it is like to fall and get hurt but they are not hysterical or overly distraught as the child might be. They understand and yet are able to take decisive action to alleviate the hurt. Therefore, such a one would not have cause to feel such feelings or express such emotions since there is no legitimate cause; but they could empathize and help in a more dynamic and wise way than a person caught in the mire of commiseration and distraught feelings along with others who are also caught in the mire of commiseration and distraught feelings. In this way, the more advanced person can assist in a higher way, show another way, and help the healing process in a more permanent way than just alleviating the current situation with palliatives of the world that do not resolve the fundamental issue that led to the suffering but merely alleviate the symptoms until the disease of feelings born of ignorance and delusion cause more sorrow in the future. In this way, ordinary people learn from the wise, how to better think about things and feel about things in a way that will tend to lead to more harmonious outcomes as opposed to more internal and external worldly entanglements and their inevitable worldly situations of suffering and grief.

> "The body was created to be subservient to the Soul; while YOU afflict the Soul for the body's pain, behold YOU SET the body above it. As the wise afflict not their garment; so the patient grieve not their Soul because that which covers it is injured." -EP

[Text emphasis by Dr. Ashby]

In the Ancient Egyptian myth of the Asarian Resurrection when Heru died, Aset cried out and when Asar died she also felt grief but only temporarily. Thereafter she reasoned and worked out a way to bring forth a higher realization, the resurrection. So too the wise initiate is to evolve so as to reach a point in conscious awareness such that their intellectual knowledge about the nature of existence is realized in fact and therefore, knowing the nature of existence renders it unnecessary to grieve over things that are not worthy or necessary of grieving about. In fact grieving over the death of loved ones or of oneself is based on an illusory belief and illusory habits in responses to that belief over many lifetimes. One does not grieve over a sunset due to the loss of the sun for one knows it will rise again the next day. Such a necessity has been based on an erroneous notion and on habit as well as socialization by the ignorant masses.

> "What is the source of sadness, but feebleness of the mind? What gives it power but the want of reason? Rouse yourself to the combat, and it quits the field before you strike." -EP

The source of sadness is feebleness of mind and feebleness is caused by error in thinking and is based on ignorance instead of wisdom. The wise do not feel sadness though they are aware of it and understand it, having once felt it before becoming wise themselves. An initiate is like a soldier and the war is between Heru and Set. Heru cannot be victorious without Aset, that is to say, the wisdom about the true nature of life and existence.

> "The impious Soul screams: I burn; I am ablaze; I know not what to cry or do; wretched me, I am devoured by all the ills that compass me about; alas, poor me, I neither see nor hear! This is the Soul's chastisement of itself. For the Mind of the man imposes these on the Soul." -EP

The impious soul is one who causes suffering to him/her self and is one who has not attained the piety of the teaching, that is to say, has not understood the deeper meaning and significance of the teaching, for there is no death and therefore nothing to mourn over about the passing of a loved one; additionally, there are no sentimental loved one's for sentimentality is an effect also of ignorance. Sentimentality may be defined as relating to worldly relationships on the basis of *Såa njset* (lack of understanding, ignorance (of the knowledge of self), dependency (for one's identity and happiness), emotionality (shallowness as opposed to substantiality based on rationality) and personal weakness (as opposed to the empowerment and independence that comes from living in accordance with wisdom). The enlightened personalities love impersonally but spiritually so they care but are not disturbed (either overjoyed or sorrowed, depressed, injured) by their caring and so their caring is stable and pure and full, like God's.

"They who abandon the body's senses, know themselves to be Light and Life. The Joy from Knowledge allows room only for the Good; in them Righteousness and Bliss have their firm seat; unrighteousness and sorrow will flee away to them who give it room." -EP

How to discover these realizations? remember this teaching whether you be in sorrow or pleasure and eventually neither the waves of sorrow nor the waves of joy will wash over and overwhelm the mind of a pious soul and this is what we call a Sheps, a noble person, a venerated person, a wise person; and this leads to becoming Akh or an enlightened person.

"Reflection is the business of Humankind; a sense of their state is the first duty: but who remembereth themselves in Joy? Is it not in mercy then that sorrow is allotted unto us?" -EP

"Good things cease to be good in our wrong enjoyment of them. What nature meant to be pure sweetness, are then sources of bitterness to us; from such delights arise pain, from such Joys, sorrows." -EP

Sorrow is caused by incorrect thinking and understanding. The wrong enjoyment of things is the source of pain at their loss; for is it legitimate to enjoy the company of a loved one, sentimentally, egotistically, as if it will go on forever, even while knowing that all humans must eventually die? Is it rational? No, but it is human error; but also it is human triumph to overcome the delusions of life, think correctly about things and be sorrowful about things that truly deserve "sorrow-ness", like the loss of the opportunity to attain enlightenment; From the perspective of the wise souls this may be a true motive of sorrow, the loss of opportunity to listen to the teaching and apply its wisdom and avoid more reincarnations and the pains and sorrows of more lives to come; all due to a life of pursuing fulfillment in the world of time and space for lack of knowing about other ways and lack of capacity to pursue the higher ways. Yet, though their path will be filled with suffering, even this is not a motive for sorrow as those souls will eventually find their way in time and we can also take solace, if we need to, from the knowledge that to whatever extent we have reached them with some element of wisdom, that that will help them to some degree.

So while emotional catharsis can be good for the masses of those not seeking enlightenment, for those who are initiates, for them, they are to follow a path that reduces delusion and concomitantly reduces the need to rely on sentimentalities and emotional displays since the feelings that would otherwise elicit those worldly emotional displays are for them neither impelling or compelling them to act in such ways. Moreover, the worldly minded do indeed need cathartic outlets for their feelings whereas the wise, having worked out the mysteries of life, do not need such release valves in order to cope with a stressful world, for their life is not fraught with inordinate troubles and sufferings born of worldly egoistic ignorant notions. Their mind has been purged to such to a degree that those aryu cannot either harm them psychologically nor compel them to become involved with situations, relationships, etc. that would lead to pain and sorrow.

Question 13-Are there any therapeutic benefits to crying?

<u>**ANSWER**</u>

Happiness is termed: *Awet ab* -expansion of heart- joy. Happiness is expansion of the mind, freedom, peace and *heru ab* - inner peace and contentment- joy. Sorrow is a kind of contraction of the heart, a tightness, a constriction of freedom and the state of unrest. How did sorrow occur and how is true happiness discovered?

Indeed, crying can be therapeutic and it can relieve stress that has been built up and it is not advisable for one to tell others not to cry IF they need to. But what is the source of stress or the need to cry and is there a reason why crying, or the expression of the feeling of sorrow should be natural to the human condition in all levels of spiritual evolution? IF a person were to change their perspective whereas they would not build up undue stress would there still be a need for crying?

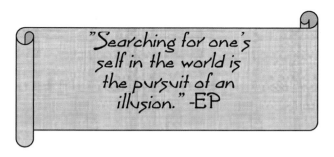

"Searching for one's self in the world is the pursuit of an illusion." -EP

Let us keep in mind that crying is an emotional expression of a feeling and that this is the deeper issue we are concerned with. The evolved personality [one who has discovered the inner fulfillment of knowing the self and all as universal, immortal and infinite and the objects of the world as manifestations of that same universal essence] does experience closeness, affection, caring and love for and from others; the difference is that the experience of peace and fullness [satisfaction, contentment] is not sentimental or dependent upon time and space [physical proximity or spending time in a physical living condition] with particular people or objects of the world exclusively; in other words, it is not dependent upon [beholden to, compelled by, controlled by] time and space, which is illusory and ephemeral. That is to say, the evolved personality may enjoy worldly pleasures but that enjoyment is an expression of their inner fulfillment, a reflection of the spirit of the divine that is everywhere and in all things and therefore, there would be no need for elation at the acquisition or sorrow at the loss of objects manifesting in time and space; so if the objects are taken away there would be no need for feelings of loss because there is fullness whether the object is there or not; for, the presence or absence of objects, being the same manifestation of the same divine spirit, is neither lost nor added to when appearing or disappearing in physical forms of the world of time and space. The evolved personality, therefore, recognizes the need that some people still have for companionship, closeness, affection, etc. as they are seeking to fulfill an emptiness felt due to the lack of inner fulfillment through self-knowledge. Accordingly, it is the duty of the Kemetic psychologist or clergy, to assist those at this level of spiritual development, to apply the teaching to their worldly pursuits in the best way possible, eventually leading them to a place of decreasing dependency and eventual enlightenment.

For unevolved personalities, since there is nothing internally to lean on, people lean on each other and on the world for happiness, and fulfillment of desires; the problem is that the world is changeable and therefore illusory and ultimately perishable so that fulfillment remains perpetually elusive and therefore always leads to sorrow in the end. Consequently, having understood this predicament, a wise person does not repudiate or disparage the worldly pursuit of desires but they do recognize it as a falsehood and therefore, relinquish that pursuit, knowing where that road leads to; and instead they pursue a path of higher reality and higher truth. One of the foremost qualities a serious initiate must develop is adherence to the truth. In this case this means not following a path of falsehood, of lies, but rather living for and out of higher truth as best as that is known and understood at any given time; then, if an even higher truth or realization arises then the present belief system must also be relinquished in favor of the higher and so on until the highest is reached. Complacency and stagnation, or relative comfort at a particular level of initiatic practice or of life, are enemies of an initiate and the initiatic process and its positive movement.

THE CONTRADICTION OF CRYING

We may ask ourselves: do people in say Scotland, cry when someone in China dies, do people in Colombia cry when someone in Russia dies? or in South America or In Europe etc.? Probably not and we may ask why? Because they don't know them; there is no close relationship. Therefore, if crying is elicited by knowing someone closely then, again, is that normal or what is it about the way of knowing that is troublesome? Let's look at this issue objectively and philosophically. If crying is a legitimate abiding feature of human existence should there not be sorrow and crying whenever someone dies anywhere? Otherwise is this not conditional and relative and therefore ego based and not reality based? Another example is ⸢⸢⸣⸣ *zecha*-memory, (to call to mind, commemorate). Very often, when a loved one dies people start to get over it until the memories flood back into the mind with memories of the loved one but that is not the only thing that happens. Along with the memories come the learned responses (aryu) [from socialization and cultural traditions] and the energy behind them (sekhem) that cause and support the learned response of crying to occur. If people lose a loved one and they are supposed to cry and grieve why do they not cry continuously and forever after the death? Why do they get over it and move on? And if they can get over it to any degree and move on to any degree, what does that imply? It means that sorrow is changeable, illusory and a learned response since some feel it to varying degrees and others don't and all get over it eventually. This means that sorrow is not endemic but dependent on the mind and aryu. Furthermore, if people can get over grief and sorrow over varying periods of time, why not get over it in less time or in a short time or in no time at all? Why not go all the way and avoid the need for grief and sorrow altogether?!!!

A mental and *aryu* structure (karmic basis) that is developed in a certain way founded in ignorance can be caught in the grips of sorrow while another mental and aryu structure can be free. So if one can get over sorrowful situations over time then it means that the time can be shortened or lengthened depending on the mental and *aryu* structure; so why not get over it as soon as possible instead of over a longer period of time? The more study (*shedy*), understanding (*Saa*) and application (*ari maat/shedy*) of the teaching (*sebait* Ancient Egyptian Spiritual Philosophy) the sooner the erroneous notions (*khemn*/ignorance) are dispelled (*kaf*) to the degree that if there is an effect on the mind it is brief such that the mind is aware of feelings but not gripped by them but also sufficiently aware that it is possible to still understand and sympathize with others who are still caught in the grips of egoistic ignorance and suffering but not be caught with them; In this way someone who has risen above the egoistic ignorance is best able to help those who are still suffering over that which is not worthy of feeling sorrow over, as opposed to commiserating and reinforcing sorrow and being unable to offer comfort and insights into a higher perspective. An initiate must resolve to relinquish the worldly culture, and the ego/emotionally based socializations behind and fully adopt the culture of the mysteries; only in this will they find the success that has been related in the ancient texts; otherwise, as the admonition to the priests and priestesses states, what is the purpose of reading it, and then go back to doing things the way one's heart (ego) desires?

If you feel sorrow for a departed family member, who dies, what about the passing is sorrowful and worthy of grieving? Is it rational when people cry over a sentimental movie or the death of a character in a play? Those who do are deeply caught in a matrix of time and space illusion, the veil (*nems*) of Aset. This is not a delusion perpetrated by her has but it is an illusion (*bes*) that souls (*bau*) have created and have come to believe in and rely upon for their sense of identity and fulfillment, not having beheld the nature of her bare essence (*nemms an*). Shall we rely on the world of illusion and temporality or shall we have faith (*nehti*) in the goddess and take refuge in her teaching (*sebait*)?

ARYU IN THE HEART

Firstly, it is important to realize that any emotional manifestation in life is determined by the aryu that the personality has accumulated. How did those aryu come to be there? Through your belief and understanding and agreement about your relationship to the world which you accepted and allowed to be lodged in the container of your heart through many lifetimes. And through many lifetimes you have believed that your feelings are real or that they are normal or legitimate, beneficial or cathartic or useful, etc. but in what context and with what philosophical evaluation, what understanding? Before we explore the answers to that question it is important to note that the Ancient Egyptian term *saa* which means understanding, also is used for the concept of "perception" and "feeling". Therefore, to understand is to feel and to feel is to understand; meaning, one's level of understanding [intellectual capacity, wisdom, and clarity of thinking] allows for what one feels and vice versa. Understanding may also be understood as the ability to have insight into reality and have the clarity and will to live by that truth regardless of personal ego feelings or desires. So, one's feelings are based on one's level of understanding [about life and the nature of existence] and therefore, to have higher divine understanding necessarily is to be beyond the effect of illusory worldly feelings. So what we understand leads us to either happiness or sorrow, or to being caught in the world of time and space or being liberated like the proverbial hawk whose wingspan encompasses the entire universe (*Ur Uadjit*). The rekhyt (ordinary people) seek to experience and understand the world and its vicissitudes in a futile pursuit to discover happiness and or fulfillment in life. The Asaru (temple initiates) seek to understand and feel the freedom and peace of the absolute truth, which is abiding and transcending worldly feelings; such is experienced during dreamless deep sleep, though unconsciously, and at a certain level consciously through meditation, when the gross elements of aryu that cause gross ignorance and gross feelings and emotions are sufficiently cleansed/purified through *rech* [wisdom practice] and *uashu* [devotional practice].

ENLIGHTENED BEINGS HAVE FEELINGS TOO

Now, having said the above, it is also important to understand that enlightened human beings still have feelings and emotions and may display the latter from time to time in ways that may on the surface appear to be worldly but that assessment fails to take into account that feelings and emotions, for a person that has risen above them, are merely displays of worldly experience which, along with other displays, are by them seen as illusory manifestations of a false reality; this means that they are not affected by either the emotionality of others or their own in the same way as ordinary people are. Furthermore, they neither believe in their own displays of emotions, be they joyous or sorrowful, nor do they lean on such for their feeling of well-being, self-worth or contentment; so they do not depend on their emotions for catharsis, for, they are internally free from the need for such.

GENDER AND FEELINGS AND EMOTIONS

Now, there are some important principles to be understood in reference to the architectural differences between men and women, especially as concerns the nervous system, which is determined by the *shai* (destiny[7]) and *renenet* (harvest[8]) of aryu through *uhem ankh* reincarnation[9]. In general, males communicate and interact in relationships more in terms of "actions" while the females communicate and interact more in terms of "feelings". Women's bodies are designed by nature to be more in touch with feelings than the architecture of men is designed to be more in touch with feelings. Men are more in touch with the mind be it operating at Anpu (instinct) level or Djehuty (bright intellect) level. So while men and women both have the capacity to access feelings, emotions, and intellect, and women may have a greater innate facility in accessing and emoting feelings while men may have greater facility in accessing and emoting thoughts. Men experience

---

[7] Result of the calculation/determination of the movement of the soul [based on the impelling and compelling force] determined by the remnants/sum total of the actions of the past
[8] The soul harvests the aryu or remnants/sum total of the actions of the past
[9] the calculation/determination of te movement of the soul is carried out by *meschenet* - the force of future birth. *meschenet, shai and renenet* are aspects of the mind and cosmic forces that guide the movement of souls as they pass from life to life -*uhem ankh.*

feelings and can choose to be more sensitive or in touch with them in varying degrees depending on the individual and his *aryu*, though men in general have more capacity to control emotions related to the feelings. The same is true for women and the intellectual capacities. Therefore, this apparent difference should not be taken to mean that men are better because they can control their emotions more, as the current state of the world readily attests. Women generally have a lower threshold for emotional display; yet, nevertheless, the enlightenment of men and women is the same though the threshold of feelings and emotions may be different, both before and after enlightenment is attained, and therefore, the comparative quality or quantity of display of emotions between the genders is not a correct procedure for determining a relative standard of enlightenment; rather any such comparison, if it were attempted, should be within the genders themselves; In any case, the standards have been set by the ancestor priests and priestesses who left a legacy of sanity, wisdom, and balance for all men and women to follow. However, for both genders, the positive movement towards enlightenment generally manifests as greater detachment and dispassion, greater sensitivity to one's own feelings and that of others, a reduction of emotionality, sentimentality, emergence and displays of feelings and emotions based on irrationality (sorrow over things that do not deserve being sorrowful over-including the death of loved ones); conversely, there is a rise in balance, peace, and wisdom.

IF CRYING IS OK, TO WHAT DEGREE AND FOR WHOM?

Elsewhere it has been suggested that: " *I believe crying is alright as long as you don't allow your emotion to get totally out of control.*" The question here would be for whom is it alright, for all or some? And at what point is it to be considered as "out of control"? Who or what determines when the "out of control" point has been reached? If it is for some and not for all, that is to say, if crying (feeling sorrow) is beneficial for some and not for others, and it is not universally applicable, then this falls under the universal definition of being something relative and therefore illusory and untrue. IF we were to say that crying is good for all then that would be a universal truth, an abiding truth but since this does not meet that test, since some do not need to cry, some only sometimes and others more or less or not at all, we are forced to conclude that crying is not an absolute or abiding reality and only applies to those who are at a certain level of spiritual evolution (of course this excludes people who are experiencing mental illness or are deranged; we are speaking about personalities that fall under a standard that is considered normal (from a worldly perspective) for the population as a whole). Therefore, if this is so, then who should cry, and when does that crying become "out of control"?

The answer is that since crying is an aberration from an enlightened spiritual perspective, and since the enlightened spiritual perspective is abiding, that is to say true in the sense that all who come to understand the nature of life and creation and achieve higher knowledge of the inner self and reach a level beyond the necessity of sorrow, then it follows that those who experience worldly egoistic sorrow are experiencing an aberration from a higher normal state of being. Furthermore, it means that such a lower state is to be tolerated only to the extent that it is needed to facilitate coping on the way to becoming fully free of the afflictions that are causing it. In the teaching of Hetheru and Djehuty did Sekhemit (Sekhmet) give any quarter, did she exhibit any forbearance, and was there any compassion for the fiendish serpents that attacked her? Did Lord Djehuty say, hey Sekhemit, there are some fiends over there that want to kill you, why don't you go and negotiate a truce with them, see if we can appease them and let them do some evil deeds and see if they let you alone, let them slap you around a little and see if they leave you alone for now and let's get away from them. There are three answers to this question which operate in all three realms of existence [TA (earth plane), PET (heavenly plane), DUAT (causal plane)]: NO, NO, and NO!!! So, from the higher perspective, and from an advanced perspective an initiate adopts the role of Sekhemit and not literally, you don't go around biting people's heads off, or shooting evil people or cutting or flailing yourself when you fail to meet the Maatian standard or do deeds based on worldly desires and ignorance, etc. Sekhemit is the power of built up aryu when all your shedy, all your uaa, all your maat ari and *uashu* reach a critical mass, overwhelming the negative within and without and allowing the Heru (aspiration for higher self) and the Asar (soul) within to emerge victorious; The victory occurs when the rage of *Sekhemit* fire (eye of intuitional vision) becomes active and negative thoughts and feelings and ignorance and illusions of the mind can no longer escape the eye of insight, which burns them up as easy as the dawning sun dispels the darkness of the night and dissolves the dew[10] of the morning no matter how long or how many nightmares may have been experienced through the night (lifetimes of ignorance).

Hence, as a teacher, you may tolerate sorrow or any form of worldly egoism, but internally, as an initiate and especially as a member of the clergy, one would not accept the validity, substantiality, legitimacy or tenability of any worldly egoistic affliction of the personality (anger, hatred, greed, jealousy, envy, desire, sorrow, etc.). These are the "natural" enemies of Heru and as our aspiration is Heru, we are opposed to those all the way. This is a discipline of applying the teaching according to this philosophy; yet, when Sekhemit turned back into Hetheru there was no longer any need for further displays of *Sekhemit,* for there was no way for the fiends to ever hurt her again, for, all illusion was dispelled at that point because she had regained the knowledge of Self wherein the worldly egoistic delusions of "normal" human existence has been dispelled and therefore there was no longer a receptive personality to heed or be affected by egoistic notions, desires or feelings - in other words, the back of the fiends (afflictions of the mind) had been broken. At that point, Sekhemit was not needed to engage in a physical and vicious

---

[10] built up residues, condensation of aryu (thoughts, feelings, desires)

fight since at that point all that was needed if Hetheru were confronted with a fiend of egoism, was a look from her enlightened eye. So too an initiate must follow this logic in day to day life, facing the foes, the ignorance, and the feelings and emotions of egoism, lurking behind every corner. This confrontation is handled with *shedy*, your *uaa*, your *maat,* and *uashu* but it all begins with correct *saa* of the *sebait*. On this all depends; if the aspiration is based on a *saa* that is faulty or is *teken* (shaky/wobbly) then the *shedy* practice will be mediocre and consequently faulty.

The bottom line: even advancing personalities and even sages experience feelings and display emotions. Spiritual evolution does not mean becoming absolutely stoic as a stone. It does mean that the power (sekhem) of any negative effects from emerging aryu is reduced to a point where it cannot impel or compel the personality to act in ways that are in contradiction with Maat which includes becoming too happy or becoming too sad (elation/depression) -so remaining within a range of balance that maintains sanity and also maintains stress levels within a normal range. Therefore, this also means not eating one's, own heart. Consequently, it also means balance of mind and clear thinking.

Question 14- A Follow-up Question: TIME AND PREPARATION TO HANDLE FEELINGS AND EMOTIONS

"When I asked this question it was in a time of weakness – which addresses the line about feebleness of the mind. I had just received some news from my daughter which made me reflect on what Sebai Maa said in reference to his father passing. My state of mind was of sadness. It is easier to control the sadness when you have time to prepare. "

ANSWER

You have acknowledged that "*"Things" just happen"* in life and you expressed the idea that " *It is easier to control the sadness when you have time to prepare."* The fact is that things always happen in life and if they are not presently happening it is because they are setting up so as to happen at some point in the future. If you mean that it is easier if you have a few days before someone's death that is not always possible because death can occur at any time and not on our schedule; Therefore, this solution is not viable. However, in relation to the teachings, time to prepare occurs every time an aspirant listens to the teaching, reflects upon it, understands it, meditates upon it and applies it in day to day life; This is the only time available and it is sufficient time as long as the teaching is correctly received, understood and practiced when life presents the "inevitable opportunities" to experience the cycles of life (birth, death, reincarnation). Then, having been armed with the wisdom of the teaching, there must be vigilance; you must expect the changes that the world brings and be watchful, *nehas,* about the thoughts of the mind and the feelings that are emerging so you can control them and not be overwhelmed and deluded by them.

Thus, there are two special occasions where time is to be taken to prepare for the challenges of life. The first is when there is no active crisis to be handled. Secondly, the next most important time to handle the feelings and emotions is when the feelings emerge. When it is noticed that feelings are emerging in the form of thoughts and or desires or impulses, that is the time to take stock and apply the wisdom and will-power gained during the time of practice when there was no crisis at hand. When a crisis hits it is a time to wait and watch, to watch the thoughts and feelings and allowing the eye of wisdom to supervise the event, no matter how many times it may occur. That is not a time for rash actions but a time of reflection and recalling the teachings and observation of mind and its movements. This discipline will empower the coping capacity and eventually lead to victory, as Hetheru discovered.

HOW TO HANDLE AND PROCESS FEELINGS AND EMOTIONS

The aspirant should make an effort to suppress the emotions, the outward expression of feelings for practical reasons: outward expressions do not resolve the issue, but often exacerbate the issue, and reinforce the negative aryu from which it emerged; But the feelings themselves should not be suppressed [or may be suppressed to the extent that they can be handled and processed internally] but rather, they should be moderated, tempered with the eye of wisdom. That eye of wisdom is the philosophy, processed and understood in such a way that it diffuses the intellectual underpinnings of strong feelings [feelings cannot be allowed to hold sway on an ignorant or weak mind]. Furthermore, by facing those strong feelings and letting them process through and then allowing a new feeling memory [aryu] to be retained in the unconscious, this process allows the power of negative feelings to be transformed into power now for strong positive feelings [eye of Hetheru, the solar eye that burns unrighteousness] when the right eye, the eye of Hetheru, that is to say, also the eye of Sekhemit, opens, then the negative has no chance, it has no possibility to take over, it is through, it is rendered impotent and referred to thus, as a "child of impotent revolt." And this is what ideally is meant by the term "Hem" in its special definition as "Seer" or one who sees beyond the veil, who has the power to burn up the evil (erroneous) thought that leads to unrighteousness [ignorance of the knowledge of self]. This is what it means to confront the feelings, that is to say, *aryu* which constitutes the foundation of the worldly ego. And if practiced correctly, this discipline leads to the victory of Heru (spiritual aspiration) over Set (worldly ego). Finally, it is important to understand that the handling of feelings and emotions by an advanced personality, may be more detached and dispassionate than lesser advanced personalities but that does not mean that the advanced personalities care less about the plight of humanity; Their caring is more qualitative and therefore more profound and helpful IF it is accessed by those who need it most.

THE MYTHOLOGY VERSUS THE PHILOSOPHY AND MYSTICISM OF SORROW AND HAPPINESS

In reference to the Teaching surrounding Aset's crying in the Asarian Resurrection, it is important to make some distinctions when approaching the study of *Matnu* ⟨hieroglyphs⟩-myth. For ordinary people the myth and its humanlike situations are appropriate as they are trying to develop a relationship with the divine characters. For an initiate, they are not allowed to apply the egoistic aspects of a mythic teaching as a literal interpretation and example for their personality or to validate or excuse their own egoistic desires, feelings or other lower emotional manifestations. Often people emphasize such aspects while minimizing others that were demonstrated in the mythic teaching, like the nature and duration of the displays of feelings and emotions as well as the action to overcome the issues. In other words, oftentimes people ignore the ⟨hieroglyphs⟩ *maut* or moral of the myth, and the disciplines it enjoins, in favor of the easy path of validating their egoistic notions and closely held desires as opposed to agreeing with, adopting and practicing the teachings for self-control, balance, meditation, detachment and dispassion, wisdom, silence, peace, selflessness and humility. The *maut* of a myth is more important than the plot of the myth. The plot, that is to say, the situations and events of a myth are a means to the end of understanding and making effective the *maut*. The mythic aspect of the teaching is to be viewed as a reflection of but also an explanation of the mysteries of the human personality and human interactions with other humans but also with the gods and goddesses. Additionally, it is a means whereby the mythic sages relate the gods and goddesses to human beings by relating to the plight of the mythic beings. However, there is another side, the philosophical side and having graduated from the ranks of common folk and shemsu, an initiates is to look beyond the plot of the myth and its sentimental or egoistic aspects and instead emphasize the philosophical/mystic aspects. In this light, mythologicaly, Aset did suffer sorrow but only briefly, showing her humanity to the common folk and temple followers; More importantly, she displayed skill, alacrity, determination, towering intellectual capacity, guile, and patience in handling *Set*. Then she relied on understanding and turned the sorrow to action, working out not only the resurrection of her loved ones but also their rise to power and enlightenment; this is what the sage strives to do for all who seek out that same wisdom.

> In terms of mysticism, Aset's personal cry of grief turned to a cry out to the Divine, wisdom's (within all of us) lamentation for aspiration (Heru within all of us) and call to the spirit (*Ra*) and the capacity of the higher self for redemption, to stop creation of egoistic life and death and time itself and cause the Supreme Divine within to take notice and compassion for and extend divine grace to the accosted soul (accosted by Set/ego). That supposedly dead and dismembered soul (Asar) and it's downtrodden and persecuted aspiration (Heru) are reconstituted and revived by wisdom, enlivened by lucid intellect (Djehuty) and empowered by spirit (Ra-akhu).

This process is what occurs when *shedy* (Neterian spiritual disciplines-Egyptian Yoga) is engaged, when *uaa* (meditation) is practiced, when *uashu* (adorations) are offered and when *maat* (living by truth) is accomplished. To do otherwise is to: *"stop the ears from listening to the words of right and wrong (Maat)."*

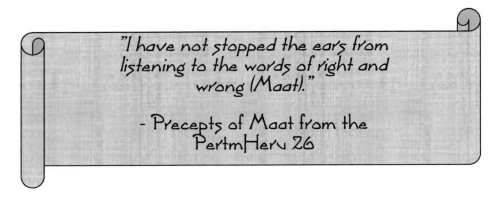

"I have not stopped the ears from listening to the words of right and wrong (Maat)."

- Precepts of Maat from the PertmHeru 26

So, in a more advanced condition, it should not matter whether a person might have a lot of time or no time to confront the situations of life because all situations of life are illusory and are to be confronted with a state of mind framed and buttressed by the teaching and there are no mental sabbaticals when one week a person is relaxed and carefree and then they get bad news that throws life out of kilter or that is surprising or shocking, requiring time to cope or come to grips with it. An initiate strives to train the mind in such a way that all situations are to be handled with the same perspective and awareness [of the illusoriness of the world] and though at the outset there may be some initial tempered and muted human emotional reaction, such reaction is neither in control of the personality nor does it compel the personality to suffer, engage in unwarranted emotional displays or lose awareness of the higher reality of the teaching; and that is the manifestation if full enlightenment has not been attained yet, and this is the benefit of the initiatic training and the teaching up to this point; let alone if full enlightenment has been achieved. In order for the training to be successful, the philosophy must be correctly understood, accepted and applied in the correct way; then the transformative effect may proceed, rendering the personality healthy, strong and wise with the capacity to handle the world of illusory situations and eventually lead itself to a beatified state.

Figure 13: Trilinear translation of verse 26 of the Pert M Heru Book of the Dead by Muata Ashby

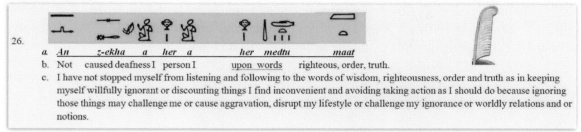

26.
a. *An   z-ekha   a   her   a   her   medtu   maat*
b. Not   caused deafness I   person I   upon words   righteous, order, truth.
c. I have not stopped myself from listening and following to the words of wisdom, righteousness, order and truth as in keeping myself willfully ignorant or discounting things I find inconvenient and avoiding taking action as I should do because ignoring those things may challenge me or cause aggravation, disrupt my lifestyle or challenge my ignorance or worldly relations and or notions.

Finally, there are other reasons for displays of emotion or the partaking in apparently worldly activities by more advanced personalities: habit and or spiritualization of the activity. If prior to attaining higher consciousness a person did certain practices then some can remain after the advancement but the nature and quality is different and the susceptibility to them is different (as explained earlier). Therefore, for example, a sage may or may not cry when confronted with a given situation. If a sage were to cry, it could be for effect, out of habit or out of compassion or deep feeling, though the crying is without sentimentality or delusion. Nevertheless, he/she would not be affected by the cause or the act in the same way as an ordinary person would nor would we expect to see hysteria or distraught behavior or wild mood swings such as depression either; This is another reason why the actions of the gods and goddesses and the sages can only be compared or used for modeling to a certain degree but cannot be accepted as a direct likeness to ordinary people because they are fundamentally different from the ordinary. In other words, ordinary people have certain things in common with sages and the gods and goddesses but not other things, namely, the effective knowledge of Self, which after all, makes all the difference in the world. Enjoyment of music is an example of a worldly activity that may be enjoyed by an advanced personality; But, where the lyric might say "I love you", a worldly minded person may think about a love affair with a spouse or a lover, whereas, while the wise person might have seen it that way also before, now they also see images of the gods and goddesses and feelings of Divine Love ensue. The experience might even trigger a *syh* (spiritual ecstasy), a temporary psychic transport into undifferentiated cosmic consciousness. Additionally, the experiences that the sage can have are not delimited by the limitations of experiences that can only occur with one person or even many persons and they are also not necessarily circumscribed by time and space or the physical constitution, as they are for an ordinary person. Thus, though the apparent experiences of an advanced personality may seem similar to those of worldly folk, there is a vast depth which is not immediately appreciated unless the worldly minded sets out to discover the deeper nature of the sage and of themselves. So, we may say that the apparently worldly actions of sages, such as Aset (Initiate who practiced intense disciplines to become a goddess)[11], should not be emulated unless they are taken in the context of sagely knowledge that is also operative at the same time. In such a case then it is permissible to emulate such a model, as long as the higher practice and not only the lower is imitated, for, if the emulation is of a degraded nature, focusing on and limited to the apparently lower manifestation of emotions for the purpose of validating egoistic notions, it will not lead to enlightenment and concurrently, if it is taking into account the higher philosophical context, then it will be beneficial.

THE PROOF OF THE TEACHING

The philosophical insights above are, yet, merely words and prove nothing, for it would be like saying such and such is true because it said so in the Bible! With the mysteries, such is not the case. The proof of the teaching is contained in the experience of the sages and the experience that can be discovered by any aspirant who follows the instructions and disciplines. So it is important that if you are choosing to be a practitioner aspirant/initiate or purveyor of the teaching at any level of the Neterian clergy you must unreservedly accept the teaching that has been given. Otherwise, you will do a disservice to yourself and the people you intend to serve. How? By holding back; By not accepting the teaching a human being can hold back, that is to say, delay the onset of enlightenment. But, since all are innately enlightened, already, there can only be a delay and not permanent prevention because human existence is ephemeral and this is why we are told, in an Ancient Egyptian Harpers song, that:

Something, which we have seen in a dream,
Is the earthly side of life.

- Ancient Egyptian- Harper's Song, c. 1160 BC

Nature removes the obstacles placed by people who actively prevent themselves from adopting, accepting and practicing the teaching: through death and reincarnation as well as suffering. Therefore, it behooves one to accept the teaching in principle and even if it cannot be fully adopted and practiced at present, the unconditional acceptance eventually paves the way for its effectiveness. However, one who places conditional

---

[11] See the book Mysteries of Isis by Dr. Muata Ashby

acceptance on the teaching, adopting only those tenets that are comfortable or that maintain the delusions desired by the individual, such a one will find limitations on their attainment as they are upholding an incorrect notion of life and the nature of existence and therefore also are engaged in *wrong enjoyment of things,* which leads to reinforcing the ignorance and delusions of life.

Additionally, as stated earlier, it is important to understand that while existing in a human body along with its remaining aryu, a sage can have displays of emotion that are not tied to their enlightened state. This means that after attaining enlightenment feelings and emotional patterns can remain, though in a more purified and muted state, which the sage her/himself may allow to continue but which have no hold over them. Why would they allow such to continue? They would do that for the purpose of natural expression of the aryu and better capacity to relate with other human beings during the time while on earth (service to humanity). Here, the term " natural expression" refers to normal feelings and emotions and not what the masses consider to be normal, feelings and emotions that lead to exuberance, elation, depression, dullness, and the afflictions of Set: Anger, hatred, greed, lust, jealousy, envy, etc., that cause strife, conflict, war and are actually the source of all human misery.

HOW SHOULD THIS TEACHING BE APPLIED BY SPIRITUAL ASPIRANTS?

Indeed, if your crying will be based on the idea that they are dying and do not exist anymore, or that you feel loss at not having their company that you enjoyed, or that your happiness is based on their presence, being able to touch, talk with, spend time with them, etc. then indeed that crying is "worldly egoistic", or "setian", as opposed to "asetian". If we define worldly egoism (setian) as opposed to wise/enlightened ego (asetian-related to Aset(Isis) Wisdom), the setian is an identity and belief system based on lack of knowledge of self and holding the notion of "I am an individual, mortal being in a world with other mortal relations", etc. If that crying is based on the notion that "I am miserable because my loved ones are gone and I cannot love them and they do not enjoy life anymore, etc." then, indeed this is egoistic in terms of egoism that causes sorrow and pain in life; for, crying based on the aforesaid is irrational {erroneous -is it rational to mourn death when we already know all must die and death is not the end of things} since the aforesaid parameters are all untrue, therefore what is there to cry about, to mourn over? Another form of the problem is fear; fear operates in the way that people think that if they adopt this teaching that they become less human or feel less and the reverse is true, for, the sentimental love is that which leads to sorrow while the love based on wisdom leads to deeper, more profound caring and connection that promotes peace instead of sorrow (for all). IF a person were to want to remain at a certain level of egoism {at least for this lifetime - but death will force a change} that is worldly as opposed to a level of egoism that is sagely (more purified ego), they may do so by choice but what would be the purpose now that you have heard the truth? If a person consciously allows their self to remain with the ignorant notions that have been contradicted, they will maintain an internal conflict that will prevent understanding subtler aspects of the philosophy and the capacity to access deeper regions of the inner higher reality being alluded to; if they consciously hold themselves back from accepting the teaching, at least in principle, in the beginning, all further progress will be limited and furthermore, their capacity to lead others will also be limited. As for initiates, as they have heard the teaching and as have signaled, by their request for initiation, a desire to be initiated and rise to the level of temple initiate and priest(ess)hood practitioner, then they are directed to fully accept the teaching in principle and apply it in day to day life and work to verify it through the means that have been outlined (Shedy practices). They are further directed to live the philosophy to the best of their ability, applying it to the best of their understanding and not harboring or holding on to erroneous notions to the extent possible. So, being that they have harbored these notions for a long time they will not be able to adopt this teaching immediately, and since they may still have lingering sentimental notions they are allowed to cry if they still need to, but they may not do so with the notion that it is based on truth or that they will remain at a lower level of egoism. If the cry, they are to do so as long as they have a handkerchief in one hand and the Pertmheru (Ancient Egyptian Book of the Dead) in the other. Every time they want to or do indeed cry or hold on to the ignorant notions of worldly life, they should look at the Pertmheru, and when they experience the truth of this philosophy, then they should put the pertmheru down and look within themselves and then see if it is still necessary to cry at that point, in that same way, or at all. They are to follow this directive and in so doing will eventually remove the proverbial veil of illusion that plagues the heart and pains the soul. As to the statement, **"*certain that I will cry when my Mother, children or any of my love ones die.*"**; this statement implies a tacit acceptance of and agreement with the feelings and constitutes a verbalization of the process of creating new worldly aryu that reinforces the feeling of crying out of sorrow over sentimental notions of loss. Therefore, it needs to be reexamined and treated with the wisdom as outlined herewith. Having applied this teaching it may be found that spiritual advancement does occur and yet when the time comes, the desire to cry may remain but again, it will not be in the same way nor will it constitute as detrimental a problem from an aryu point of view.

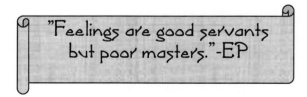

"Feelings are good servants but poor masters." -EP

Through this discipline, the feelings become a source of strength instead of a source of weakness, for, when feelings are impure, the energy that they wield can propel the personality into situations and emotional states that are detrimental (sorrow and suffering); this is called "eating one's own heart" [a personality that can experience undue and or unwarranted grief, sorrow or self-imposed grief and sorrow born of delusion and ignorance]. Conversely, purified feelings can lend their support to courses of action arrived at through wisdom; here the contradiction sometimes observed, is of people who are supposedly wise but that yet commit egoistic or seemingly impulsive or even irrational acts, would not occur. In this way, the feelings become servants of the evolved personality rather than a degrading force in life. The empowered personality would not be as susceptible to the world's uncanny ability to wear down and twist the mind into accepting the degraded condition of running after enjoyments of the world for the sake of personal fulfillment or acquiescing to degraded conditions of life for the sake of experiencing physical love, personal comfort, companionship or upholding foolish and or irrational ideological notions for the sake of sustaining egoistic notions of social order (political, religious, economic, etc.) because there would be no delusion about finding oneself or fulfillment in the world of time and space; in other words, the purified mind would not have egoistic feelings producing egoistic desires that bind a person to the pursuit of desires and the inevitable sorrow that the pursuit leads to. For such a person, those situations that have been engendered prior to the dawning of wisdom, understanding, and purification, would now be treated in a more enlightened way, a way that disentangles the personality, a way that is more detached, dispassionate and wise, freer and with self-control born of will-power and purified feelings and energy freed for supporting the understanding arrived at through the wisdom teaching instead of empowering desires based on ignorant notions and feelings.

Through ignorance, the soul has attached to itself aryu or feelings from experiences in time and space and those feelings cloud the intellectual capacity to see (understand) the higher nature of Self. The mind has been "infected", afflicted with varied flaws or defects that allow the emergence of defective thought processes. These defects are referred to as *inj-Set* (mind afflicted by fetters of Set(egoism)). The main affliction is ignorance of the knowledge of the Higher Self, manifesting as erroneous understandings about the nature of God and the universe, the state of seeing oneself as an individual, mortal and limited individual and disconnected from nature and the universe. They lead to egoistic thought and desire manifestations with varied levels of emotionality, including anger, hatred, greed, jealousy, envy, etc., which lead to pain and sorrow as well as the reinforcement and sometimes intensification of the egoism. First, a person must become virtuous because this purifies the person's gross or base impurities of mind and actions and thus, also their *Aryu* (karmic) basis. The practice of uashu (devotional practices) purifies feelings and the practice of rech cleanses the subtle impurities from the mind. This process purifies the emotions and the thought process, producing positive aryu. Negative

Aryu leads to negative situations but also to mental dullness and it is hard to understand the teachings when the mind is in a dull state, full of base thoughts, desires, and feelings- this is the opposite of *Rech-ab*, it may be referred, as stated earlier, as *inj-Set* (mind afflicted by fetters of Set). This process leads to desires of the deluded mind or *shesp-ab;* the desires of the heart lead to *utjez-ka* "mind's own ideas and thoughts lifted up, raised up unworthily, with pride, conceit, haughtiness, and arrogance" i.e. egocentricity. This process leads to *shemsu-ab* or "egoistic will", [self-willed people who follow the desires of their *khemn-ab* ignorant heart] while disregarding the dictates of wisdom and its purveyors.

Now, having relinquished ignorance, and having attained the higher level of *saa*, with it's attending divine will (*sekhem ab*), the ignorance of the aryu in the Ab is recognized and even if some remain in the mind and even if it emotes it will not have power over the personality to compel it to act like an animal led by the senses and instincts (the state of ignorance and caught up in the world of human desires). Therefore, a person not being compelled either to believe in or to act upon worldly illusions is free from being affected by those illusions and a person in this state can relinquish worldly desires or participate in them without entanglement. Such a person whose mind is purified, whose eye of understanding is ⟨hieroglyphs⟩ *Beq*, lucid and not ⟨hieroglyphs⟩ *uhmet ab,* (dull -ignorant) or ⟨hieroglyphs⟩ *neshesh,* agitated (shaky, unsteady). This is what is referred to in the *Pertmheru* (Pert-m-Heru) (Book of Enlightenment (Ancient Egyptian Book of the Dead)) text as *mat* (renewing) the heart before the gods and goddesses, having gained *sekhem* (power) over the heart, and having attained ⟨hieroglyphs⟩ **or** ⟨hieroglyphs⟩ *maakheru* or "true of speech" status.

CONCLUSIONS for this Question

> "Those who gave thee a body, furnished it with weakness; but The ALL who gave thee Soul, armed thee with resolution. Employ it, and thou art wise; be wise and thou art happy." -EP
>
> "Beware of irresolution in the intent of thy actions, beware of instability in the execution; so shalt thou triumph over two great failings of thy nature." -EP
>
> "Vain and inconstant if thou art, how can thou but be weak? Is not inconstancy connected with frailty? Avoid the danger of the one, and thou shalt escape the mischief of the other." -EP

    With this essay, I have striven to espouse how the teaching relates to the issue of sorrow and grief in life. Whether or not a person is happy depends on their state of mind and the state of mind depends on the level of understanding about the nature of the soul and the Higher self/God and the Universe. As the proverb says, if one applies resolution towards the teaching one becomes wise and if one becomes wise then one is automatically happy. So, being happy is a state of mind that arises when irresolution and ignorance are not present; It is not a chance occurrence or a state of mind affected or controlled by the world of time and space, other people or the ups and downs of life. I have also laid out the path an initiate should follow in order to confront and overcome this egoistic feeling and emotions. This is a philosophical path with an exacting precision that must be understood carefully and exactly as well as applied precisely and you are now beginning to see the inner world of the wise and why so many fail to achieve what is to be achieved. As concerns this teaching, I have been trying to convey the severity, and depth of what initiatic and self-mastery studies are and should be about and this is the further opening of the door to what it means to be an initiate, and even more so, a cleric of Shetaut Neter (Egyptian Mysteries). It is also why there should be care taken about who is called initiate, priest or sage. Again, though the path is precise, its understanding can be nuanced but still, it requires precision and then still the application of it must be competent if not adept. It begins with faith in the teaching, the teacher and yourself and ends with stalwart souls living the meaning of their higher creed. This is what you must begin to see for your lives and your practice of the teachings and it is what you must work on diligently and relentlessly, such conviction, without which the peace of wisdom, even before attaining enlightenment, would be elusive and thereafter, in time, the attainment of the greater heights would be obscured. This (initiatic training-through the study of this teaching) is the big leagues and not the realm of child's play or a pastime for idle complacent aspirants who take the teaching and apply it when convenient, when it does not impinge on their enjoyment of illusory pleasures they are so used to and find comforting or only when they get slapped around by the world, enough so they seek refuge in the place they know deep down is true, the teaching, but which they have been thus far unable to fully pledge their lives to. This is the divine resolution that led Aset and Heru to ultimate victory and it is available for all who determine it as their path that will lead them to true happiness and away from sorrow and weakness. When this teaching is understood and lived an initiate will be able to "proudly" proclaim, as stated in the PertmHeru Chapter 9, victory over the iniquity (Apep) of ignorance and it's compelling of the soul to error, worldly desires, and suffering.

CHAPTER 9 THE CHAPTER FOR REPULSING APEP WHOM IS THE EMBODIMENT OF EVIL.

I Asar _____ speak now to Apep. You are the evil of unrighteousness, which strikes like a serpent and thereby draws human beings to their ruin. Listen, I have lived a righteous life and I have discovered my greatness. I am not like one of those weak people who are powerless against your schemes and tricks of temptation and delusion.

Your poison of desire, falsehood, hatred and fear cannot enter me. For I am so subtle, due to my purity, that I am as if hidden from you, like Amun, the Hidden Spirit which pervades all.

- Generally referred to as Chapter 7. Based on Papyrus in Turin museum.

Question 15-Even after years of practicing the teachings I still feel desires to be in a relationship even after being married with children and now divorced. Is it bad of me and if I get into another relationship will it stop my chances to attain enlightenment?

Dr. Ashby, thank you for your teachings over the years as I have realized the truth of them over the years in my own life and previous relationships with a wife and girlfriend before that. I developed many patterns of behavior such as what you described and I realize now that I got into those relationships because of my need to be with someone and not because they were good persons. I had a child with my wife thinking that she cared for me and that having a child would solidify our bond. She was looking for financial support more than a caring relationship and when I was laid off in 2009 with the economic crash we started having lots of fighting about money and that affected sex and just everyday relations. We had less sex and were constantly as you mentioned, walking on eggshells and my child suffered because of it and it was painful getting a divorce. I finally had to face that I was staying not because it was right but because I did not want to be alone and also I felt shame as my friends and family tried to keep us together because they felt bad as if the world was not right unless people are married and supposedly happy also. So if I stayed married it would be for them and not for me and my son would suffer just for my inability to face my reality. Finally, I got the strength to do what I needed to do. I have been divorced for a few years now but I still have feelings of desiring to be with someone. I have studied your teachings for years even before my divorce and recognized the syndromes you talked about in lectures. I know it is illusory and that I have engendered or gone along with the biological urges to be with someone and that I grew up in ignorance so I fostered many mental impressions about this issue, believing in what my family said and friends and the community, etc. Even though, every year I seem to desire more to be with someone and based on the teachings I don't know what to do? I want to attain enlightenment as per the Ancient Egyptian wisdom. If I get into a relationship again will this help or hurt my spiritual desires? Is it possible to resolve the desires for worldly relationship and then move on with my spiritual life? If I get into a relationship it seems I will create more aryu of worldliness and put off my chances to achieve enlightenment? Should I refrain or give in to my desires? What should I do to resolve the issues and stay on course with the teachings?

__ANSWER:__
If one will engage in a relationship how should that be pursued and what kind of partner to look for?
While the responses to worldly stimuli and the reactions and desires related to them are mostly an effect of biology and conditioning and un-realization of the goal of the

teachings it is important to note that even sages had and have worldly impulses but the difference is in their response to these; they do not attach validity or necessity to these for their happiness, self-esteem or personal satisfaction or feeling of fulfilment in life; so they have no hold on a sage and do not obstruct his/her activities in life or cause undue burdens or stress or constitute compelling urges on a sage; It is true that not all aspirants can reach such a high stage in the same way or at the same time and some travel the path of being single while others the path of marriage and householder life. So even sages once upon a time had worldly lives, degraded thoughts, and naive illusions. It is important to work through the challenges of the world by whichever means is most effective. This is a process in which mystical study can be coupled with worldly engagement. If you choose the path of worldly engagement you should take care to always remember it is illusory, since one day you will find that your fulfillment came not in satisfaction through worldly fulfillments but rather from fulfillment through the understanding and feeling that the process has helped to extinguish the irrational worldly desires.

Indeed, there are three main areas that cause relationship/marital strife: 1-financial issues, 2-sexual issues and 3-issues related to children and child rearing.

Definitely, if relationships are engaged with worldly intent or abandon instead of with insights and disciplines enjoined by the teachings, then for sure it will lead to setting back the advent of enlightenment even by lifetimes. In the context of this statement the word "Abandon" means the idea that you abandon all caution or restraints and this is not advised; it is the idea like, it's all or nothing and if you cannot do the teaching then indulge in any and every worldly pleasure without thinking of the teaching or any consequences. None of that is advised here. Also, living life while abstaining but without resolving the issues has a similar effect because in your mind you will be desiring and also anxious about losing the opportunity before getting older and dying, etc.

Therefore, if such path is deemed necessary pursue it with the ideal of discovering its wisdom and not just for its pleasure or satisfaction, since as you know pleasures or satisfactions are fleeting and illusory and addictive, like a fire upon which gasoline is poured; there will be no quenching it and it will expand. Without this perspective, you would indeed be drawn again to the very thing you say you want to avoid while being psychologically caught again and perhaps even more strongly caught up in the matrix of egoistic feelings and desires.

So what to do? Instead of being caught in the world of desires you want to be finished with and not lingering on in a deluded lustful quandary seeking enlightenment and the world at the same time. Whether you engage the world or not as an initiate the duty is to realize the illusoriness of life. You would not be the first aspirant to have these feelings and to have sought counsel on this very issue in a similar stage of life. There are those who have had similar experiences to yours and feel they are through with relationships and still producing more progeny after having been married and having children. If you do not feel that way yet that is not a strike against you or a sign you are a "bad" aspirant or anything like that. It is a sign that more work needs to be done and perhaps the best way to work through it is with the partner of the sage, the world-the school of hard knocks. So continuing to study and practice while engaging with the world in an Maatian orderly and not reckless manner can be a viable option as opposed to sitting around and having your mind be disrupted while trying to follow the teachings but having the desires and urges and quandaries interfere when trying to meditate or attend lectures and that is a kind of contamination that is not helpful to the spiritual evolution. So which path is best to follow?

If engaging the worldly relationships is found to be useful in that regard then it is acceptable and even encouraged. So "Go for it." But go for it with the teaching in mind and not with abandon; go for it with Maatian balance and not with worldly sentimental values. Do not try to please your mate all the time, do not seek validation for everything you feel or do, spend time alone and on retreat regularly and maintain healthy distance so as not to fall into the delusions of relationships, that you will be perfect soulmates walking into the sunset together forever and ever, etc.

Realize the value of a partner and seek someone with similar values and goals in life for attaining the realization expressed in the teachings. However, also realize that you may be in a partnership now but your ultimate destination is a singular place where you are one with all, including your partner but not in an egoistic or sentimental sense. If you live sentimentally then that is all you will attain and as we know at the time of death all that blows away. If you live life for the teaching, be it in or out of a relationship, then you will eventually grow beyond worldly perspectives and transcend it and arrive at the higher destination of life even before death. If this occurs it will be a boon for your partner, your family, descendants, community and indeed the world.

Find a partner who also wants to attain enlightenment and who is not seeking a relationship for sentimental values or deluded notions. Find someone with whom you can have a philosophical conversation, with whom you can attend spiritual conferences and will understand when you need time alone on retreat and practice meditation in silence and you can also practice the teachings by helping that person have what they need to move along on the spiritual path as well. In so doing you can be in a relationship that will be helpful and not hurtful to your spiritual evolution. Be aware that this is not a panacea. Since neither you nor your partners are enlightened and there are remnants of worldly sentimental desires that will come up and cause issues in the relationship and in your own personalities. However, if you have the intent of helping each other face and work through those issues, with the teachings, then they can be handled in a manner that is harmonious with the teachings.

Question 16-Dr. Ashby, why does it seem like when I am in a relationship it doesn't seem to last because something always goes wrong and we end up arguing a lot or frustrated with my partner?

<u>**ANSWER:**</u>

This is an issue related to sabotaging. –I'm not saying this is something that you're doing purposely or maliciously, but it occurs because of negative *aryu* which we might often term psychological issues, due to maladaptations to situations when growing up or psychological trauma that has not been resolved and which has caused a situation of incorrect relating in life. All that is lumped in under the wisdom about negative aryu of the past; *Aryu* is the sum total effect of the past thoughts, feelings, desires, and experiences of the past that have contributed to shaping your current outlook on life and manner of handling life situations. This sum-total effect emerges from the content of aryu in the unconscious mind be it positive or negative. It can be something that happened when you were in school, or at camp, or while visiting relatives for the summer, or the army or with your father, a death in the family or whatever experience it might have been from a past life trauma, etc.

Those issues might be and are likely the cause of present day issues relating to being unable to carry on a viable relationship. Perhaps you lost your father at an early age so you sabotage relationships so that they do not develop and you can avoid the fear of losing them too. Perhaps you are afraid of having children so when your partner brings up the subject you start a fight over how they forgot to pay the electric bill last month or some other minor fault. Another possibility is that since you grew up without a father who took care of his responsibilities and was there to impart wisdom while you were growing up you never learned what it means to be a man, to stand up for yourself; so you might grow up as a misfit male personality or a woman seeking love through seriously flawed men instead of well adjusted, balanced persons with integrity and ethics, who have self-esteem and want to share and grow in a relationship in a balanced partnership where the partners complement and help each other grow and discover the purpose and meaning of life.

Perhaps you grew up with a mother that was traumatized by her parents and she never received love and affection so she grew up to be cold or as an authoritarian and or domineering parent since that was her way of showing love, to avoid receiving affections and did not know how to love and be affectionate with you; so in your present relationship you do not know how to love and feel love for yourself so you too cannot love and show affection for others and your partners feel this and ask for it and you leave them because you feel bad and cannot find it in yourself to either give or receive love and affection, or caring, from others. Other people might have a syndrome that they experienced that as love and caring so they expect to be treated as their parents treated them so if they are treated differently they don't know how to handle it so they leave or sabotage those relations that they can't handle since the aryu of the past is still haunting them in the present. This same aryu is part of the content of aryu that is preventing a person from growing spiritually as well. So working through the relationship issues can also be part of the spiritual work needed to attain spiritual enlightenment.

It's complicated also because viable relationships require two people to be sufficiently mature for being in a viable relationship and maturity incorporates or includes sanity. In this context, sanity implies a personality that has adjusted and reconciled the psychological issues of past negative aryu. So, if you have psychological issues, then you're not completely sane, which means that your aryu is going to be directing your life with negative inputs to your present thoughts and feelings and ideas about yourself and relating to others. Since the negative aryu is stronger than the positive you don't have control over all your conscious actions, only some. So, through your traumatized mind (mind operating with unresolved psychological issues caused by negative aryu) is impaired your ability to see and act with truth(facing reality) is compromised. One of the ways that this can manifest is that you're sabotaging the relationship because you're afraid of having that relationship since it might lead to shared experiences that bring you back to the unresolved trauma, to recall a trauma that occurred that has not been worked out, that you have not resolved and adjusted your personality in order to carry on a balanced life without its negative effects. In other words, the lessons from the trauma have not been learned and integrated into the personality as an event of the past that you learned from so you can move on with life with wisdom because of the situation of trauma. Instead, the trauma is unresolved and causing obstructions to life as well as repeating itself, re-traumatizing life and the personality is neither healing nor growing as it should.

In short, you don't want to feel pain or you want to avoid it so you sabotage relationships often unconsciously. How does sabotaging occur? It could be by fighting or starting a fight so that you don't get close, to avoid intimacy, so you can prevent a friendship from developing because as it develops it might remind you, unconsciously, of a lifetime of the past that hurt you so you want to avoid experiencing that hurt again. And then you feel justified in thinking that your relationships are bad. You can't have friendship and all friendships are futile and you mess up your relationships, squandering opportunities to have friendships throughout life. Everyone is bad, and in reality, it's really you. But it can be complicated because the other person can be afflicted by their own issues too. So both partners in the relationship are immature and afflicted and therefore unfit to carry on a relationship. Therefore, the afflicted relations are rocky and full of negative drama;

distracting and sometimes entertaining but in the end serving the purpose more of meting out suffering as opposed to being venues of growth and enlightenment. In such a condition you're not thinking straight and the turmoil of your unconscious mind (afflicted with negative aryu) is blinding your conscious mind. You're conscious personality is so weakened by the whole negative affair that you have no control over your personality, or you have less control, while your unconscious feelings and desires hold sway over you and direct you to situations and outcomes that are negative. From a Kemetic Mystic Psychology point of view, it is the negative aryu that has confined, defined and conditioned the awareness of self which in reality, deep down is infinite spirit, but the conditioning causes them to believe they are individual being so that is what we call a soul. Due to that feeling of individuality the human souls seek to couple themselves with another soul so as to feel whole and extended beyond their individual and limited awareness of themselves. This process of individuation is what sustains the mental issues and troubles of life.

WHAT TO DO?

So it all comes down to regaining purity, purity of heart which is purity of mind, working through and working out and resolving the negative aryu so that you will not be affected and controlled by the negative aryu. This is what it comes down to. It also means having enough clarity and self-will for choosing a sane person to have a relationship with. If you have a relationship with a person who's as afflicted as you, then it's going to be doubly hard. If one person is afflicted and the other person is not, at least you have that going for you. But if you're both "screwed up", as I said, it's going to be doubly hard to disentangle the insanity between yourselves and the repercussions of other people's issues projected on the other person who might then think those issues are their own when in reality they belong to the other.

On the road to healing one should take care to realize it takes time when one is on a healing track, meaning one is using a viable teaching and following righteous instructions to work through the issues. Sometimes people can feel that they had a breakthrough. Words like miraculous or fantastic or earthshaking are not appropriate to describe it. It's a milestone on the journey and real success is measured in long-term balanced and sensible relating based on ethical conscience as opposed to desires, compulsions or thoughts and feelings arrived at through agitated or turbulent reflections.

Question 17-I have been having trouble in my relationship for a long while because my partner has been putting pressure on me to take a job I did not want and recently the pressure has let off and I feel a breakthrough has occurred. Am I right?

ANSWER:

Since such issues do not resolve without specifically working to resolve them or in a rapid time frame, I would caution that what can also be happening is that you're feeling an opening of free association, meaning that your partner seems to be giving you freedom instead of trying to be possessive and say you must do this or that and agree with what I want, etc. This temporary reprieve can be out of frustration that has been repressed but which may return when there is provocation such as the next financial stress or argument or upset situation.

On one hand, the feeling of relief is due to the temporary lifting of stress. On the other hand the cause of being in a relationship that causes stress remains in the personality but at a subtle and dormant level that gives the illusion of being resolved, but in reality, since it is not resolved at the deeper level, it is only waiting to reemerge and bewilder a person when that occurs since they thought the issue had been dealt with.

In any case, these issues are in your personality, in the pathology that's going on due to the negative aryu of the past that is expressing as maladapted behavior born of ignorance of how to satisfy unrighteous desires and feelings. The experience of relief may be seen as possibly a new experience, a new opening, a new freedom that is resonating with a part of you that you can feel, perhaps even unconsciously, that you can open up, like a window of freedom in yourself.

This is something that happens often in relationships, that people are possessive and that they behave and act in a way that is in response to the possessiveness of other people. So both acting un-righteously due to immaturity and ignorance of what is righteous and worthy of pursuing in life. This syndrome operates acutely, especially in men, it has a very deleterious effect when they feel that they're caught or trapped or controlled. At the same time, they want to control and trap women as they themselves roam around with their own freedom.

Of course, the reasons for these issues are manifold but are mainly due to being caught in the snare of thinking and feeling in accord with the lower nature instead of the higher supporting the complication in relationships of desiring to be paired with someone else due to feeling a void that a relationship is thought to be the solution for. Nevertheless, the relationship will not fulfill that desire and will provide the issues of the other person, which will lead to complications and the myriad of frustrations and disappointments that people experience in relationships. Also, that happens because of their feeling of inferiority, their feeling of trauma, of feeling bad because of something that happened in the past that makes them feel like they should be in some kind of controlled situation, a relationship because they can't feel freedom independently on their own. So that is one source of fighting, and they don't know why they're fighting or why they're upset in the relationship. There are various kinds of aberrant behavioral permutations that could happen. It is important to realize that dependence, even on a loved one, and even if that person is good to you, is a kind of degraded way of life.

You have stated that you feel you are being granted some freedom. You also stated that your partner was up to now very possessive. This is a pathology that afflicts men and women. They can become abusive if their possession, "their woman" does not behave as they want. Many women have possessive issues also because and they can't let go even though the situation may involve cheating or violence. Men have to really be messed up for an ordinary woman to really want to leave them.

Question 18-Is it possible to be free in a relationship?

ANSWER:

The guideline is that the best path in life is the one that leads to freedom; freedom of feeling, freedom of thought and freedom of action. In life most people are not free but that is because of their beliefs that hold them to certain limitations, be they cultural beliefs, beliefs about what relations are supposed to be like, beliefs about their own shortcomings or misgivings that cause them to be needy or desirous of things they think will make them happy because they do not have a feeling of wholeness within themselves. So with that empty feeling or feeling of desire they search in the world for something to make them feel whole. But in order to get that in a world of constant changes and consequences, they have to bind themselves to a course of action, person(s), or objects and to get or hold on to those they become bound and in essence, slaves to those items. So freedom of feeling, thought and action are restricted by the desire to acquire or hold on to the perceived item, situation, etc. they perceive as the thing to make them whole and satisfied. Since that can never happen, since everything in the world is changeable and other people have their desires and emotions and issues, there can never be a complete achievement of that goal and in the end people will always remain unfulfilled on that path. So the answer is learn to live ethically, that is, by truth, which leads to the realization of discovering inner balance and inner peace without the need for outside objects, people or circumstances to discover wholeness.

In a seemingly harmonious relationship there are limitations on freedom and if you have a negative relationship, there are more limitations there as well. You can't freely express in any romantic relationship because you might upset the other person and they may withdraw their affections for you, or you might get into a fight etc. So when you choose to bind yourself to people, objects or situations in the illusory world (everything is changeable and impermanent) you are enslaving yourself and curtailing your own freedom of movement, expression, thought and feeling in exchange for a perceived goal that is illusory and short-lived.

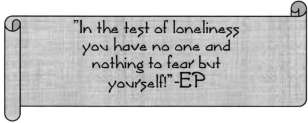

"In the test of loneliness you have no one and nothing to fear but yourself!" -EP

   The best course in life is if you can have a choice based on internal wholeness. If you are not needy but want to partner up with someone you can do so but with someone who is also not needy and not doing it to fill a void based on their own immaturity and psychological deficiencies and dependencies but rather to share their life and gifts based on their higher level of wholeness; with such a person you can pool resources to achieve things that individuals working alone cannot, like having children or building an organization, collaborating on a beneficial project for humanity, etc. In such a relationship, between mature individuals, the sum will equal more than the parts and the relations will be more than just shallow worldly goals and petty desires the can easily cause hurt feelings and frustrated egos. So, if you're entering into relations because of fear or because of deficient need, or because you need to be with someone because you might appear weird otherwise or because you're afraid of being alone, etc., then you're not really making a free decision.   You're making it out of immaturity, fear and ignorance. Most people who do that have "issues", thus, they have to work through those in their relationships; they have ups and downs and frustrations and fighting and need counseling. This is the rocky path for the immature who get together with others who are immature but both of whom are unable to work through their issues in other ways; this is the school of life, the school of hard knocks. If you're able to come to a place where you're doing it out of freedom, then you still have to make the decision of is this the right person at that point. Is the person mature, well-adjusted and comfortable with themselves, with good self-esteem and not narcissism of co-dependency? Are you interested in someone because part of them attracts you but another feature is that they have self-loathing issues because they do not like some physical feature they have, or their parent told them they are trash or they hate themselves because they feel unworthy as a human being, fearful or feeling inferior in facing the world or they hate themselves for some other reason? Are they moody or subject to depression? Do you like them anyway and think your relating with them will help them and change them? –in which case you must realize you are suffering from a complementary co-dependency psychological issue as well. Or are you with them because you need to be with someone or because they are attractive, a feature that will fade away in time? Is that person attractive but ethically and morally bankrupt but you are with them out of lust? Does the person have some good qualities like having a career, but they smoke and eat meat and live an unhealthy lifestyle and you desire them because they like you and you are afraid to find someone better so as not to be alone? When you compromise your ethics to be with someone and if the relations turn sour then you blame that person instead of your own fault in entering into the relations without maturity and or the wrong reasons and goals.

The first choice in a mate is ethical conscience and then, after that determination, then the other superficial aspects can be considered. Ethical conscience means they live by truth, not fooling themselves and not pursuing illusions in life. Ethical conscience means a healthy vegetarian diet, supplements, a job or career that is rewarding and helpful to humanity. If you want someone because they have lots of money then that delusion will lead to its own downfall as money cannot buy happiness or cure all errors of life or fill the void of the heart. How many people get divorced when they go bankrupt? If money was not holding them together would they still get divorced? Would they have married in the beginning if there was no money involved? If people seem to be harmonious when there is money and disharmonious when there are hard times then what does that say about the illusory harmony and supposed love they professed for each other in the beginning? It was all sentimental delusional romantic sentimentalities in an attempt to get a perceived goal but not based on ethical conscience; so being based on lack of ethics and deficient character, it leads to frustration, unhappiness, and failure.

If you make a choice to be with a person who has "issues", then it still means that you are also afflicted with "issues" and that means you're going to have a relationship with issues. So if you're making a choice from a sanity and maturity, well-adjusted personality standpoint, to be with someone who is sane or someone who is balanced, someone with whom you can contribute to something more than just your pathologies, then that's going to be a different kind of choice. That means that you have to be free and balanced internally, for yourself, already, before entering into a relationship, in order to be able to make that kind of decision.

Of course, this is an ideal but the path is to look for a person with most of these qualities and then consider looks and other features later. Choose someone who is working towards these goals and then you can also help each other move towards perfecting the goals even better than you could on your own. Then you will have a relationship that is not co-dependent but instead a spiritual cooperative.

Finally, one more point is that being autonomous (mature, well adjusted, with normal and not narcissistic egoistic self-esteem) doesn't mean always doing your own thing, or being alone but it means making a choice about what you're doing out of truth (Maat) instead of egoistic desires (Set). So if you choose to be around someone else or be with them in a relationship, as long as it's your choice, meaning it is a choice made with honest considered reflection not influenced by notions outside of ethical conscience, then you're still autonomous. You're still a sovereign person. But if you're not doing it with sovereignty, which means that you're acting out of immaturity, fear or ignorance, you will lose your personal freedom. When you're sovereign, it means that you are whole within yourself whether you're doing something or not, with someone or not, rich or not, having a career or not. If you feel bad, because you're not doing something with someone else or because you're alone or whatever, then you're not sovereign; you're dependent. You are in a state of immaturity, in a state of pathology.

Question 19-Why would one be in a relationship if one did not have an interest or want to be in one? You have talked about becoming fully independent from feelings, or desires, or interest in being in a skewed relationship.

ANSWER

I think the answer to your question as you've stated it is obvious from the perspective of sanity and well-adjusted personality. If you don't have any interest, then you wouldn't pursue it. However, your question is not really that. I think your question is what circumstances would a person who is spiritually oriented and who developed a well-adjusted personality, a balanced personality, an independent personality, why would they seek a relationship? The answer is that one can be independent and well-adjusted and still have unfulfilled needs of a social nature, of a worldly nature, like procreation or like having a family and all those kinds of things.

But if those desires and those needs are overwhelming and they are the guiding forces in life, even to such a degree as to select a partner even when the partner is an unrighteous personality or they want to enter into a relationship because the "biological clock is ticking" and disregarding the ethical nature of the partner, then they are not really independent or well-adjusted personalities. So, in the immature and not well-adjusted personality, those desires are guiding the personality; that lower aryu has control of the personality and the person cannot act with an ethical conscience but rather with emotional impetus, the same impetus that is played on by the marketing and advertising and government propaganda.

For instance, if you have a rider on a horse, if the horse leads the rider wherever it wants to go, then the rider is not really directing things, not in control. The rider can use the lower forces, which is the horse and the muscle and the energy and direct it to where he wants to go.

Having a relationship in a sense is like that also. You're having a relationship not only to fulfill personal and egoistic lower desires and needs. You're actually also doing it to fulfill higher ones as well. If you are not able to do that completely independently, then the world has setup a system to assist that process of learning and growing through pairing up with a partner or partners to help each other, to discover certain things about yourself through working together or through helping the other person, through sacrifice. Also on the other side, the negative side, there are learning opportunities through disagreement, fighting and through the hurt that is experienced through the negative aspects of relationships. So it's all those experiences that lead to a certain self-discovery and eventual real independence and freedom from the need to pair-up with someone in a relationship.

It can happen slowly if it's not guided through the teaching. If it's guided through the teaching, it can be positive and a more rapid process and experience. On the other hand, if a person is so well-adjusted and psychologically and spiritually integrated, they may have also grown beyond the needs that require any romantic relations to be fulfilled. So they don't need children or a spouse with which to fulfill either themselves or a life desire.

Those who are not well-adjusted and psychologically and spiritually integrated are compelled by their desires that they see as necessary to be fulfilled in order to feel personally fulfilled or to feel self-worth. Such a non-well-adjusted personality might have thoughts and feelings such as: If I'm not in a relationship, I'm not happy. Somebody doesn't like me and I can't be happy. I can't be comfortable. I have to be in a relationship. I have to be with someone. I have to do this. I have to do that. But from a worldly standpoint, that's considered normal.

I think people who have engaged in relationships without maturity and ethics that way have demonstrated that it's not okay and the so-called normality is really a normalization, in the society, of psychopathology due to immaturity, unresolved psychological traumas, and desires, lack of ethical conscience and presence of spiritual ignorance. So due to those deficiencies that kind of less than optimal relationship doesn't really work well. It's a self-delusional kind of lifestyle that eventually blows up and/or leads to frustration and sorrow in the end. And then people self-delude themselves further, thinking: "Oh, if I only could have this other person, it will work out better." In order to be in a positive relationship you need not be in a relationship, that is, you should not need the relationship to define who you are or your self-worth as a human being. Then you can have a relationship on a higher order that leads to fulfilment of higher goals in life and the chance for achieving happiness derived from fulfilling the goals of life that are helped by but not defined by any kind of worldly relationships. You have to be already a whole person, meaning, having a well-adjusted personality, even without having a partner, in a sense; that's a mature way of coming together. From a higher standpoint also, this kind of relationship has the potential of becoming a "spiritual relationship".

The immature way is finding whoever you can and hooking up and becoming attached and deluding yourself that in entering into the relationship you are becoming whole or that you're complete with the other person. What happens when the other person disappoints you or does not make you happy as you thought or leaves you or dies?

Ultimately, as a person grows older, a person is supposed to be growing out of childish ideas and concepts and egoistic notions. By the time you get to the higher part of the cycle of life when you're older, when your children have grown up and maybe your partner has even died or your partner may still be there, you're 80 years old or whatever, then what? Are you going to continue to act childishly and ignorantly like you're 40 or act like you were when you were 20? Thinking now about what if your partner dies? You are 80 and your partner was 85 and your partner dies; are you going to act like an older person going with people half their age? Are you going to go seek a 35-year-old partner so that you can feel young and whole again? That's not sensible and it denotes a co-dependent and immature, psychologically and emotionally compromised personality. Most people die still feeling desires and needs never fulfilled so they reincarnate to do it all over again.

If there are certain lingering desires, for example if a person has become more elevated in a wisdom sense but yet there are some lingering desires, some lingering non-fulfillment from a worldly perspective, it is not wrong to seek a relationship but the relationship should be done in a way so that it is pursued with ethical conscience in order for it to lead towards fulfillment of the mature and spiritual needs of life instead of the base or worldly "normalized" desires and supporting the psychological deficiencies and pathologies of human life.

The relations of a higher order need to be pursued with the idea that the relationship itself is not the goal or source of fulfillment. The development of fulfillment in life, as contributed by relationships is that it occurs because the relationship helped the person work through personal issues, which is what brings increasing fulfillment in life.

In an ideal Kemetic relationship you're working through the relationship in a manner such that at some point you would not even need to be in a relationship. It doesn't mean that you get a divorce, if you're already in a relationship, but it means that you would be in such a place of inner wholeness that it wouldn't matter whether you're in a relationship or not. That's the kind of perspective a person following the Kemetic marriage philosophy needs to have.

So it is not wrong to have a relationship. What is detrimental is to have a relationship based on delusions and egoistic notions that are driving the relationship perspective, the egoistic and immature reasons for seeking at all, and the ignorant conduct of the relationship.

Question 20- I grew up in the culture somehow always knowing either something was wrong with me or with the way me and my friends do our relationships. I grew up thinking I have to find a mate and have kids and house and so on. I have been studying the work of Dr. Ashby and some books and do not know why I think but I think I need a spouse?

ANSWER

If you reflect deeply on the philosophy and the evidence of your life's relations you will come to understand that you don't really want a husband or wife or marriage but rather you are really seeking the perceived pleasure, happiness, and satisfaction or sense of completeness that is believed to be possible through those mediums. What you really are looking for is to have the pleasure, happiness, and satisfaction or sense of completeness. This is the point. Instead of going directly for that most people seek those through some medium of exchange like a spouse, children, money, real estate, power, etc. So in the process then one has to deal with the issues that those mediums may have, the drama, the psychological problems others may have, their delusions, desires or unpredictable behaviors. Some people shun those but then they go for relations with cars, boats, a job, or other objects that are also fleeting or can be stolen, and in the end will be lost at the time of death; so relationships are not just with people but with animals and nature as well. Why not seek for pleasure, happiness, and satisfaction or sense of completeness, the fulfillment of life, by becoming a sane and balanced person who is capable of providing those for oneself? This is the promise of living by Maat philosophy. Then, a person who is self-fulfilled will not be seeking relations with spouses, children, co-workers, etc. for personal fulfilment but on a higher order, for the purpose of achieving higher goals that would be difficult even for fulfilled individuals, such as creating a great civilization, like that of Ancient Egypt, where all can live in peace and pursue the higher purpose of life, attain enlightenment and expand consciousness to the reaches of self-knowledge and the expanse of Creation. Therefore, Kemetic Relationships are about a wider context than romantic relations-this is about all relations and also about a way of relating that is founded in ethical conscience that fosters honor for all involved and peace for all.

Question 21-You have spoken about independence and I got a divorce from my wife 5 years ago and have not felt a desire to be with anyone else, just my children. Am I not independent?

<u>ANSWER</u>

That happens to many women and men when they get divorced or they get separated or the spouse dies etc., so they go along with their children. For practical reasons, their energies and attention is taken up with their children so the other desires (aryu) become dormant. They don't have a practical outlet for meeting a prospective spouse or because of the hurt of the lost relationship, it takes time for them to get over it, move on and find someone else. So that doesn't really prove anything, in other words. To say that you are alone for some years doesn't prove that you're independent really. For instance, you went through a certain situation in life that caused you to have a great burden of responsibility of caring for children on your own. But all things being equal and having all the opportunities, you might have likely made the choice to go back in some other relationship if you didn't have the same circumstances. So a real test is when opportunities arise and what choices you will make or if you suffer loneliness or desires to be with someone either romantically or just for companionship or to experience carnal pleasures. Then the real test will tell if you are independent or not or how independent you really are.

Sometimes people will come together so that they can afford to pay the rent or for other practical reasons, they become romantically involved on one level but also repudiate each other on other levels, subconsciously; then they win the lottery and they separate. They go their separate ways because they don't really want to be together. In this case, they were together only due to practical reasons and when the situation changed they did what they would have done otherwise.

Question 22-Are you saying people should not be in any relationships at all?

<u>ANSWER</u>

There is a humorous saying that in order to get through the journey of life you need a ship to make the voyage and that ship is a relationship. All human beings are like seedlings with the potential to grow to be strong trees. Just as a plant needs caring and protection to grow until it can protect itself so too the human needs a strong social support network. If the social network is not strong but based on egoism, competition, and pleasure-seeking then that support will not be strong enough to produce ethically conscious, independent and well-adjusted individuals who can grow out of the childish need for social networks for their self-worth and instead be able to live lives of conscience and strong ethical will. So relationships are necessary for all but the nature of those relationships determines how a person will tend to develop in life and the nature of the culture and society they will be part of will be determined by all its individuals as well. The healthy social network leads to a healthy human being and healthy society. The unhealthy social support network supports what is diseased dependency, vile, ignorant, diseased and corrupt in human beings and the societies they create.

If self-development were done before entering into relationships, then actually any relationship that you might have, not just romantic paired relationships, would be more beneficial. There are certain people who are more suited for a monastic lifestyle and certain people who are more suited for being in a paired relationship. There are different types of relationships also, not just a paired relationship. There are different kinds of associations, some being platonic.

Most people, due to the inhuman development of people in the abnormal society that is now world culture, fostered by diseased, pathological social upbringing, have developed that unrighteous form of relationship need. Society has fostered and has helped that need, has nurtured that need, so it's very, very difficult to become free of it and so it's very understandable the state in which most people find themselves both intellectually and "feelingly" compromised and degraded and unfit for relationships. So the next best thing also is to use the relationship in such a way as to be thinking about this ancient philosophy and wisdom so they will mature and lead themselves to freedom.

Question 23- How does the process work of aryu in relationships?

<u>ANSWER</u>

Aryu may be defined as: "the sum total of a person's past actions, thoughts, feelings, desires and their results that direct a person's present day feelings, thoughts, and desires." It can be elicited by worldly situations that bring them out, that resonate with them. For instance, you may, sometime in the future, come to know someone who is in the same kind of situation you experienced in the past or as you come together in a relationship they act in certain ways that remind you of a previous failed relationship and then they bring up the feelings and thoughts in you related to your experience of your situation. So witnessing their situation resonates with yours and reminds you of yours. That will be a test to see what is still in there, your unconscious, or how much you're going to resonate with that, how much of the aryu is going to be still remaining in your personality and how affected by the aryu memories you will be in the present. Is it going to overwhelm you again? Are you going to relive it as if it is happening now? Or did you work through it and can now look at the situation objectively and from a distance as a learning experience? Will you act forthrightly or will you go through the drama in the new relationship as you did in the old because you feel self-loathing and want to suffer or are guided by relationship miseducation, that you have to stay with a person and not get divorced no matter how toxic the relationship might be? That's how life tests you.

That's when you really know what you have attained, from being tested through life relationships. You can know internally also through higher evolution and spiritual purity as well. But if you don't have that kind of evolution, that kind of sensitivity, the world can test you and you can know that way too. Most people who think they are mature and on a higher level of spiritual evolution and purity are self-deluded and they are perplexed when the life situations demonstrate their immaturity. If they are willing to face their error they can grow. If not, the self-delusion continues indefinitely.

One aspect of growing is being tested by the world. But first, there needs to be study and growth, just like a seed needs to be protected from the elements until it grows and can protect itself. In modern society, most people do not get that education. They simply grow up and are expected to have viable relationships without being taught how or having an ethical basis to approach relationships with. It can be difficult to do all this kind of work when you're intermingling with other people. The more intimate you're intermingling, the more intensive it is on the mind and feelings and the harder it is to stabilize yourself and your personality so as to be able to see clearly the nature of your own thoughts and where you end and the other person begins so as to make sense and have clarity about your situation as well as the will to act in accordance with your ethical conscience instead of acting out of weak willed emotional impetus. So it's best to do spiritual work from the position of maturity and stability and not while experiencing relationship dramas and turbulence.

When people are not cognizant of their own entity, meaning aware and well-adjusted to their own personality in the world and they start mixing with another person or persons, the mixing is happening at different levels. It's not just physical when they are having sex. There's mental intermingling that goes on there. There's a level of feelings and emotions as well. From a physical standpoint there are the pheromones and hormones that become affected and disturbed which affect the thought and feeling process; if you touch physically, like a hug, there are changes and effects that occur. All those interactions can cause impurity (not being able to discern who you are in a pure clear experience of self) because you're not purely yourself. You're being affected by what the other person is saying or not saying, what they're doing or not doing, or how close you are or not. And then you have other worries and anxieties that may come in to play. The person might become upset or has stopped talking to you, or didn't touch you the way they did before. There are a lot of other issues coming in that a single person doesn't have to deal with. However, on the other side, sometimes you don't deal with the issues internally and then you think that you dealt with them and have grown beyond them, and that can hold a single person back since they do not have a venue to experience the lessons needed.

Therefore, relationships do have a place to help people grow which is most advantageous when people who are coming together are not doing so out of lower egoistic needs and illusory desires. So it's not a blanket statement that nobody should ever be paired up or have a relationship. It depends on your level of illusion, where you are, what your needs are and the kind of lessons that are needed in life and the best way to get them. No matter how skilled or powerful the teacher, if you are not ready to learn something by means of being taught, then you have to learn through experience, the hard way.

There are stories about aspirants who are like that. They can even counsel others on these issues too. They're celibates for years, and then all of a sudden somebody comes along making passes at them and wiggling the body all around, and then they go wild, overboard and headlong into worldly experiences, sometimes more strongly than if they had not deprived themselves. Deprivation occurs when there is lingering desire. If there is maturity and growth beyond the experience such that there is no lingering desire about pursuing more of those experiences, then refraining from an experience is no deprivation. It happens with food, too, people abstaining from eating this or eating that, and then it gets put in front of them, and then they go wild. They go for more.

Some of these issues are very complicated, so the teaching has to be sufficiently intricate to handle the issues and also up to the task of working with different personalities in different levels. It's a big predicament. It's hard to transform yourself as human beings. It's the hardest thing there is to do. Yet when there is a certain level of readiness, when a person has been through a certain amount of hard knocks and have developed a certain minimal level of maturity, they can be ready to listen to an enlightening teaching and have the will to act on the wisdom they have received, while overriding the egoistic desires they have learned are illusory and leading to pain and sorrow. Learning is when a person not only intellectually knows something is bad for them but also when they develop will to resist the temptation to engage in the experience. Any people know something is wrong and cannot stop themselves from pursuing the experience anyway because their will is weak. In other words, the negative aryu in their unconscious is stronger than their ethical conscience and can override it and not only impel them towards the action but also compelled them, forced them, to pursue it even when they know it is wrong. This kind of mind is caught up by setian control, that is, the grip of egoism.

Question 24-You have spoken about aryu but can you summarize the teaching of aryu and how it operates to control the personality and determine the destiny of a human being and how can this process be changed through maat philosophy?

ANSWER

Above: The Judgment of the Heart of Scribe Ani

Aryu is a fundamental tenet of maat philosophy. In the Judgment of the Heart of scribe Ani the teaching of aryu is boldly described as the heart being the container of aryu, therefore, it is the unconscious mind. The aryu that is weighed in the scales of Maat (ethical conscience) is the sum total aggregate potential of present and future thoughts, feelings and desires based on actions, thoughts, and feelings of the past, that determines the character of the human being. Therefore, the character is being weighed against a standard; that standard is a benchmark, a criterion that the human character must reach in order to successfully pass the test of the balance of ethical conscience in life. If the character has a tendency towards unrighteousness then there is a potential for unethical behavior and feelings which determine the heart as being heavier than the feather of Maat, and needing more time and space worldly experiences, and sufferings so as to clear sufficient negative aryu (of ignorance, self-centeredness, unrighteousness, etc.) so as to allow the personality to awaken to ethical conscience and purity of heart. If the content of the heart is found to be equal to the standard of maat it is deemed to be ethical and worthy to proceed on, to live a heavenly existence while attaining final perfection and union with the divine. If the content of the heart (character) is found to be lighter than the feather of Maat (Maatian standard) then that character has been found to contain lucid and ethically pure content of aryu. It means the finding that the person has discovered absolute truth [un-maat] or identification with spirit (final perfection, oneness with Asar (Osiris)).

As you know, aryu is the sum total effect of the past experiences, thoughts, and feelings from the current and previous lives. What influences the perception of that experience of aryu of the past is resonance. When you have accumulated aryu of the past it involves perhaps hundreds of millions of different experiences. Some are different and some similar but not all are recalled at the same time because otherwise the mind would be overwhelmed and the mind really works with one thought at a time. However, the mind can feel more than one aryu at a time and this is what brings conflicts in life when the personality is driven by conflicted emotionality as opposed to rationality (not rationalization) and healthy emotions. People can like something about a person and hate some other aspect of the same person, at the same time, and not know why, etc. This is how the sum total of positive and negative aryu can operate in the character of a person, manifesting in the conscious level of mind as a single, multifaceted irrational "feeling" about a person, situation or object.

One way of having a perception of the experience of aryu is if the aryu is so strong that it pressures the mind to think related ideas. So if you have lots of aryu related to desiring a car for your 18th birthday, for example, then the aryu will bubble up thoughts related to that as you get closer to 18; the bubbling thoughts that come to the surface from the unconscious will add to the storehouse of past aryu (in the *Ab* or unconscious mind) and make them stronger to the point that on the 18th birthday you will not be able to control yourself and you must get a car some way somehow. Furthermore, the thoughts will lead to perceiving cars everywhere (on TV, in magazines, in the street, on the radio, when talking to friends, etc.) and visualize yourself driving one, etc., etc.; all of which makes the unconscious storehouse of aryu stronger and more compelling even to the point of forcing rationalizations (mental act of forcing thoughts to conform to one's own ideologies or desires despite world realities or proofs to the contrary) to facilitate the desire: example: The force of aryu is to get a car so anyone or anything obstructing that becomes an object of hate. So if you want the car but did not save for it but your father does not want to give you money to get it he is the bad person and not you. As exacerbation, this aryu resonates with other similar ones where your father refused to get a toy, or pay for a trip, etc. and all those add up to rationalize: "my father never gets me "anything"" and hates me, even when the father took care of the mortgage and other family expenses and might have given other gifts, though not the ones really desired. This is only one example and there are other intervening aspects. Perhaps the father took you to ball games and family picnics that were fond times. So the feelings of "father loves me" and father hates me fester in the unconscious mind at the same time while growing up. Later as an adult, a person tends to remember fond memories and suppress negative ones so the illusory rationalization might be: "my father cared for me" but he was a mean guy. In even later life the illusory rationalization might be: "my father was a good guy and I see now why he did some of the things he did". The rationalizations are based on experiences loaded, as aryu, in the unconscious, through the misinterpretation of them and commingling them with personal ignorance, desires and feelings all leads to a conglomerate called a person's character, that is not based on reality or pure truth but on memories filtered by egoism.

Another way this issue may operate is: in the course of ordinary life a person is confronted with varied experiences and some of those experiences have the same or similar energy of the storehouse aryu. So you may not be thinking of a car at present and your desire for it but one passes by and it resonates with the unconscious desires and reminds you of the desires and imaginary feelings of having a car and since you have agreed with these thoughts and feelings they re-embed in the unconscious, adding to the ones that were already there, making them stronger and more compelling.

In the context of co-dependency, the aryu urges a person, impels them to seek after a desired person, object or situation that the content of aryu as determined as desirable, that will bring pleasures or satisfaction to the personality because the personality feels low self-esteem and perceives that it needs those things to alleviate the angst of low self-esteem or self-loathing. This syndrome operates even if those things are unattainable or conflicting with other desires of the personality. Nevertheless, the personality pursues them and this can lead to internal conflicts leading to pathologies like: "if I can't have you nobody can" even rising to the level of murder/suicide. Or, even if the personality is repeatedly shown that the object, person or situation is rejecting them or that the situation is a source of pain, as long as the content of aryu impelling and compelling the personality is stronger than the positive wisdom aryu, the personality will continue pursuing the negative object, person or situation. They will continue buying a different car because the next one will be the one to bring happiness; they will continue calling the old girlfriend or boyfriend, trying to ingratiate themselves or finding one like her and if it does not work out it can lead to anger against the person and or increasing self-hatred and disgust, personal misery and despair leading which are mild pathologies leading to more severe and self-destructive stages; They continue compromising their own ethics and morals and self-respect to ingratiate themselves even when the gestures are continually rebuffed; yet they will continue trying to create a situation, like being rich even when they see rich people who are not happy, etc. etc.

How can one change the aryu and thereby change the condition of the character of the personality? Through the study of wisdom, a person must understand the illusoriness of aryu. This does not get rid of it but allows a person some space to start opposing it so when the resonances occur the procedure is to apply wisdom in the mind to counteract the rising [awakened] aryu. Then the next step is to disagree with the new resonating experiences and not allow them to add to the storehouse. So the rising aryu gets dissipated and spent and no new aryu is added; rather, wisdom aryu is created which will eventually be strong enough to counteract and balance out against the negative aryu of worldly desires. Then a human being will not be compelled by that worldly aryu but will be in command to allow actions that are based on truth rather than blind feelings and desires of the ignorant ego.

Now, understanding this wisdom means realizing that what you associate with, what you think about, what you allow yourself to feel and agree or disagree with is going to influence the content of aryu in the unconscious mind and it is that content that directs life and not the conscious mind. The conscious mind is a slave to the unconscious just as the tip of an iceberg is a slave to where the body of the iceberg below the surface wants to go. A person who acts based on the dictates of and resonances with the unconscious aryu is a reactionary personality without free will. A person who is neither impelled nor compelled to follow the dictates of the unconscious aryu is a person with free will.

So, the associations, relations, and situations of life contribute to the storehouse of aryu in the unconscious mind. Therefore, to transform that storehouse you need to work with those relationships, associations, and situations you allow yourself to be involved with in life. Thus, if you want to associate with family and you like romances and or sentimental family relations, that influences you and prevents you from achieving higher thoughts and feelings of detachment and dispassion. If you believe the world is real and the people and objects in it are abiding realities and you live with that notion, that notion contributes to your aryu of individuality and perceptions of self as part of a conglomerate of matter, time and space (egoism); and that influences your aryu such that you cannot think about the concepts of transcending time and space, in an initiatic context.

So you see how this concept works and what must be done to counteract the syndrome of egoism so as to be free from the mass cloud of illusion formed by unrestricted negative/ignorant aryu based on reactions to world stimuli and egoistic feelings based on emotionality as opposed to reason. It is necessary to study an authentic mystic/mystery teaching and work on the mind to cleanse/counteract the negative/ignorant aryu of the past, with wisdom studies, with rituals of right feeling to reinforce the wisdom with detachment and dispassion to create a buffer between the past aryu and new experiences and resonances, and with a discipline of reflection to consider what new aryu is to be allowed to become part of the unconscious. These disciplines and others work to cleanse the unconscious and lead to true free will and spiritual enlightenment.

Psychological studies have shown that only 5% of thoughts are conscious and 95% are coming from the subconscious and unconscious. That modern finding correlates with the ancient wisdom of aryu which resides in the AB or heart (unconscious). In terms of human relationships, this wisdom, as explained above, means that the relations that most people have are illusory because they are based on compelling forces arising out of their own ego's unconscious unknown desires and feelings. So a person one may be in love with would otherwise be hated if the aryu were configured differently. Therefore, it is hard to face the reality that most people do not love each other for who they are essentially but due to a myriad of other factors operating in the unconscious of both persons in the relationship. In fact, lets go further and realize that the people you love are loved because of aryu experiences and desires that an relate to culture as well as psychological impressions, aryu, of the past and not because you have made up your mind to care for another person consciously. So most relations, attachments, affections or repudiations, scorn, or rejections are not due to conscious and carefully thought out decisions but rather due to unknown, irrational, feeling based impressions of the past that rise to the surface of mind with uncontrolled force of will to impel and compel the weak and ignorant personality to engage in unconsidered relationships. Out of these relationships, with their vicissitudes, dramas and brief periods of happiness punctuated by defining periods of sorrow, frustration and disappointments, a human being eventually, perhaps even after thousands of reincarnations, face the reality of the futility of discovering abiding satisfaction and inner fulfillment through such relations and develops an interest in pursuing thoughtful, wise and ethical self-development that can lead to the capacity to exercise self-will and spiritual enlightenment instead of futile worldly pursuits. At least, when this prospect commences there is the possibility to transform the present relations into thoughtful ones out of thoughtless, mindless, instinctual and reactionary relations. Such a prospect can work to help those engaged in developing positive, real human spiritual relations as opposed to the unconscious relations based on uncontrolled, instinctual forces arising from impure aryu.

Additionally, as if all of the above were not sufficient for one human being to handle, there are other impinging factors that complicate and contribute to the shape and feel of the aryu that is experienced. Gender tendencies are well known physiological predispositions experienced due to physiological reasons. Firstly there is the issue of hormones that initiate animal biological imperatives such as the imperative of procreation, that forces human sexual and conjugal relations. They may be thought of also as aspects of instinctual behaviors. These relate to gender. Males tend towards rationality and women tend towards emotionality. When men perceive that women are approaching them in an emotional way (even if it is not) they tend to pull back or even withdraw from the interaction and if severe enough from the relationship; they complain about being nagged at or nitpicked to an unbearable point. When women perceive that men do not understand their point or are not connecting on an emotional level they tend to pursue the men by insisting their point be listened to or that men should share their feelings. If men do not respond the pursuit escalates and even to the point of screaming at which time men completely tune out and or shut down and leave the scene, sometimes, if the pattern continues long enough, to stay away for long periods, to seek out other "less troubling" mates, etc., just to avoid the confrontations. All of these experiences complicate and contribute to the content of aryu that composes the character of males and females. So without a balanced, respectful, orderly process, founded it Maatian dispassion and detachment as well as ethical conscience of one's actions thoughts and feelings in the acts of communication the characters, thoughts, and feelings can deteriorate along with the relations and their capacity to lead to personal and relationship satisfaction and personal spiritual growth and enlightenment. In order for the higher goals of life to be attained, the urges coming from the aryu as well as the biological imperatives are to be overcome through the study and practice of the Maatian wisdom.

Finally, it is important to understand that aryu directs the destiny of life, be it negative or positive; this means that if a person were to work to transform the content of aryu then that person, instead of the aryu, becomes the architect of their own destiny and master of their own fate instead of being controlled, like a puppet on strings, by ignorance, irrationality, and delusion.

Question 25-Greetings, I have been a follower of Kemetic spiritual wisdom and also Kemetic Marriage philosophy for some time and I am wondering if it is ok for me to seek a relationship. I do not want to become unnecessarily entangled with someone but I still do feel a desire to be in a relationship with someone.

ANSWER

If you really want to engage in a relationship I usually recommend at least a year of dating, of hanging out and getting to know each other. This means remaining on a platonic level and starting a friendship and having the other person find out about your life and you find out about theirs including about their ethics and religious perspectives on life, etc.

This should go on until a process goes on that you come to know the person but taking care to never allow the friendship to become sentimental or co-dependent such that if you find out there is something unacceptable about them that you could not break up with them and go separate ways and rather hold on for egoistic reasons that are not permitted by Maatian ethics (Maat Philosophy). Things come out, about issues in the personality, about past issues, etc., when you start relating. After a while, when the novelty of dating for the first time wears off and deeper aspects and complexities of the personality come out, then you have to decide if you want to live with what you discover. Is it in line with ethical conscience? is it beneficial to your practical and spiritual life? Are you compatible in your goals of life? Will this person impede your human and spiritual evolution or be a help and honest partner? (Meaning they will act with honor and righteousness when it comes to your welfare and not out of egoism, sentimentality or ignorance). This standard is not just a judgment about what they seem to think consciously; it relates to a person's capacity to follow through on their goals or to what extent are they thwarted by their unconscious obstructions that will cause frustrations in their life that you will partake in and at times even be a source of comfort for. If that is a case will they be able to work through their issues and grow or will they use you as a crutch or balm to sooth their failures or inadequacies? Some of this can be related to traumatic events in early life but also it can be related to the kind of upbringing: middle class, rich household, poor household, etc., that was experienced while growing up. It's about discovering their character and upbringing because that contributes to their aryu, the sum-total of the effect of their thoughts, feelings, and desires of the past, that you will be exposing yourself to and participating in as you move forward together. As you examine their character you can examine yours to see if you would be a positive partner to them and if you can work together to help each other on the path of life.

So you're trying to see if there's compatibility, spiritual compatibility with the religion and if there might be issues that are going to be a problem. There are many issues to consider as sources of trouble in relationships. If there is an ethical conscience in the relationship then the small and petty issues will be resolved without unnecessary drama and the important issues will be handled with maturity. This is an ideal.

All those things need to be determined before going forward, and it requires somewhat of a test of time. Invite the prospective partner to important events and functions in your life and you go to theirs and that kind of thing. Expose them to your lifestyle and philosophical convictions but don't try to convert or force anything on them. Let things proceed naturally and see how it goes; see if there is genuine and not forced (because you think you want to be together) compatibility and agreement on life goals. In other words, you take care of making sure your actions are in line with Maat and she will take care of determining if the relationship is viable and if this is a proper partner to have a relationship with; so you can sit back and let things work out and not worry about the outcome since that is to be determined by truth and not egoism (setian desires, inadequacies, misconceptions, fears, ignorance, codependences, etc.).

Consider that in terms of having peace, harmony and also capacity to build success in life, everything depends on maturity because you can have one person who is younger physically who is more mature than the person who is physically older. So one person can be less physically mature, but they are more spiritually and morally mature than the other person who is physically older. The point is that maturity depends on the content of aryu in the unconscious mind, which is not necessarily dependent on physical age. Therefore, it depends on the other person's aryu. That's really your main consideration or concern, what is the content of the aryu of the other person? Is that going to be detrimental? Is it mature? Is the person going to bring drama or insanity into your life that you don't want or need? Or is it going to be balanced? Balanced does not mean without challenges or brief periods of struggle but it means not being the type of person that succumbs to all tragedies or troubles in life and acts the way television taught in soap operas or ignorant families that cry or act out or blame or accuse others of everything and not face their errors, or make a fuss about everything like insolent petulant children, even as grown-up's.

Is it going to be helpful? Can you be helpful to each other on the journey of life and the spiritual quest to attain enlightenment? These are the questions. If it's going to be detrimental or if it's going to be unnecessary drama, if you're going to be fighting frequently even over stupid things and nonsense, then you would want to depart such a relationship. Due to the hidden unconscious aryu, people do things they are not in control of and don't know of so the lack of control over feelings, emotions, and actions makes them feel and act in contradictory ways that can drive each other crazy.

So, if you have learned the Kemetic Marriage philosophy well and you have become sufficiently purified through your spiritual practices and studies to be able to exercise your will in your life to competently determine who you will be relating with based on ethics before emotions and sentimental attachments develop, then you have a chance to select a good partner. This means, before you allow yourself to fall in love with a person before you allow your emotions to become attached, the intellect has to be the gatekeeper and approve first. The intellect and your ethical conscience have to first tell you if it's okay or not to engage in the relationship; Then and only then should you allow your emotions to develop towards the person. Then if any attachment develops it will be within the purview of ethics and sanity instead of blind following of one's ignorant heart and "falling" in love with a less than optimal person. Then those remaining feelings you may have, for being attached or in a paired relationship, will have a better chance to be resolved and eventually those impediments to spiritual evolution that are pulling towards worldly relations and desires, will be resolved and the pathway to spiritual success will be opened. This is the true purpose of human relationships and the ultimate goal when conducted with sanity, maturity and ethical conscience.

One suggestion would be for you to practice reading this volume on the ideal of Kemetic relationships, with your prospective partner. Treat it as a study session. Meet weekly to read and converse about it and share your thoughts and feelings on it and hold regular discussions about it and try working out what it could mean in your lives and over time you will have the answers you need.

Question 26-Greetings Dr. Ashby My question is about having a relationship in the context of being a follower and practitioner of maat philosophy.

I had a relationship previously and then for years while studying the teachings I thought I could realize I did not need a relationship but in the last few years I found that the teachings were not enough to fulfill me and I realized I still had desired to be in a relationship. Then I found a good hearted person who also studies the teaching and they were also desiring to be in a relationship. But after some time now I find I am sometimes annoyed in the relationship and maybe I do not want the relationship in the same way as I thought. It's not about them, it's about me. What should I do?

ANSWER:

Firstly, I would like to quote a university study about major irritants in relationships between men and women:

Some couples were asked to rate their top relationship irritants. The University of Louisville psychologist Michael Cunningham reported the following:

Women's complaints about men:
- *forgetting important dates, like birthdays or anniversaries*
- *not working hard at his job*
- *noisily burping or passing gas*
- *staring at other women*
- *being stubborn and refusing to give in*

Men's complaints about women:
- *the silent treatment*
- *bringing up things he's done in the distant past*
- *being too hot or too cold*
- *being critical*
- *being stubborn and refusing to give in*

The irritants listed above are, of course, all illusory items that people deal with because they want something for themselves out of relationships so they put up with the irritants in an effort to get that which they perceive as their desires. The listing is what affects most people but those who are studying this teaching should be getting past many of those issues and should not be acting as regular common uninitiated folk. Another point is that just because people are studying Maat it does not mean they have worked through their issues or attained higher ethical conscience since the aryu can still be preventing them from achieving their stated goals. This applies to you as well as your partner. Having said that, until people become ready to deal with the underlying issue, that is the desiring for illusory things, itself, they will continue to be in relationships and putting up with things they should not have to as dignified souls instead of acting like squalid animals putting up with the excrements of ordinary human life. This idea of excrements comes out of the Ancient Egyptian Pert-m-Heru [Ancient Egyptian Book of The Dead] text where the initiate rejects the excrements of life. People, like animals, put out excrement but unlike ordinary animals, people put out at least three forms of excrement, the physical feces, the negative or egoistic speech, and the negative or egoistic thoughts that translate into "excrementitious" actions, some of which involve or are directed to others. So there are more reasons to pursue detachment instead of seeking relationships with those who are emotionally, mentally and ethically immature or even degraded or even disturbed. Yet most people accept those as part of life. Since, at the ordinary human level most people are not acting out of their soul wisdom, with intuitional enlightened knowledge of self in all, life is not about improving or seeking a higher way of existence and life remains about those lower values from beginning to end even when people convince themselves they are acting out of altruistic desires. Those same people go on through life seeking joy and fulfillment in ignorant and deluded ways that lead to discovering frustration and more delusion. Even those who say they are happy in ordinary relationships are deluded for they are convincing themselves of that while ignoring the obvious inconsistencies and foibles of human existence that abound in relationships perhaps more than in most sectors of human life.

Therefore, as long as those desires are there persisting you may as well use this opportunity, with a person who is above average in terms of ethical conscience and spiritual aspiration, to relate in such a way that will have the effect of sublimating the desires of you both from being related to lower thoughts, desires and feelings that lead to illusory but annoying irritants, to a path that leads to resolving those desires and promotes reduction and absence of irritants because life will be about higher things instead of the things that lead to irritations and frustration due to the lower way of living dedicated to attaining things that are unattainable. The illusory irritants listed above may never be completely resolved through the relationships but working to resolve the issues that give rise to them within oneself leads one to clear the personal egoistic supports of negative aryu sufficiently enough to open a window to the inner peace and wisdom of the higher self that gives rise to the true and abiding satisfaction and fulfilment that is what people are really searching for but cannot find in the illusory idea of being coupled with someone and being happy all the time and walking into the sunset and living forever after with the soulmate in heaven, etc.; This is perhaps the grandest of all illusions in worldly relationships, that cause more frustrations and distractions in life, the romantic, sentimental view of relationships based on the idea that human beings and the human experiences and ways of relating to modern culture are correct. If ever that delusion should have been dispelled it should have been after the first 1000 years of western culture (beginning with classical Greek civilization). Not one person has ever discovered fulfillment and abiding happiness through sentimental, romantic relationships so why should anyone continue pursuing that prospect? They do it out of personal ignorance (negative aryu) and cultural ignorance that is passed on from generation to generation.

Indeed, think about it, when you are deciding to engage in a relationship you are engaging with another person who is not in control of their thoughts, feelings, and emotions and you are trusting that they will always have your best interest at heart not realizing they are being controlled by forces that even they do not know about so how are they going to provide for your happiness and fulfilment?

Consider how fickle and therefore, illusory, ordinary human desires are and how they lead people into actions that do not yield the results they desired, hoped for or expected. The teachings were not enough so you desired a relationship and the neteru (cosmic forces coursing through the universe) complied and brought you what you said you wanted. Isn't this the same as your previous relationship? What happened to that? This points to the illusoriness of mind, desires, and feelings. They are illusory but when they have been given power, they take on a force that impels and compels people to carry on in illusory relations and pursuing illusory goals that are in the end distractions but entertaining like a magic show where the magician has created an illusion and during the time of the illusion it is compelling and captivating but in the end you still have to leave the magic show and go home and face the realities of life.

Now, consider that indeed it may be you who have the issue and not the other person and consider also that if you leave this person and go along for some time, if you have not dealt with the deep-rooted issues of the desires then you will be right back in this position when the current realities fade and then the illusory longings return once again in the future and then your mind will convince you that you need to be in a relationship again, and after that, again and again, etc. As long as the aryu has not been dealt with the situations will repeat in the same lifetime and in the next as well as the one after that one, and so on.

So, what is necessary is to deal with this current relationship in the most Maatian way possible and that means not overindulging in sentimentalities, or spending too much time together fostering egoistic forms of relating and or expecting others to be with you to make you happy all the time, etc. Spend time on your own doing your thing. Have a personal and separate private life and also have a part of life that is shared for the benefit of both. This minimizes the lower forms of interacting and producing egoistic physical ways of relating for pleasure but also for irritation. Remember the adages: "absence makes the heart grow fonder" and "familiarity breeds contempt". When together make a point of discussing these issues and others covered in this volume and journal your reflections and resolutions and resolve to face the issues and do the best you can to overcome them in the future.

You will never find someone who is perfect in every way because that is an egoistic notion; if you did find such a person it would be according to egoistic notions that actually would reinforce the ego leading to a downfall when the relationship ends due to death of one or the other. A perfect relationship from the Maatian perspective is with others who are ethically conscious, seeking to live by truth (what is correct, factual, verifiable and real including the reality of higher consciousness) and also forthright, who will tell you like it is and listen to you when you tell it like it is, with openness and goodwill. Since most people have lower egoistic remnants active in the personality, as good as they may try to be, they cannot either sometimes or anytime hear it like it is about themselves and you may not want to tell it like it is for fear of creating disharmony in the present even when not doing so will eventually blow up in a disagreement and possible fight later on that will not resolve issues but produce resentments and more negative aryu.

Therefore, the best thing is to work towards a Maatian ideal realizing that the remnants of negative aryu will come out every so often but that is illusory and to be allowed to pass like a cloud in the sky. Also, work on infusing into the unconscious, new positive aryu of realizing that the relations at the surface, worldly level are illusory and so desires related to that are also illusory. Further, work with this relationship and have discussions about the issues and work to become more forthright and clear about feelings and reflections to avoid and dissipate new negative forming aryu. Also, work to promote the positive aspects of relations that you have in reality come together to pursue, not having children or giving pleasure or making the other happy, etc. which are all illusory, not fulfilling (in the way one imagines) and are also fleeting in the end. You came together to work on helping each other work towards discovering the meaning of life and just as two heads are better than one, so too, two bodies are better than one when it comes to paying rent, putting on events, having philosophical discussions and reflections when studying the teachings given by the spiritual teacher, helping each other have quiet time to do you r individual spiritual practices by maintaining the premises quiet or taking messages for the other during those times or helping each other develop good ideas for projects that you can accomplish to help the world and yourselves to move towards enlightenment and peace. This is the real purpose of having a relationship and out of this way of living, personal pleasure and happiness can develop that is not ego based and is healthy. Ultimately those higher positive pleasures are a support for real friendship and peace of mind that is the foundation of a personality that can practice the advancing aspects of the spiritual philosophy of Shetaut Neter (Ancient Egyptian Mysteries), owing to having peace and balance at home and in the personality, having worked for that by applying these Maatian principles in the relationships to lead them to produce an outcome of Maat (truth, justice) and Hetep (inner peace) by avoiding the conflicts due to following illusory desires, thoughts and feelings.

Question 27- I think I understand the maat philosophy of relationships but I don't think I can accept it. How is it possible to be dispassionate about loved ones and my kids?

ANSWER

Indeed, if you think you understand then it means you have some intellectual notion about the illusoriness of relationships of all kinds. Yet you are not able to accept the teaching or live your life in accord with it. That is the real question; what is stopping you from understanding reality, understanding an actual truth and yet not be able to accept and act on it? The answer is aryu. No matter how true anything is and no matter what evidences are presented, the unconscious impressions of a person will absolutely prevent them from accepting it or acting on it if the content of that aryu is opposite to it. In this way many people have developed negative thoughts, feelings and energies reinforced over perhaps millions of years and there is a lot of momentum-force behind all that, which is reinforced every day when interacting with family and loved ones in an erroneous manner. The treatment for that condition is a steady dose of truth and a steady practice or effort towards accepting and acting on it. Then as the negative content (lies, incorrect notions, passions, desires) of the unconscious become more neutralized and purified and more positive and correct, true information is taken in, then the tide changes and the person can have more clarity, integrity and will power to live by truth.

Question 28-How different were relationships in precolonial Africa in general and in Ancient Egypt and what can we learn and practice from that in modern times versus the modern culture that we have adapted to in the present day?

ANSWER
Well, first of all, I should say, when we say African perspective, many of us think of Africa in general. And that's understandable, especially by those who are in the Afrocentric movement or speaking specifically about Africa. Africa has many nations as we know today which we did not really have in previous years like for instance in the Middle East, Asia Minor was called the Middle East. A lot of those nations did not exist

prior to, say, World War II or World War I when the Europeans came in and carved up the countries from lands that previously belonged to the Ottoman Empire, a situation which is now making a lot of strife today. The same thing happened in Africa and generally throughout the colonialism and neocolonialism periods.

But speaking about the ancient period, there were some main important nations and one of them was Ancient Egypt, another one was Nubia. Since prehistoric times coming down to the common era (referred to as the birth of Jesus/Christ-year "0"), since that time that ancient cultural influence of Ancient Egypt affected other cultures and the religions, including other African religions like Yoruba, to the Greek, the Christian, and the Hindu, Buddhist, and others. One of the most important influences was in the area of ethical conscience with the monumental wisdom of Maat Philosophy. In terms of relationships, with the foundation of Maat, I see Kemet as the epitome, shall we say, of the African conception of a relationship. This includes all relationships even though we're currently speaking of relationships between men and women; so also by extension, it means relationships between parents and children, friends, family, communities and of course a relationship with God.

In terms of the male and female relationship, again, the Kemetic philosophy is very clear in the context of balance. The foundation of relationships is *Maat* and people think of it as truth. But one of the primary aspects of *Maat* is a balance. The Ancient Egyptian, the Kemetic culture, is perhaps the only known culture, in human history, wherein it is found that, between genders, there was more balance and justice between the gender relations than in any other culture that we have known about before or since. That includes the current society that we're in, the Western culture (the United States or European culture), which is dominant in the world today. Perhaps besides Ancient Egypt, maybe Bhutan exhibited some of the same quality of relationships. Or maybe India in the mythic Rama Raja era, if you will, might have had a similar kind of expression. But Ancient Egypt put that into practice for thousands of years in a historical verifiable and practical application in law and custom, in a major civilization, in a way not seen anywhere in the world. That's the difference. Ancient Egypt established a practical reality backed by law and custom. Men and women had the same rights. Even today, we have women getting paid less than men. Additionally, laws are biased in terms of gender. For instance, recently we saw in the news the report of a young man who was caught and convicted of raping a woman behind a dumpster. He got a 90-day jail sentence for such a horrific crime. What are the woman's rights in that? The answer, not anywhere equal to a man's rights.

In Ancient Egypt, these kinds of crimes, first of all, they were unheard of, secondly, the punishment for these kinds of things was severe. So it's not just in terms of the relationship themselves, it's also in terms of the character of the culture and the values the culture seeks to uphold in law. In modern times, now, we have a culture of violence, racism, and misogyny. We have a culture of drug abuse - of illegal and legal drug abuse. We have a culture of political and economic corruption along with legal double-standard in the application between rich and poor and gender and "race."

All that, over time, deteriorates the human psyche; it degrades the social fabric and the ethical conscience of people in the society as well as their leaders, leading to fascism, totalitarianism, despotism, and barbarism. In ancient times, that was not the case because *Maat* philosophy was the guiding principle of the country. That meant that you cannot have, for instance, people being left without the help of health care in such a way that they're going to bankrupt themselves trying to save a family member and at the same time being under so much stress that their relationships fall apart. In ancient times the 42 Precepts of Maat prevented having people and corporations like Monsanto putting out all kinds of pesticides, preservatives, and chemicals in farming and in foods that are destroying the environment and bringing on disease, cancer and dementia. You're going to have all kinds of problems in relationships due to malnutrition, poisonings, and stress because of the lack of ethics of the society and allowing society to be polluted for profit, by sociopaths who don't care as long as they make more money. Also, a lot of these problems lead to hormonal imbalances that affect men as well as women and children perhaps more in that context. That's going to skew the capacity for a healthy relationship.

There are many issues that Ancient Egypt had dealt with and instituted wise guidelines for society to follow. So Ancient Egypt is a model of society and, I believe, convincingly presented in my books, it was, if not the height of the potential of human society, the model for sustainable and purposeful human civilization. What we have now, in modern society, is not civilization because the purpose of this current society is greed and death (through capitalism, pollution and unhealthy lifestyle and diet) instead of enlightenment and life. Therefore, we can't really talk about having healthy relationships in a physiological, environmental, social, economic and political setting of barbarism, which is what we have today. In barbarism, you don't have democracy or justice in the society. This is mayhem. That's why the society is tipping over into environmental, economic and psychological perdition. In order to have proper relationships today, people have to move away from modern culture and its values and move towards ancient ethics and truth as well as the values of life and enlightenment instead of greed, celebrity, personal pleasure-seeking and egoistic pursuits as goals of life.

A question has also been asked about ancient times about, were men and women openly courting one another or were their relationships arranged?

I have not seen evidence of specific boyfriend/girlfriend activities except in rare accounts of relationships between lovers such as in love poems so we can surmise that relationships were free but as we see from marital contracts they were also structured in a family oriented context backed by personal responsibility enforced by law. We also have records from the ***PertmHeru*** or Egyptian Book of the Dead wherein married couples are depicted helping each other through the netherworld to discover God.

Figure 14: Ancient Egyptian Man and woman, as equals, performing a ritual before the tree goddess-Tomb of the Nobles

So, the men and women in Ancient Egypt had equal rights and they were considered as equals in the society. So they could interact but in a context of righteousness, order and truth instead of, as people nowadays like to romantically promote, following the heard or falling in love indiscriminately, etc. That delusion is the novelty, the irresponsible and ignorant manner of engaging in relations with other human beings, who are, for the most part, immature and living out of the animal nature rather than the higher altruistic sensibilities. So it was not like the way things are in modern society where men are pretty much allowed to run around and the women are expected to not be promiscuous and all that kind of thing even though most young people and many "physically" adult people, all run around and act promiscuously at some point.

There is a difference between freely associating with others in relationships versus promiscuity. One is driven by relationship while the other by physical animal urge as well as psychological degradation, seeking fulfillment via physical relations and seeing that as a primary expression of love and or caring. So, if people wanted to come together by choice, they could do so, and they could set up a marriage agreement between themselves if they wanted to enter into a marital relationship. This was recognized by the courts and it was binding. But also, there was no stigma about divorce either. If a woman wanted to get divorced, if a man wanted to get divorced, they could do so but upholding the provisions of the marriage contract. This, in a way, shows the enlightening or the enlightened nature of the society. It doesn't have all the hang ups and all the nonsense of deluded western culture or modern society. By contract, you had to take care of your children. You had to take care of your spouse if there were some agreement to do so. And then one's spouse cannot be left destitute etc., so these are important features of how a truly enlightened society applies ethics in a format that promotes the conduct of relationships in a way so that they may have the opportunity to move towards enlightenment.

The motivation for putting out this book on relationships was kind of an evolutionary process because I've been counseling people over the years and as I see the nature of society deteriorating, I see that we are dealing with relationships in a bubble. This is what I was really getting at. If we're talking about living in a diseased society essentially - a society where most of the people, over 50 percent, are using drugs of some kind, the legal ones or illegal ones, alcohol, cocaine, or pain killers, or whatever it might be, then the capacity to live by sanity, let alone ethical consciousness, is extremely difficult. In the United States, for example, most of the people are self-medicating and that is skewing your awareness, your consciousness, and your capacity. You have corruption of all kinds in the government and in corporations so the society also lives with unrighteousness and egoism as well. Overall, this is an anti-righteous society what we call *An-maat*. *An-maat* means "against *Maat*" or the opposite of *Maat*. So if you're trying to have a relationship in that kind of society, first of all, if you have injustice in the society, you're going to have extra levels of stress and that translates into relationships at fundamental levels. Just to give an example, how many people in society claim to love each other, and everything is going good and they have jobs and a house etc. Then one loses a job and the bills become a strain and stress develops leading to fighting, accusations, and divorce; like the song of the Black Eyed Peas group or the song by Roberta Flack: goes: "Where is the Love". When there is extreme stress, what happened to the holding hands and smiles and plans for the future and kind words, etc.? Since there is lacking deeper ethical foundations in the relationship the couple may start accusing each other, blaming, and allowing old unresolved resentments to resurface, that add fuel and fire to degrade and destroy the capacity to work against the source of stress with ethics and maturity and rather descend into childish egoistic animal instincts. And then the negative things in the relationship that are being otherwise suppressed come out. That's one example. Another example is, when people win the lottery, how they go their separate ways, indicating they were only together for practical reasons; so where is the romantic notion of soulmates and eternal love and walking into the sunset holding hands together forever, etc., etc.? It is an illusion and was from the beginning. We have to recognize that there's a delusion, first of all, in the nature of the worldly notion of the concept of relationship itself. We like to believe we can find some kind of a soul mate. The reality is that you came into this world alone and you go out alone. Your search for relationship is really the attempt to satisfy an urge for completion or wholeness of your soul which feels something missing and that something is what was lost when the personality became individual and polarized by the experience of human existence and all of its egoistic and individualistic aspects such as gender, nationality, race, etc.

That's where the issues of human need and feelings of incompleteness come from and this is a primary message of this book. We're actually looking to unite ourselves to something to complete ourselves in order to discover contentment and satisfaction. We have been deluded to think that we can find that in another person, in objects of the world, money, fame, power, etc.

Since human existence is temporary and situations of life always change there can be no full satisfaction or contentment derived from worldly situations or relationships. In other words, one problem is that everyone gets older or gets sick. Not everybody is happy all the time and, of course, in the end, everyone dies. Sometimes people are depressed; others can't make you happy all the time. They can't fulfill you all the time. So there is no abiding happiness to be derived from a relationship with another person or persons.

But the source of what that other person is, the source from which they have arisen - their soul, their consciousness - that is the supreme divine of what we refer to as the supreme self. That same supreme self is the spirit of all. If we will recognize that relating with that is the true purpose, fulfillment, destiny, and goal of life, then that ego of that person will be recognized as a delusion and their soul is recognized as the true objective of relationship.

When a person believes, that's not the goal of life, and that instead it's to have a physical relationship with someone so they can make you happy which can never happen and in any case even if it could happen, the relationship will eventually come to an end when one or the other partner dies. Through that process of a higher perspective that leads to higher attainment that is where true fulfillment may be discovered. If this ideal is understood and lived then the physical relationships with other persons, with the world, the parents, the children, and everything else, all that comes into a healthier focus. Relations are not to be seen as a goal, or objectives of life but these relationships are pathways or shall we say conduits to a higher experience of existence. That's what Kemetic relationship is really all about. What we have now is a distortion. It's like a Hollywood delusion of what our life is supposed to be or one of those Harlequin romance novels containing relationship nonsense that emphasizes delusions about relationships and manipulations of emotions with unhealthy ideas and imaginary situations about relationships that bear little resemblance to real life. So trying to apply a deluded notion to real life will not end well and this is what we see in relationships worldwide with 1st time marriages ending with divorce rates above 50% which means most marriages are failures and a great part of the reason is entering into marriage with deluded ideals about what marriage is supposed to be.

In writing this book I was considering a psychological issue that seems to be plaguing society more and more and is evident in the culture of Facebook, twitter, and selfies. I was thinking about the issue of narcissism. My thought on that is that what we really have is a - in my opinion - an issue that I would refer to as ***"narcissistic co-dependency"***. What I mean by that is that people are "all about me" and doing selfies and being on Facebook and constantly trying to tell other people what is going on in their life or what they're doing at the moment. They're trying to find, not everyone, but on a mass level, trying to find validation by showing themselves or calling attention to themselves as if that makes their life worthwhile or worthy but if others are not interested in their life then they are worthless and depressed; and the same thing operates in relationships. One person is trying to ingratiate themselves to others and their life is meaningless without the interest or approval of another. You're trying to validate yourself by having a relationship or by having children or by attaching to something outside of yourself all the time because you're not fulfilled internally, not secure in oneself and therefore one is weak and needy. At the same time, one can be also resentful and self-deprecating so at the same time seeking validation and at the same time tearing oneself down even when others try to validate you. This is narcissism and co-dependency operating at the same time and it is, of course, one of many possible mental complexes a person can suffer. Getting into a relationship with someone like this, of course, means that you too are suffering some kind of complex as well. Perhaps there is present a need to be in a dramatic relationship experiencing fights and unrest so as to not face deeper issues and there are many other possibilities.

The issue is not with a person's spirit but rather with their soul and its disconnectedness with its higher self that causes a futile search for fulfillment through relations with other deluded souls instead of with the sanity of one's own higher self. It's a co-dependence that you have that you're trying to fulfill yourself by trying to make it seem as if you're legitimate by the things you have or you're doing, or by the things you're saying, or how you look, and by having other people like you. That's how you're judging yourself, by the vicissitudes or worldly relating. That's where we really know that there's a disease because if you have to have other people's approval and their validation, it seems that you are immature or that you are psychologically unbalanced because you're not a full human being. We have a society full of psychologically diseased, narcissistically co-dependent human beings. They're all trying to fulfill themselves through delusions. They're all trying to validate themselves, their own existence. And then they're looking at lovers, family, friends, Hollywood actors, politicians, etc. trying to validate themselves by projecting their validation on to these people who are really just using them and abusing them for their own codependent reasons; why do people in Hollywood seek fame? Why do politicians seek power? Why do corporate leaders seek more wealth?

The bottom line is that you have to be a person who is self-fulfilled and/or understanding that the validation from outside is really a function of a validation inside. And so if that internal aspect is not there, then you're going to have failure all the way around and the outer world will reflect that back to you. An example of this kind of issue in modern politics is the candidate for president, Donald Trump. His validation is in projecting himself as a rich person. And if you take that away from him, he might probably commit suicide. But that's his persona. Another example is a person that might be in love with someone else and the other person rejects them or dumps them, so they go out and commit suicide because their narcissistic co-dependency was based on validation coming from that other person.

While conducting a lecture series[12] almost two years ago for our online school I wanted to show how these mental complexes reflect the music of the culture. This can be found in many eras and genres and music is a kind of poetry which provides feelings in melody and rhythm, which allows people to connect with the issues in different ways that may not be possible in ordinary interactions of life; so music is a special way to experience emotions and feelings even though it can be deluded and insecure as any other aspect of life governed by ignorance and immaturity. There's a song by a group called the Temptations. They were very famous in the 1960's and 1970's and they had a famous song called: *I Wish it Would Rain*. If you look at what the song is talking about, the singer says I wish it would rain because I'm crying and if I go outside, people will see I'm crying, but if it's raining then people can't tell I'm crying, etc. I'm just paraphrasing the theme of the song. So the point is that if it's raining, people can't tell I'm crying because my girlfriend left me. The song was a big hit and after it came out the writer of the song committed suicide because he was writing about his own life and he could not take the loss meaning his source of validation, his reason for living and feelings of self-worth were tied to the relationship with the other person and when that was lost the foundation of his personality, which was deficient and weak, crumbled and he could not live with that degraded self. This was the perfect example of what most people are going through at some point but in different degrees; some get depressed and move on while others are crushed and commit suicide but it part of the same mental complex. And if you are afflicted by that narcissism and or co-dependency, then your life is going to be measured by a diseased selfish, greedy, deluded and or otherwise degraded general social mental pathology(s) of the society at large; society is composed of individuals so if individuals are suffering mental complexes then society as a whole can also suffer delusions,

---

[12] Se the series *Kemetic Life Skills* –www.EgyptianMysterySchool.org

narcissisms, and codependencies which lead to self-destructive behavior, internal and external discriminations, biases, wars, etc.

Henry David Thoreau once wrote that most people live lives of quiet desperation. He may have been emphasizing stress due to political and economic reasons but included in that is the spiritual area of life and that also applies to relationships. People in relationships have a similar angst about being accepted and often compromise their ethics or other principles just to get that acceptance or at least an approximation of that. They live as children desperately seeking parental support and approval even as adults in supposedly adult relationships. Thus, they are easily manipulated by politicians who present themselves as father figures who will take care of them and tell them what to do. So we may say that along with lives of quiet desperation, people are also living lives of quiet unfulfillment and disappointment that they mask in smiles, or by having progeny or partying, traveling, losing themselves in their work, or upholding belief systems that dictate fulfilment, like holding on to the supposed certainties of religious dogmas or comforting racist social values that artificially uphold one's own self-worth by holding others down in relation to oneself as substitutes for ethical conscience and true human connections that can only be experienced in a context of human brotherhood and never in a context of segregation or delusions of superiority.

Now the question is how to turn these pathologies around and for that, we need family, social and cultural institutions that promote sanity and the path to true fulfillment in life and healthy relationships which means the need to create their own institutions like some societies have. Some groups and communities have done a lot of that. They have their own community centers and their own schools from beginning to end. But other societies that we're talking about, they trust the system. The mass media and the public school that is really dedicated to supporting narcissism and creating more co-dependency. You cannot just have private schools, you must have your own private schools that support your cultural values and a sane perspective of life based on ethical conscience and that is what Maat Philosophy is all about.

So we need to have these values institutionalized and systematically taught to ourselves and our descendants by ourselves and not by a wider culture that has a goal of domination, exploitation, and imperialism using our bodies as gears in the machinery of world destruction while leading us into early death after serving the corporate masters.

One of the big lessons that we learn from Ancient Egyptian (Kemetic) history and religious wisdom comes from studying the ancient Egyptian temple Hypostyle Hall. The Hypostyle Hall is a covered hall where you have lots of columns. The columns symbolize a papyrus swamp. In the ancient Egyptian mythology of the Asarian Resurrection, we learn that the goddess Aset who was hiding with her baby, Heru, in a papyrus swamp after Set had killed her husband. What this gives us to understand, mythically, is that in order to bring up a child who would eventually be the redeemer, the savior, the fully matured and not narcissistic or codependent personality to retake the rightful throne from the murderous uncle, she has to go with Heru into hiding. She has to go into a place of peace, a place without stress, where the teaching of life could be imparted to Heru and could be explored undisturbed and where health of body, mind, and soul could be the main focus. We don't have that place in modern society. Every place in the society is a place of movement, distractions, danger and a place of violence because of the diseased, degraded level of culture in the present day where most people live out of fear of being alone, fear of being unloved, unapproved, fear of being poor and also fear of having one's beliefs, that one depends on for one's self-worth, being discounted, debunked or otherwise determined to be false or even injurious. So people do not want to hear about the corruptions of their political leaders, or that their state of destitution is not because they did not work hard but because the oligarch's setup an economy to impoverish everyone else.

This idea clashes with the idea of individualism and pulling oneself up by one's bootstraps, a notion they have tied up with their self-worth, even though the rich do all they can to steal by rigging elections, rigging financial markets and rigging the general economy in their favor by subverting courts and legislators with bribes to support laws in their favor and police state policies to keep everyone in their class level of the society. Most people seem to accept the corruptions and philandering's of politicians because they themselves have illicit affairs, lie and seek to get over on others in day to day life; sometimes to survive but at others just to achieve the so-called American dream. Most people also do not want to hear that their son died in a war based on lies or that their religion is based on faith and not reality or that their not the greatest country in the world and not the only country with modern conveniences or that their country is the main agent of terrorism, world violence, and war or that their country is the purveyor of economic suffering the world over. Those ideas would shatter the illusions and expose the insecurities and fears that most people cannot face and constantly seek to prevent the truth about those issues from being faced, and mask the delusions with possessions, entertainments, technological developments, big skyscrapers, big bank accounts and big egos through celebrity culture. All of these factors constitute obstructions to healthy relationships and in fact, serve as agents of corrupting relations between human beings. The relations between human beings become tainted by those fears which manifest as an inability to trust, Incapacity to cooperate without competition or selfish interest and anger at not getting one's way or frustration due to inability to find satisfaction and lacking fulfillment. These lead to misunderstanding, disgust, and self-hatred as well as hatred of the other, be they in one's own house or even a spouse or be they in the community or a different country.

So in order to have healthy relationships we need to live in a healthy culture, like a fish that needs clean water to live in. That means we need to have our own institutions of culture including our own schools, government, police, hospitals, our own summer camps, etc. We have to have our own everything pretty much. At the same time, we cannot be trusting in, not be giving your allegiance to the diseased society and its culture of multiple pathologies including the habits of meat eating, drugs, entertainment based celebrity authorities and bankrupt political leadership. The culture of contaminated and synthetic chemical-laden processed foods that are really poisoning and rotting people's bodies and rendering people's minds afflicted with Alzheimer's and dementia along with a myriad of chronic diseases has to be rejected and replaced. We have to have the systems created and administered by and for ourselves and we have to have them institutionalized. Furthermore, it cannot be just, oh, let's go to Uncle Bob on the street. He's the wise person or elder. No; It has to be an institutionalized program, founded in ethical wisdom, where our children are protected and they're left in a specific program, managed by trained and vetted leaders of the community, to learn and develop with our values for themselves; learning our culture of life and valuing themselves and valuing others, and valuing nature itself.

If you don't have those values based on a righteous culture of truth and life (Maat), then the other values of the degraded wider society which are the values of death, destruction, and violence will be adopted and normalized; and then we wonder why the degradation and demise of society is all happening unchallenged while people say "I don't know what we're going to do about it." As long as people are still allying themselves with the popular culture of disease and death culture of personal ignorance and war, corrupt with its politics, an economic system that has exploitative and that it destroys the environment along with human lives, etc. so long there will be disease and disorder in society and in relationships.

INDEX

Other Books From C M Books
P.O.Box 570459
Miami, Florida, 33257
(305) 378-6253 Fax: (305) 378-6253

Prices subject to change.

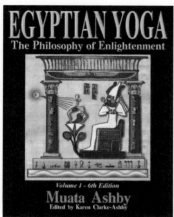

1.   *EGYPTIAN YOGA: THE PHILOSOPHY OF ENLIGHTENMENT* An original, fully illustrated work, including hieroglyphs, detailing the meaning of the Egyptian mysteries, tantric yoga, psycho-spiritual and physical exercises. Egyptian Yoga is a guide to the practice of the highest spiritual philosophy which leads to absolute freedom from human misery and to immortality. It is well known by scholars that Egyptian philosophy is the basis of Western and Middle Eastern religious philosophies such as *Christianity, Islam, Judaism,* the *Kabala*, and Greek philosophy, but what about Indian philosophy, Yoga, and Taoism? What were the original teachings? How can they be practiced today? What is the source of pain and suffering in the world and what is the solution? Discover the deepest mysteries of the mind and universe within and outside of yourself. 8.5" X 11" ISBN: 1-884564-01-1 Soft $19.95

2.   *EGYPTIAN YOGA: African Religion Volume 2*- Theban Theology U.S. In this long awaited sequel to *Egyptian Yoga: The Philosophy of Enlightenment* you will take a fascinating and enlightening journey back in time and discover the teachings which constituted the epitome of Ancient Egyptian spiritual wisdom. What are the disciplines which lead to the fulfillment of all desires? Delve into the three states of consciousness (waking, dream and deep sleep) and the fourth state which transcends them all, Neberdjer, "The Absolute." These teachings of the city of Waset (Thebes) were the crowning achievement of the Sages of Ancient Egypt. They establish the

standard mystical keys for understanding the profound mystical symbolism of the Triad of human consciousness. ISBN 1-884564-39-9 $23.95

3.   *THE KEMETIC DIET: GUIDE TO HEALTH, DIET AND FASTING* Health issues have always been important to human beings since the beginning of time. The earliest records of history show that the art of healing was held in high esteem since the time of Ancient Egypt. In the early 20th century, medical doctors had almost attained the status of sainthood by the promotion of the idea that they alone were "scientists" while other healing modalities and traditional healers who did not follow the "scientific method' were nothing but superstitious, ignorant charlatans who at best would take the money of their clients and at worst kill them with the unscientific "snake oils" and "irrational theories". In the late 20th century, the failure of the modern medical establishment's ability to lead the general public to good health promoted the move by many in society towards "alternative medicine". Alternative medicine disciplines are those healing modalities which do not adhere to the philosophy of allopathic medicine. Allopathic medicine is what medical doctors practice by an large. It is the theory that disease is caused by agencies outside the body such as bacteria, viruses or physical means which affect the body. These can therefore be treated by medicines and therapies   The natural healing method began in the absence of extensive technologies with the idea that all the answers for health may be found in nature or rather, the deviation from nature. Therefore, the health of the body can be restored by correcting the aberration and thereby restoring balance. This is the area that will be covered in this volume. Allopathic techniques have their place in the art of healing. However, we should not forget that the body is a grand achievement of the spirit and built into it is the capacity to maintain itself and heal itself. Ashby, Muata ISBN: 1-884564-49-6 $28.95

4.   INITIATION INTO EGYPTIAN YOGA Shedy: Spiritual discipline or program, to go deeply into the mysteries, to study the mystery teachings and literature profoundly, to penetrate the mysteries. You will learn about the mysteries of initiation into the teachings and practice of Yoga and how to become an Initiate of the mystical sciences. This insightful manual is the first in a series which introduces you to the goals of daily spiritual and yoga practices: Meditation, Diet, Words of Power and the ancient wisdom teachings. 8.5" X 11" ISBN 1-884564-02-X   Soft Cover $24.95 U.S.

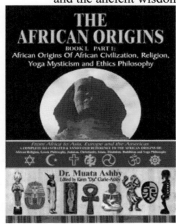

5.   *THE AFRICAN ORIGINS OF CIVILIZATION, RELIGION AND YOGA SPIRITUALITY AND ETHICS PHILOSOPHY* HARD COVER EDITION Part 1, Part 2, Part 3 in one volume 683 Pages Hard Cover First Edition Three volumes in one. Over the past several years I have been asked to put together in one volume the most important evidences showing the correlations and common teachings between Kamitan (Ancient Egyptian) culture and religion and that of India. The questions of the history of Ancient Egypt, and the latest archeological evidences showing civilization and culture in Ancient Egypt and its spread to other countries, has intrigued many scholars as well as mystics over the years. Also, the possibility that Ancient Egyptian Priests and Priestesses migrated to Greece, India and other countries to carry on the traditions of the Ancient Egyptian Mysteries, has been speculated over the years as well. In chapter 1 of the book *Egyptian Yoga The Philosophy of Enlightenment,* 1995, I first introduced the deepest comparison between Ancient Egypt and India that had been brought forth up to that time. Now, in the year 2001 this new book, *THE AFRICAN ORIGINS OF CIVILIZATION, MYSTICAL RELIGION AND YOGA PHILOSOPHY,* more fully explores the motifs, symbols and philosophical correlations between Ancient Egyptian and Indian mysticism and clearly shows not only that Ancient Egypt and India

were connected culturally but also spiritually. How does this knowledge help the spiritual aspirant? This discovery has great importance for the Yogis and mystics who follow the philosophy of Ancient Egypt and the mysticism of India. It means that India has a longer history and heritage than was previously understood. It shows that the mysteries of Ancient Egypt were essentially a yoga tradition which did not die but rather developed into the modern day systems of Yoga technology of India. It further shows that African culture developed Yoga Mysticism earlier than any other civilization in history. All of this expands our understanding of the unity of culture and the deep legacy of Yoga, which stretches into the distant past, beyond the Indus Valley civilization, the earliest known high culture in India as well as the Vedic tradition of Aryan culture. Therefore, Yoga culture and mysticism is the oldest known tradition of spiritual development and Indian mysticism is an extension of the Ancient Egyptian mysticism. By understanding the legacy which Ancient Egypt gave to India the mysticism of India is better understood and by comprehending the heritage of Indian Yoga, which is rooted in Ancient Egypt the Mysticism of Ancient Egypt is also better understood. This expanded understanding allows us to prove the underlying kinship of humanity, through the common symbols, motifs and philosophies which are not disparate and confusing teachings but in reality expressions of the same study of truth through metaphysics and mystical realization of Self. (HARD COVER) ISBN: 1-884564-50-X $45.00 U.S.   81/2" X 11"

6.　　*AFRICAN ORIGINS BOOK 1 PART 1* African Origins of African Civilization, Religion, Yoga Mysticism and Ethics Philosophy-Soft Cover $24.95 ISBN: 1-884564-55-0

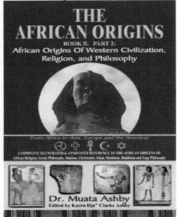

7.　　*AFRICAN ORIGINS BOOK 2 PART 2* African Origins of Western Civilization, Religion and Philosophy (Soft) -Soft Cover $24.95 ISBN: 1-884564-56-9

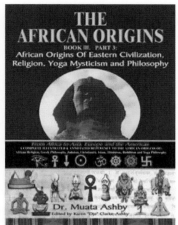

8.   *EGYPT AND INDIA* AFRICAN ORIGINS OF *Eastern Civilization, Religion, Yoga Mysticism and Philosophy*-<u>Soft Cover</u> $29.95 (Soft) ISBN: 1-884564-57-7

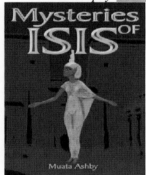

9.   *THE MYSTERIES OF ISIS:* **The Ancient Egyptian Philosophy of Self-Realization** - There are several paths to discover the Divine and the mysteries of the higher Self. This volume details the mystery teachings of the goddess Aset (Isis) from Ancient Egypt- the path of wisdom. It includes the teachings of her temple and the disciplines that are enjoined for the initiates of the temple of Aset as they were given in ancient times. Also, this book includes the teachings of the main myths of Aset that lead a human being to spiritual enlightenment and immortality. Through the study of ancient myth and the illumination of initiatic understanding the idea of God is expanded from the mythological comprehension to the metaphysical. Then this metaphysical understanding is related to you, the student, so as to begin understanding your true divine nature. ISBN 1-884564-24-0 $22.99

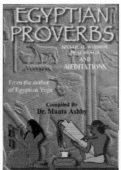

10.   *EGYPTIAN PROVERBS:*   collection of —Ancient Egyptian Proverbs and Wisdom Teachings - How to live according to MAAT Philosophy. Beginning Meditation. All proverbs are indexed for easy searches. For the first time in one volume, ——Ancient Egyptian Proverbs, wisdom teachings and meditations, fully illustrated with hieroglyphic text and symbols. EGYPTIAN PROVERBS is a unique collection of knowledge and wisdom which you can put into practice today and transform your life. $14.95 U.S   ISBN: 1-884564-00-3

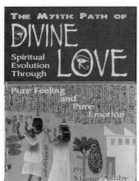

11.   *GOD OF LOVE: THE PATH OF DIVINE LOVE The Process of Mystical Transformation and The Path of Divine Love*   This Volume focuses on the ancient wisdom teachings of "Neter Merri" –the Ancient Egyptian philosophy of Divine Love and how to use them in a scientific process for self-transformation. Love is one of the most powerful human emotions. It is also the source of Divine feeling that unifies God and the individual human being. When love is fragmented and diminished by egoism the Divine connection is lost. The Ancient tradition of Neter Merri leads human beings back to their Divine connection, allowing them to discover their innate glorious self that is actually Divine and immortal. This volume will detail the process of transformation from ordinary consciousness to cosmic consciousness through the integrated practice of the teachings and the path of Devotional Love toward the Divine. 5.5"x 8.5" ISBN 1-884564-11-9 $22.95

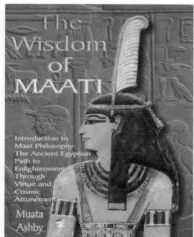

12. *INTRODUCTION TO MAAT PHILOSOPHY: Spiritual Enlightenment Through the Path of Virtue*
     Known commonly as Karma in India, the teachings of MAAT contain an extensive philosophy
     based on ariu (deeds) and their fructification in the form of shai and renenet (fortune and destiny,
     leading to Meskhenet (fate in a future birth) for living virtuously and with orderly wisdom are
     explained and the student is to begin practicing the precepts of Maat in daily life so as to promote
     the process of purification of the heart in preparation for the judgment of the soul. This judgment
     will be understood not as an event that will occur at the time of death but as an event that occurs
     continuously, at every moment in the life of the individual. The student will learn how to become
     allied with the forces of the Higher Self and to thereby begin cleansing the mind (heart) of
     impurities so as to attain a higher vision of reality. ISBN 1-884564-20-8 $22.99

13. *MEDITATION The Ancient Egyptian Path to Enlightenment*   Many people do not know about
     the rich history of meditation practice in Ancient Egypt. This volume outlines the theory of
     meditation and presents the Ancient Egyptian Hieroglyphic text which give instruction as to the
     nature of the mind and its three modes of expression. It also presents the texts which give
     instruction on the practice of meditation for spiritual Enlightenment and unity with the Divine.
     This volume allows the reader to begin practicing meditation by explaining, in easy to understand
     terms, the simplest form of meditation and working up to the most advanced form which was
     practiced in ancient times and which is still practiced by yogis around the world in modern times.
     ISBN 1-884564-27-7 $22.99

14.   *THE GLORIOUS LIGHT MEDITATION* TECHNIQUE OF ANCIENT EGYPT New for the year 2000. This volume is based on the earliest known instruction in history given for the practice of formal meditation. Discovered by Dr. Muata Ashby, it is inscribed on the walls of the Tomb of Seti I in Thebes Egypt. This volume details the philosophy and practice of this unique system of meditation originated in Ancient Egypt and the earliest practice of meditation known in the world which occurred in the most advanced African Culture. ISBN: 1-884564-15-1 $16.95 (PB)

15.   *THE SERPENT POWER: The Ancient Egyptian Mystical Wisdom of the Inner Life Force.* This Volume specifically deals with the latent life Force energy of the universe and in the human body, its control and sublimation. How to develop the Life Force energy of the subtle body. This Volume will introduce the esoteric wisdom of the science of how virtuous living acts in a subtle and mysterious way to cleanse the latent psychic energy conduits and vortices of the spiritual body. ISBN 1-884564-19-4 $22.95

16.   *EGYPTIAN YOGA The Postures of The Gods and Goddesses* Discover the physical postures and exercises practiced thousands of years ago in Ancient Egypt which are today known as Yoga exercises. Discover the history of the postures and how they were transferred from Ancient Egypt in Africa to India through Buddhist Tantrism. Then practice the postures as you discover the mythic teaching that originally gave birth to the postures and was practiced by the Ancient Egyptian priests and priestesses. This work is based on the pictures and teachings from the Creation story of Ra, The Asarian Resurrection Myth and the carvings and reliefs from various Temples in Ancient Egypt 8.5" X 11" ISBN 1-884564-10-0 Soft Cover $21.95   Exercise video $20

17.   *SACRED SEXUALITY: ANCIENT EGYPTIAN TANTRA YOGA: The Art of Sex* Sublimation and Universal Consciousness This Volume will expand on the male and female principles within the human body and in the universe and further detail the sublimation of sexual energy into spiritual energy. The student will study the deities Min and Hathor, Asar and Aset, Geb and Nut and discover the mystical implications for a practical spiritual discipline. This Volume will also focus on the Tantric aspects of Ancient Egyptian and Indian mysticism, the purpose of sex and the mystical teachings of sexual sublimation which lead to self-knowledge and Enlightenment. ISBN 1-884564-03-8 $24.95

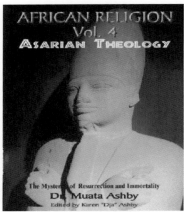

18.   *AFRICAN RELIGION Volume 4: ASARIAN THEOLOGY: RESURRECTING OSIRIS* The path of Mystical Awakening and the Keys to Immortality NEW REVISED AND EXPANDED EDITION! The Ancient Sages created stories based on human and superhuman beings whose struggles, aspirations, needs and desires ultimately lead them to discover their true Self. The myth of Aset, Asar and Heru is no exception in this area. While there is no one source where the entire story may be found, pieces of it are inscribed in various ancient Temples walls, tombs, steles and papyri. For the first time available, the complete myth of Asar, Aset and Heru has been compiled from original Ancient Egyptian, Greek and Coptic Texts. This epic myth has been richly illustrated with reliefs from the Temple of Heru at Edfu, the Temple of Aset at Philae, the Temple of Asar at Abydos, the Temple of Hathor at Denderah and various papyri, inscriptions and reliefs. Discover the myth which inspired the teachings of the *Shetaut Neter* (Egyptian Mystery System - Egyptian Yoga) and the Egyptian Book of Coming Forth By Day. Also, discover the three levels of Ancient Egyptian Religion, how to understand the mysteries of the Duat or Astral World and how to discover the abode of the Supreme in the Amenta, *The Other World*   The ancient religion of Asar, Aset and Heru, if properly understood, contains all of the elements necessary to lead the sincere aspirant to attain immortality through inner self-discovery. This volume presents the entire myth and explores the main mystical themes and rituals associated with the myth for understating human existence, creation and the way to achieve spiritual emancipation - *Resurrection.* The Asarian myth is so powerful that it influenced and is still having an effect on the major world religions. Discover the origins and mystical meaning of the Christian Trinity, the Eucharist ritual and the ancient origin of the birthday of Jesus Christ. Soft Cover ISBN: 1-884564-27-5 $24.95

19.	*THE EGYPTIAN BOOK OF THE DEAD MYSTICISM OF THE PERT EM HERU* " I Know myself, I know myself, I am One With God!–From the Pert Em Heru "The Ru Pert em Heru" or "Ancient Egyptian Book of The Dead," or "Book of Coming Forth By Day" as it is more popularly known, has fascinated the world since the successful translation of Ancient Egyptian hieroglyphic scripture over 150 years ago. The astonishing writings in it reveal that the Ancient Egyptians believed in life after death and in an ultimate destiny to discover the Divine. The elegance and aesthetic beauty of the hieroglyphic text itself has inspired many see it as an art form in and of itself. But is there more to it than that? Did the Ancient Egyptian wisdom contain more than just aphorisms and hopes of eternal life beyond death? In this volume Dr. Muata Ashby, the author of over 25 books on Ancient Egyptian Yoga Philosophy has produced a new translation of the original texts which uncovers a mystical teaching underlying the sayings and rituals instituted by the Ancient Egyptian Sages and Saints. "Once the philosophy of Ancient Egypt is understood as a mystical tradition instead of as a religion or primitive mythology, it reveals its secrets which if practiced today will lead anyone to discover the glory of spiritual self-discovery. The Pert em Heru is in every way comparable to the Indian Upanishads or the Tibetan Book of the Dead." $28.95 ISBN# 1-884564-28-3 Size: 8½" X 11

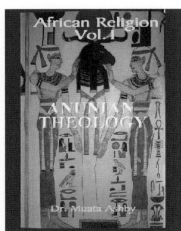

20.	*African Religion VOL. 1- ANUNIAN THEOLOGY THE MYSTERIES OF RA* The Philosophy of Anu and The Mystical Teachings of The Ancient Egyptian Creation Myth Discover the mystical teachings contained in the Creation Myth and the gods and goddesses who brought creation and human beings into existence. The Creation myth of Anu is the source of Anunian Theology but also of the other main theological systems of Ancient Egypt that also influenced other world religions including Christianity, Hinduism and Buddhism. The Creation Myth holds the key to understanding the universe and for attaining spiritual Enlightenment. ISBN: 1-884564-38-0 $19.95

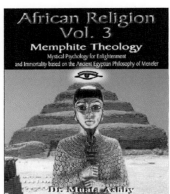

21.   *African Religion VOL 3: Memphite Theology: MYSTERIES OF MIND* Mystical Psychology & Mental Health for Enlightenment and Immortality based on the Ancient Egyptian Philosophy of Menefer -Mysticism of Ptah, Egyptian Physics and Yoga Metaphysics and the Hidden properties of Matter.   This volume uncovers the mystical psychology of the Ancient Egyptian wisdom teachings centering on the philosophy of the Ancient Egyptian city of Menefer (Memphite Theology). How to understand the mind and how to control the senses and lead the mind to health, clarity and mystical self-discovery. This Volume will also go deeper into the philosophy of God as creation and will explore the concepts of modern science and how they correlate with ancient teachings. This Volume will lay the ground work for the understanding of the philosophy of universal consciousness and the initiatic/yogic insight into who or what is God? ISBN 1-884564-07-0 $22.95

22.   *AFRICAN RELIGION VOLUME 5: THE GODDESS AND THE EGYPTIAN MYSTERIESTHE PATH OF THE GODDESS THE GODDESS PATH* The Secret Forms of the Goddess and the Rituals of Resurrection The Supreme Being may be worshipped as father or as mother. *Ushet Rekhat* or *Mother Worship*, is the spiritual process of worshipping the Divine in the form of the

Divine Goddess. It celebrates the most important forms of the Goddess including *Nathor, Maat, Aset, Arat, Amentet and Hathor* and explores their mystical meaning as well as the rising of *Sirius,* the star of Aset (Aset) and the new birth of Hor (Heru). The end of the year is a time of reckoning, reflection and engendering a new or renewed positive movement toward attaining spiritual Enlightenment. The Mother Worship devotional meditation ritual, performed on five days during the month of December and on New Year's Eve, is based on the Ushet Rekhit. During the ceremony, the cosmic forces, symbolized by Sirius - and the constellation of Orion ---, are harnessed through the understanding and devotional attitude of the participant. This propitiation draws the light of wisdom and health to all those who share in the ritual, leading to prosperity and wisdom. $14.95 ISBN 1-884564-18-6

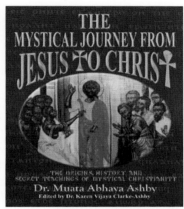

23.   *THE MYSTICAL JOURNEY FROM JESUS TO CHRIST* Discover the ancient Egyptian origins of Christianity before the Catholic Church and learn the mystical teachings given by Jesus to assist all humanity in becoming Christlike. Discover the secret meaning of the Gospels that were discovered in Egypt. Also discover how and why so many Christian churches came into being. Discover that the Bible still holds the keys to mystical realization even though its original writings were changed by the church. Discover how to practice the original teachings of Christianity which leads to the Kingdom of Heaven. $24.95   ISBN# 1-884564-05-4 size: 8½" X 11"

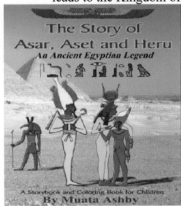

24.   *THE STORY OF ASAR, ASET AND HERU:* An Ancient Egyptian Legend (For Children)   Now for the first time, the most ancient myth of Ancient Egypt comes alive for children. Inspired by the books *The Asarian Resurrection: The Ancient Egyptian Bible* and *The Mystical Teachings of The Asarian Resurrection, The Story of Asar, Aset and Heru* is an easy to understand and thrilling tale which inspired the children of Ancient Egypt to aspire to greatness and righteousness.   If you and

your child have enjoyed stories like *The Lion King* and *Star Wars you will love The Story of Asar, Aset and Heru.* Also, if you know the story of Jesus and Krishna you will discover than Ancient Egypt had a similar myth and that this myth carries important spiritual teachings for living a fruitful and fulfilling life. This book may be used along with *The Parents Guide To The Asarian Resurrection Myth: How to Teach Yourself and Your Child the Principles of Universal Mystical Religion.* The guide provides some background to the Asarian Resurrection myth and it also gives insight into the mystical teachings contained in it which you may introduce to your child. It is designed for parents who wish to grow spiritually with their children and it serves as an introduction for those who would like to study the Asarian Resurrection Myth in depth and to practice its teachings. 8.5" X 11"   ISBN: 1-884564-31-3 $12.95

25.   *THE PARENTS GUIDE TO THE AUSARIAN RESURRECTION MYTH:* How to Teach Yourself and Your Child the Principles of Universal Mystical Religion.   This insightful manual brings for the timeless wisdom of the ancient through the Ancient Egyptian myth of Asar, Aset and Heru and the mystical teachings contained in it for parents who want to guide their children to understand and practice the teachings of mystical spirituality. This manual may be used with the children's storybook *The Story of Asar, Aset and Heru* by Dr. Muata Abhaya Ashby.   ISBN: 1-884564-30-5 $16.95

26.   *HEALING THE CRIMINAL HEART.* Introduction to Maat Philosophy, Yoga and Spiritual Redemption Through the Path of Virtue   Who is a criminal? Is there such a thing as a criminal heart? What is the source of evil and sinfulness and is there any way to rise above it? Is there

redemption for those who have committed sins, even the worst crimes?   Ancient Egyptian mystical psychology holds important answers to these questions. Over ten thousand years ago mystical psychologists, the Sages of Ancient Egypt, studied and charted the human mind and spirit and laid out a path which will lead to spiritual redemption, prosperity and Enlightenment.   This introductory volume brings forth the teachings of the Asarian Resurrection, the most important myth of Ancient Egypt, with relation to the faults of human existence: anger, hatred, greed, lust, animosity, discontent, ignorance, egoism jealousy, bitterness, and a myriad of psycho-spiritual ailments which keep a human being in a state of negativity and adversity   ISBN: 1-884564-17-8 $15.95

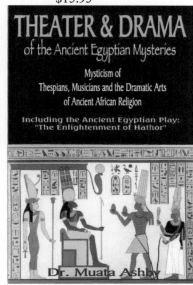

27.   *TEMPLE RITUAL OF THE ANCIENT EGYPTIAN MYSTERIES--THEATER & DRAMA OF THE ANCIENT EGYPTIAN MYSTERIES*: Details the practice of the mysteries and ritual program of the temple and the philosophy an practice of the ritual of the mysteries, its purpose and execution. Featuring the Ancient Egyptian stage play-"The Enlightenment of Hathor' Based on an Ancient Egyptian Drama, The original Theater -Mysticism of the Temple of Hetheru 1-884564-14-3 $19.95 By Dr. Muata Ashby

28.   *GUIDE TO PRINT ON DEMAND: SELF-PUBLISH FOR PROFIT*, SPIRITUAL FULFILLMENT AND SERVICE TO HUMANITY Everyone asks us how we produced so many books in such a short time. Here are the secrets to writing and producing books that uplift humanity and how to get them printed for a fraction of the regular cost. Anyone can become an author even if they have limited funds. All that is necessary is the willingness to learn how the printing and book business work and the desire to follow the special instructions given here for preparing your manuscript format. Then you take your work directly to the non-traditional companies who can produce your books for less than the traditional book printer can. ISBN: 1-884564-40-2 $16.95 U. S.

29.   *Egyptian Mysteries: Vol. 1,* Shetaut Neter What are the Mysteries? For thousands of years the spiritual tradition of Ancient Egypt, *Shetaut Neter,* "The Egyptian Mysteries," "The Secret Teachings," have fascinated, tantalized and amazed the world. At one time exalted and recognized as the highest culture of the world, by Africans, Europeans, Asiatics, Hindus, Buddhists and other cultures of the ancient world, in time it was shunned by the emerging orthodox world religions. Its temples desecrated, its philosophy maligned, its tradition spurned, its philosophy dormant in the mystical *Medu Neter*, the mysterious hieroglyphic texts which hold the secret symbolic meaning

that has scarcely been discerned up to now. What are the secrets of *Nehast* {spiritual awakening and emancipation, resurrection}. More than just a literal translation, this volume is for awakening to the secret code *Shetitu* of the teaching which was not deciphered by Egyptologists, nor could be understood by ordinary spiritualists. This book is a reinstatement of the original science made available for our times, to the reincarnated followers of Ancient Egyptian culture and the prospect of spiritual freedom to break the bonds of *Khemn*, "ignorance," and slavery to evil forces: *Såaa* . ISBN: 1-884564-41-0 $19.99

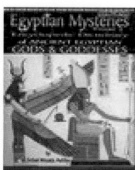

30.   *EGYPTIAN MYSTERIES VOL 2:* Dictionary of Gods and Goddesses This book is about the mystery of neteru, the gods and goddesses of Ancient Egypt (Kamit, Kemet). Neteru means "Gods and Goddesses." But the Neterian teaching of Neteru represents more than the usual limited modern day concept of "divinities" or "spirits." The Neteru of Kamit are also metaphors, cosmic principles and vehicles for the enlightening teachings of Shetaut Neter (Ancient Egyptian-African Religion). Actually they are the elements for one of the most advanced systems of spirituality ever conceived in human history. Understanding the concept of neteru provides a firm basis for spiritual evolution and the pathway for viable culture, peace on earth and a healthy human society. Why is it important to have gods and goddesses in our lives? In order for spiritual evolution to be possible, once a human being has accepted that there is existence after death and there is a transcendental being who exists beyond time and space knowledge, human beings need a connection to that which transcends the ordinary experience of human life in time and space and a means to understand the transcendental reality beyond the mundane reality. ISBN: 1-884564-23-2 $21.95

31.   *EGYPTIAN MYSTERIES VOL. 3* The Priests and Priestesses of Ancient Egypt This volume details the path of Neterian priesthood, the joys, challenges and rewards of advanced Neterian life, the teachings that allowed the priests and priestesses to manage the most long lived civilization in human history and how that path can be adopted today; for those who want to tread the path of the Clergy of Shetaut Neter. ISBN: 1-884564-53-4 $24.95

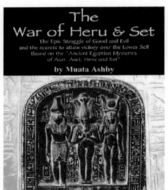

32.   *The War of Heru and Set:* The Struggle of Good and Evil for Control of the World and The Human Soul This volume contains a novelized version of the Asarian Resurrection myth that is based on the actual scriptures presented in the Book Asarian Religion (old name –Resurrecting Osiris). This volume is prepared in the form of a screenplay and can be easily adapted to be used as a stage play. Spiritual seeking is a mythic journey that has many emotional highs and lows, ecstasies and depressions, victories and frustrations. This is the War of Life that is played out in the myth as the struggle of Heru and Set and those are mythic characters that represent the human Higher and Lower self. How to understand the war and emerge victorious in the journey of life? The ultimate victory and fulfillment can be experienced, which is not changeable or lost in time. The purpose of myth is to convey the wisdom of life through the story of divinities who show the way to overcome the challenges and foibles of life. In this volume the feelings and emotions of the characters of the myth have been highlighted to show the deeply rich texture of the Ancient Egyptian myth. This myth contains deep spiritual teachings and insights into the nature of self, of God and the mysteries of life and the means to discover the true meaning of life and thereby achieve the true purpose of life. To become victorious in the battle of life means to become the King (or Queen) of Egypt. Have you seen movies like The Lion King, Hamlet, The Odyssey, or The Little Buddha? These have been some of the most popular movies in modern times. The Sema Institute of Yoga is dedicated to researching and presenting the wisdom and culture of ancient Africa. The Script is designed to be produced as a motion picture but may be addapted for the theater as well. $21.95   copyright 1998 By Dr. Muata Ashby ISBN 1-8840564-44-5

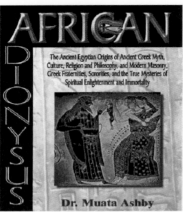

33.   *AFRICAN DIONYSUS: FROM EGYPT TO GREECE:* The Kamitan Origins of Greek Culture and Religion ISBN: 1-884564-47-X FROM EGYPT TO GREECE This insightful manual is a reference

to Ancient Egyptian mythology and philosophy and its correlation to what later became known as Greek and Rome mythology and philosophy. It outlines the basic tenets of the mythologies and shoes the ancient origins of Greek culture in Ancient Egypt. This volume also documents the origins of the Greek alphabet in Egypt as well as Greek religion, myth and philosophy of the gods and goddesses from Egypt from the myth of Atlantis and archaic period with the Minoans to the Classical period. This volume also acts as a resource for Colleges students who would like to set up fraternities and sororities based on the original Ancient Egyptian principles of Sheti and Maat philosophy. ISBN: 1-884564-47-X $22.95 U.S.

34. *THE FORTY TWO PRECEPTS OF MAAT, THE PHILOSOPHY OF RIGHTEOUS ACTION AND THE ANCIENT EGYPTIAN WISDOM TEXTS* <u>ADVANCED STUDIES</u> This manual is designed for use with the 1998 Maat Philosophy Class conducted by Dr. Muata Ashby. This is a detailed study of Maat Philosophy. It contains a compilation of the 42 laws or precepts of Maat and the corresponding principles which they represent along with the teachings of the ancient Egyptian Sages relating to each. Maat philosophy was the basis of Ancient Egyptian society and government as well as the heart of Ancient Egyptian myth and spirituality. Maat is at once a goddess, a cosmic force and a living social doctrine, which promotes social harmony and thereby paves the way for spiritual evolution in all levels of society. ISBN: 1-884564-48-8 $16.95 U.S.

35. *THE SECRET LOTUS: Poetry of Enlightenment*

Discover the mystical sentiment of the Kemetic teaching as expressed through the poetry of Sebai Muata Ashby. The teaching of spiritual awakening is uniquely experienced when the poetic sensibility is present. This first volume contains the poems written between 1996 and 2003. **1-884564--16 -X $16.99**

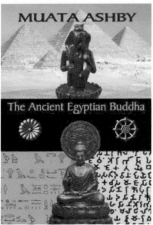

36. The Ancient Egyptian Buddha: The Ancient Egyptian Origins of Buddhism

This book is a compilation of several sections of a larger work, a book by the name of African Origins of Civilization, Religion, Yoga Mysticism and Ethics Philosophy. It also contains some additional evidences not contained in the larger work that demonstrate the correlation between Ancient Egyptian Religion and Buddhism. This book is one of several compiled short volumes that has been compiled so as to facilitate access to specific subjects contained in the larger work which is over 680 pages long. These short and small volumes have been specifically designed to cover one subject in a brief and low cost format. This present volume, The Ancient Egyptian Buddha: The Ancient Egyptian Origins of Buddhism, formed one subject in the larger work; actually it was one chapter of the larger work. However, this volume has some new additional evidences and comparisons of Buddhist and Neterian (Ancient Egyptian) philosophies not previously discussed. It was felt that this subject needed to be discussed because even in the early 21st century, the idea persists that Buddhism originated only in India independently. Yet there is ample evidence from ancient writings and perhaps more importantly, iconographical evidences from the Ancient Egyptians and early Buddhists themselves that prove otherwise. This handy volume has been designed to be accessible to young adults and all others who would like to have an easy reference with documentation on this important subject. This is an important subject because the frame of reference with which we look at a culture depends strongly on our conceptions about its origins. In this case, if we look at the Buddhism as an Asiatic religion we would treat it and its culture in one way. If we id as African [Ancient Egyptian] we not only would see it in a different light but we also must ascribe Africa with a glorious legacy that matches any other culture in human history and gave rise to one of the present day most important religious philosophies. We would also look at the culture and philosophies of the Ancient Egyptians as having African insights that offer us greater depth into the Buddhist philosophies. Those insights inform our knowledge about other African traditions and we can also begin to understand in a deeper way the effect of Ancient Egyptian culture on African culture and also on the Asiatic as well. We would also be able to discover the glorious and wondrous teaching of mystical philosophy that Ancient Egyptian Shetaut Neter religion offers, that is as powerful as any other mystic system of spiritual philosophy in the world today. ISBN: 1-884564-61-5 $28.95

Reginald Muata Ashby

37. The Death of American Empire: Neo-conservatism, Theocracy, Economic Imperialism, Environmental Disaster and the Collapse of Civilization

This work is a collection of essays relating to social and economic, leadership, and ethics, ecological and religious issues that are facing the world today in order to understand the course of history that has led humanity to its present condition and then arrive at positive solutions that will lead to better outcomes for all humanity. It surveys the development and decline of major empires throughout history and focuses on the creation of American Empire along with the social, political and economic policies that led to the prominence of the United States of America as a Superpower including the rise of the political control of the neo-con political philosophy including militarism and the military industrial complex in American politics and the rise of the religious right into and American Theocracy movement. This volume details, through historical and current events, the psychology behind the dominance of western culture in world politics through the "Superpower Syndrome Mandatory Conflict Complex" that drives the Superpower culture to establish itself above all others and then act hubristically to dominate world culture through legitimate influences as well as coercion, media censorship and misinformation leading to international hegemony and world conflict. This volume also details the financial policies that gave rise to American prominence in the global economy, especially after World War II, and promoted American preeminence over the world economy through Globalization as well as the environmental policies, including the oil economy, that are promoting degradation of the world ecology and contribute to the decline of America as an Empire culture. This volume finally explores the factors pointing to the decline of the American Empire economy and imperial power and what to expect in the aftermath of American prominence and how to survive the decline while at the same time promoting policies and social-economic-religious-political changes that are needed in order to promote the emergence of a beneficial and sustainable culture. **$25.95soft** 1-884564-25-9, Hard Cover **$29.95soft** 1-884564-45-3

38. The African Origins of Hatha Yoga: And its Ancient Mystical Teaching

The subject of this present volume, The Ancient Egyptian Origins of Yoga Postures, formed one subject in the larger works, African Origins of Civilization Religion, Yoga Mysticism and Ethics Philosophy and the Book Egypt and India is the section of the book African Origins of Civilization. Those works contain the collection of all correlations between Ancient Egypt and India. This volume also contains some additional information not contained in the previous work. It was felt that this subject needed to be discussed more directly, being treated in one volume, as opposed to being contained in the larger work along with other subjects, because even in the early 21st century, the idea persists that the Yoga and specifically, Yoga Postures, were invented and developed only in India. The Ancient Egyptians were peoples originally from Africa who were, in ancient times, colonists in India. Therefore it is no surprise that many Indian traditions including religious and Yogic, would be found earlier in Ancient Egypt. Yet there is ample evidence from ancient writings and perhaps more importantly, iconographical evidences from the Ancient Egyptians themselves and the Indians themselves that prove the connection between Ancient Egypt and India as well as the existence of a discipline of Yoga Postures in Ancient Egypt long before its practice in India. This handy volume has been designed to be accessible to young adults and all others who would like to have an easy reference with documentation on this important subject. This is an important subject because the frame of reference with which we look at a culture depends strongly on our conceptions about its origins. In this case, if we look at the Ancient Egyptians as Asiatic peoples we would treat them and their culture in one way. If we see them as Africans we not only see them in a different light but we also must ascribe Africa with a glorious legacy that matches any other culture in human history. We would also look at the culture and philosophies of the Ancient Egyptians as having African insights instead of Asiatic ones. Those insights inform our knowledge about other African traditions and we can also begin to understand in a deeper way the effect of Ancient Egyptian culture on African culture and also on the Asiatic as well. When we discover the deeper and more ancient practice of the postures system in Ancient Egypt that was called "Hatha Yoga" in India, we are able to find a new and expanded understanding of the practice that constitutes a discipline of spiritual practice that informs and revitalizes the Indian practices as well as all spiritual disciplines. $19.99 ISBN 1-884564-60-7

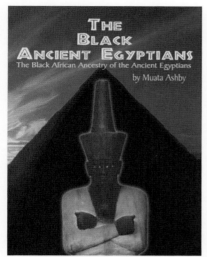

39. The Black Ancient Egyptians

This present volume, The Black Ancient Egyptians: The Black African Ancestry of the Ancient Egyptians, formed one subject in the larger work: The African Origins of Civilization, Religion, Yoga Mysticism and Ethics Philosophy. It was felt that this subject needed to be discussed because even in the early 21st century, the idea persists that the Ancient Egyptians were peoples originally from Asia Minor who came into North-East Africa. Yet there is ample evidence from ancient writings and perhaps more importantly, iconographical evidences from the Ancient Egyptians themselves that proves otherwise. This handy volume has been designed to be accessible to young adults and all others who would like to have an easy reference with documentation on this important subject. This is an important subject because the frame of reference with which we look at a culture depends strongly on our conceptions about its origins. in this case, if we look at the Ancient Egyptians as Asiatic peoples we would treat them and their culture in one way. If we see them as Africans we not only see them in a different light but we also must ascribe Africa with a glorious legacy that matches any other culture in human history. We would also look at the culture and philosophies of the Ancient Egyptians as having African insights instead of Asiatic ones. Those insights inform our knowledge about other African traditions and we can also begin to understand in a deeper way the effect of Ancient Egyptian culture on African culture and also on the Asiatic as well. ISBN 1-884564-21-6 $19.99

40. The Limits of Faith: The Failure of Faith-based Religions and the Solution to the Meaning of Life

Is faith belief in something without proof? And if so is there never to be any proof or discovery? If so what is the need of intellect? If faith is trust in something that is real is that reality historical, literal or metaphorical or philosophical? If knowledge is an essential element in faith why should there be so much emphasis on believing and not on understanding in the modern practice of religion? This volume is a compilation of essays related to the nature of religious faith in the context of its inception in human history as well as its meaning for religious practice and relations between religions in modern times. Faith has come to be regarded as a virtuous goal in life. However, many people have asked how can it be that an endeavor that is supposed to be dedicated to spiritual upliftment has led to more conflict in human history than any other social factor? ISBN 1884564631 SOFT COVER - $19.99, ISBN 1884564623 HARD COVER -$28.95

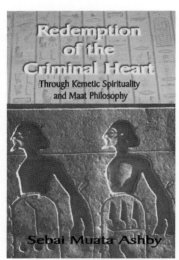

41. <u>Redemption of The Criminal Heart Through Kemetic Spirituality and Maat Philosophy</u>

Special book dedicated to inmates, their families and members of the Law Enforcement community. ISBN: 1-884564-70-4
$5.00

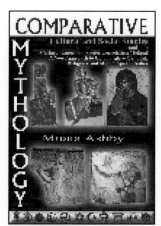

42. COMPARATIVE MYTHOLOGY

What are Myth and Culture and what is their importance for understanding the development of societies, human evolution and the search for meaning? What is the purpose of culture and how do cultures evolve? What are the elements of a culture and how can those elements be broken down and the constituent parts of a culture understood and compared? How do cultures interact? How does enculturation occur and how do people interact with other cultures? How do the processes of acculturation and cooptation occur and what does this mean for the development of a society? How can the study of myths and the elements of culture help in understanding the meaning of life and the means to promote understanding and peace in the world of human activity? This volume is the exposition of a method for studying and comparing cultures, myths and other social aspects of a society. It is an expansion on the Cultural Category Factor Correlation method for studying and comparing myths, cultures, religions and other aspects of human culture. It was originally introduced in the year 2002. This volume contains an expanded treatment as well as several refinements along with examples of the application of the method. the apparent. I hope you enjoy these art renditions as serene reflections of the mysteries of life. ISBN: 1-884564-72-0
Book price $21.95

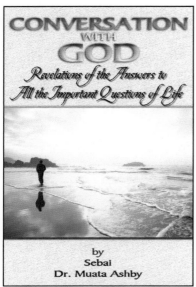

43. CONVERSATION WITH GOD: Revelations of the Important Questions of Life
$24.99 U.S.

This volume contains a grouping of some of the questions that have been submitted to Sebai Dr. Muata Ashby. They are efforts by many aspirants to better understand and practice the teachings of mystical spirituality. It is said that when sages are asked spiritual questions they are relaying the wisdom of God, the Goddess, the Higher Self, etc. There is a very special quality about the Q & A process that does not occur during a regular lecture session. Certain points come out that would not come out otherwise due to the nature of the process which ideally occurs after a lecture. Having been to a certain degree enlightened by a lecture certain new questions arise and the answers to these have the effect of elevating the teaching of the lecture to even higher levels. Therefore, enjoy these exchanges and may they lead you to enlightenment, peace and prosperity. Available Late Summer 2007 ISBN: 1-884564-68-2

44. MYSTIC ART PAINTINGS

(with Full Color images) This book contains a collection of the small number of paintings that I have created over the years. Some were used as early book covers and others were done simply to express certain spiritual feelings; some were created for no purpose except to express the joy of color and the feeling of relaxed freedom. All are to elicit mystical awakening in the viewer. Writing a book on philosophy is like sculpture, the more the work is rewritten the reflections and ideas become honed and take form and become clearer and imbued with intellectual beauty. Mystic music is like meditation, a world of its own that exists about 1 inch above ground wherein the musician does not touch the ground. Mystic Graphic Art is meditation in form, color, image and reflected image which opens the door to the reality behind the apparent. I hope you enjoy these art renditions and my reflections on them as serene reflections of the mysteries of life, as visual renditions of the philosophy I have written about over the years. ISBN 1-884564-69-0 $19.95

45. ANCIENT EGYPTIAN HIEROGLYPHS FOR BEGINNERS
This brief guide was prepared for those inquiring about how to enter into Hieroglyphic studies on their own at home or in study groups. First of all you should know that there are a few institutions around the world which teach how to read the Hieroglyphic text but due to the nature of the study there are perhaps only a handful of people who can read fluently. It is possible for anyone with average intelligence to achieve a high level of proficiency in reading inscriptions on temples and artifacts; however, reading extensive texts is another issue entirely. However, this introduction will give you entry into those texts if assisted by dictionaries and other aids. Most Egyptologists have a basic knowledge and keep dictionaries and notes handy when it comes to dealing with more difficult texts. Medtu Neter or the Ancient Egyptian hieroglyphic language has been considered as a "Dead Language." However, dead languages have always been studied by individuals who for the most part have taught themselves through various means. This book will discuss those means and how to use them most efficiently. ISBN 1884564429 **$28.95**

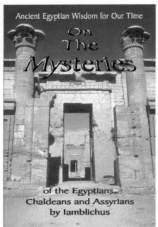

46. ON THE MYSTERIES: Wisdom of An Ancient Egyptian Sage -with Foreword by Muata Ashby
This volume, On the Mysteries, by Iamblichus (Abamun) is a unique form or scripture out of the Ancient Egyptian religious tradition. It is written in a form that is not usual or which is not usually found in the remnants of Ancient Egyptian scriptures. It is in the form of teacher and disciple, much like the Eastern scriptures such as Bhagavad Gita or the Upanishads. This form of writing may not have been necessary in Ancient times, because the format of teaching in Egypt was different prior to the conquest period by the Persians, Assyrians, Greeks and later the Romans. The question and answer format can be found but such extensive discourses and corrections of misunderstandings within the context of a teacher - disciple relationship is not usual. It therefore provides extensive insights into the times when it was written and the state of practice of Ancient Egyptian and other mystery religions. This has important implications for our times because we are today, as in the Greco-Roman period, also besieged with varied religions and new age philosophies as well as social strife and war. How can we understand our times and also make sense of the forest of spiritual traditions? How can we cut through the cacophony of religious fanaticism, and ignorance as well as misconceptions about the mysteries on the other in order to discover the true purpose of religion and the secret teachings that open up the mysteries of life and the way to enlightenment and immortality? This book, which comes to us from so long ago, offers us transcendental wisdom that applied to the world two thousand years ago as well as our world today. ISBN 1-884564-64-X $25.95

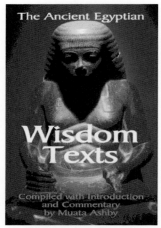

47. The Ancient Egyptian Wisdom Texts -Compiled by Muata Ashby

The Ancient Egyptian Wisdom Texts are a genre of writings from the ancient culture that have survived to the present and provide a vibrant record of the practice of spiritual evolution otherwise known as religion or yoga philosophy in Ancient Egypt. The principle focus of the Wisdom Texts is the cultivation of understanding, peace, harmony, selfless service, self-control, Inner fulfillment and spiritual realization. When these factors are cultivated in human life, the virtuous qualities in a human being begin to manifest and sinfulness, ignorance and negativity diminish until a person is able to enter into higher consciousness, the coveted goal of all civilizations. It is this virtuous mode of life which opens the door to self-discovery and spiritual enlightenment. Therefore, the Wisdom Texts are important scriptures on the subject of human nature, spiritual psychology and mystical philosophy. The teachings presented in the Wisdom Texts form the foundation of religion as well as the guidelines for conducting the affairs of every area of social interaction including commerce, education, the army, marriage, and especially the legal system. These texts were sources for the famous 42 Precepts of Maat of the Pert M Heru (Book of the Dead), essential regulations of good conduct to develop virtue and purity in order to attain higher consciousness and immortality after death. ISBN1-884564-65-8 $18.95

48. THE KEMETIC TREE OF LIFE
THE KEMETIC TREE OF LIFE: Newly Revealed Ancient Egyptian Cosmology and Metaphysics for Higher Consciousness The Tree of Life is a roadmap of a journey which explains how Creation came into being and how it will end. It also explains what Creation is composed of and also what human beings are and what they are composed of. It also explains the process of Creation, how Creation develops, as well as who created Creation and where that entity may be found. It also explains how a human being may discover that entity and in so doing also discover the secrets of Creation, the meaning of life and the means to break free from the pathetic condition of human limitation and mortality in order to discover the higher realms of being by discovering the principles, the levels of existence that are beyond the simple physical and material aspects of life. This book contains color plates **ISBN: 1-884564-74-7**
$27.95 U.S.

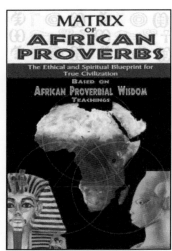

49-MATRIX OF AFRICAN PROVERBS: The Ethical and Spiritual Blueprint
This volume sets forth the fundamental principles of African ethics and their practical applications for use
by individuals and organizations seeking to model their ethical policies using the Traditional African values
and concepts of ethical human behavior for the proper sustenance and management of society.
Furthermore, this book will provide guidance as to how the Traditional African Ethics may be viewed and
applied, taking into consideration the technological and social advancements in the present. This volume
also presents the principles of ethical culture, and references for each to specific injunctions from
Traditional African Proverbial Wisdom Teachings. These teachings are compiled from varied Pre-colonial
African societies including Yoruba, Ashanti, Kemet, Malawi, Nigeria, Ethiopia, Galla, Ghana and many
more. ISBN 1-884564-77-1

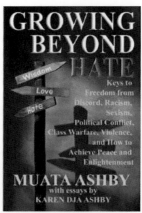

**50- Growing Beyond Hate: Keys to Freedom from Discord, Racism, Sexism, Political Conflict, Class
Warfare, Violence, and How to Achieve Peace and Enlightenment**---INTRODUCTION: WHY DO WE
HATE? Hatred is one of the fundamental motivating aspects of human life; the other is desire. Desire can
be of a worldly nature or of a spiritual, elevating nature. Worldly desire and hatred are like two sides of the
same coin in that human life is usually swaying from one to the other; but the question is why? And is there
a way to satisfy the desiring or hating mind in such a way as to find peace in life? Why do human beings go
to war? Why do human beings perpetrate violence against one another? And is there a way not just to
understand the phenomena but to resolve the issues that plague humanity and could lead to a more
harmonious society? Hatred is perhaps the greatest scourge of humanity in that it leads to

misunderstanding, conflict and untold miseries of life and clashes between individuals, societies and nations. Therefore, the riddle of Hatred, that is, understanding the sources of it and how to confront, reduce and even eradicate it so as to bring forth the fulfillment in life and peace for society, should be a top priority for social scientists, spiritualists and philosophers. This book is written from the perspective of spiritual philosophy based on the mystical wisdom and sema or yoga philosophy of the Ancient Egyptians. This philosophy, originated and based in the wisdom of Shetaut Neter, the Egyptian Mysteries, and Maat, ethical way of life in society and in spirit, contains Sema-Yogic wisdom and understanding of life's predicaments that can allow a human being of any ethnic group to understand and overcome the causes of hatred, racism, sexism, violence and disharmony in life, that plague human society. ISBN: 1-884564-81-X

Printed in Great Britain
by Amazon

36657101R00142